641.5945 Orsini, Joseph E.
ORS

~~NEW~~   Italian family
                    cooking.

$27.50

DATE			

Italian Family Cooking

Also by Father Joseph Orsini

FATHER ORSINI'S ITALIAN KITCHEN

FATHER ORSINI'S PASTA PERFETTA

Italian Family Cooking

UNLOCKING A TREASURY OF RECIPES AND STORIES

Father Joseph Orsini

ST. MARTIN'S PRESS ☙ NEW YORK

THOMAS DUNNE BOOKS.
An imprint of St. Martin's Press.

Book design by Fritz Metsch
Illustrations by Clair Moritz-Magnesio

Library of Congress Cataloging-in-Publication Data
Orsini, Joseph E.
    Italian family cooking: unlocking a treasury of recipes and
    stories/Joseph Orsini.—1st ed.
        p. cm.
    ISBN 0-312-24225-5
    1. Cookery, Italian. I. Title.
TX723.O7483 2000
641.5945—dc21   99-056353
                                                       CIP

First Edition: March 2000

10 9 8 7 6 5 4 3 2 1

Giuseppe Orsini

Carmela Amore Orsini

TO MY BELOVED DECEASED FAMILY MEMBERS AND FRIENDS

Giuseppe Orsini, my father

Carmela Orsini, my mother

Dominick Orsini, my nephew

Oreste Orsini, my brother

John Orsini, my brother

Marie Orsini, my sister-in-law

Leo Orsini, my brother

Reggie Conti, my friend

Contents

Acknowledgments

There are many special people who helped and supported me in writing this book. Those listed below deserve an award for putting up with me.

CARMEL O. FERRANTE ✎ My niece, who patiently edited the galley sheets to conform with the rules of syntax and grammar. She has retired from teaching English, but once a teacher, always a teacher.

MARY MARCK ✎ Her professionalism in word processing is incomparable. Her long hard hours of work are most appreciated. You see, I write all my books in longhand, so I need a person like Mary to type for me.

PETER WOLVERTON ✎ My editor, whose great patience and talent made this a better book.

JOHN MURPHY ✎ My publicist, whose experience and contacts sent me running all over the place to push my book.

MARY ORSINI ✎ My sister-in-law in whose kitchen all the recipes were tested and shared. Mae did all the cleaning up and never complained.

ALL MY FAMILY MEMBERS AND FRIENDS ✎ They generously gave me their family treasures (recipes) to share with you. They are named throughout this book.

THE FRUGAL GOURMET ✎ He gave me advice and support by telephone and fax during the process of writing the book.

HELEN BARBERIO ✎ Who patiently proofread my original manuscript and suggested changes that cleared up obscure sentences and directions.

I know, I know. It sounds like a movie script. An Italian version of that great old movie about Catholic priests, *Going My Way.* Bing Crosby and Barry Fitzgerald played the roles of unforgettable Irish Catholic priests. That was fiction, but this story is true. There is a Father Joe Orsini. He is an Italian-American Catholic priest. We call him Father Joe. He is not only a dedicated priest and a gourmet cook who writes cookbooks, but he is also one terrific guy. He has cooked on my show and we became instant friends. I have been a guest at his dining room table. I'll never forget his sauce or his pasta with perfect meatballs, authentic Italian sausage, gorgeous-looking pinwheels of lean flank steak stuffed with imported Italian cheeses, savory bread crumbs, flecks of hard-boiled egg whites (he left out the yokes so my cholesterol levels wouldn't rise), and tasty Genoa salami. I'm salivating right now as I remember that wonderful meal.

I consider Father Joe my private chaplain. He is and continues to be a spiritual inspiration for me and a few of my friends and associates. Did you ever meet someone who lifts your spirits by just being there? Father Joe is also the kind of guy who combines his brilliant academic background with street smarts. You shake hands with him and you feel as if you have been to confession, and right afterward you sip a glass of good Italian wine with him and ask him, "What are you cooking today?"

Not too long ago, Father Joe started a food company. It's called "Father Orsini's Italian Specialties." He asked me to be a member of his company's board of directors. I hesitated because I'm involoved in so many things. Then I found out that Father Joe has dedicated all of his *personal* income from his books and the food company to charities, especially to the nuns of the saintly Mother Teresa of Calcutta's order of Sisters. I couldn't refuse to be a part of that kind of enterprise. I told you this is one sharp guy. And what a cook! He was taught how to cook by his beloved Mamma. On one of my *Live with Regis and Kathie Lee* shows, I asked him how he got started in cooking. He told me that once his mother realized that he was serious about becoming a priest, she marched him into the kitchen, put an apron on him, and taught him how to cook. "After all" she said, "you won't have a wife to cook for you, so just watch me and do what I do." So from his Italian mom, he learned the basics of Italian cooking. Over the years, he perfected his cooking skills by countless research trips to Italy.

Now, not only does Father Joe know how to cook, he knows the food and where it came from. In the first chapter of this book, I was astonished to learn about the American roots of Italian cooking. When another Italian, Christopher Columbus, made his historic discovery of the New World, he opened the way for Native American foodstuffs to change the cuisines of the Old World. Father Joe tells us, "Columbus could have made a fortune in Italy had he been able to patent or register the culinary innovations that he introduced into his native country. The new American foods he brought back were rapidly fused with ancient culinary practices and traditions and are still an essential part of the Italian diet and can be found all over the world." The most important foods from the Americas that have been Italianized are tomatoes, potatoes, numerous varieties of beans, new kinds of squashes, corn, sweet and hot peppers, turkey, and chocolate.

In his book Father Joe documents the fact that pasta was being made and used in Italy long before Marco Polo brought back noodles to Venice from his voyage to China. He tells us about the "marriage" of pasta with tomatoes that probably took place in Sicily, the invention of the pasta fork, the history of olive oil, Italian wines, and a detailed, almost poetic explanation of the most important Italian cheeses. And that just scratches the surface of this fascinating and informative cookbook.

Not only do you get great Italian recipes, but the anecdotes and true stories that introduce most of the recipes will make you chuckle and ponder. Father Joe writes in such a way that you can almost picture many of the people he has met during his lifetime. He slowly introduces you to the uniquely Italian style of human relationships. First you become friends, then *compare* and *compari* (God-parents), and finally members of the extended family. And the sharing of good food and wine is the cement that holds everything together.

Father Joe also recounts some poignant memories of the past, but he doesn't get stuck there. He has an entire chapter of recipes that make terrific use of microwave ovens to help us in our fast-paced modern lives.

Can a cookbook make you feel better? This one can and will. In his epilogue Father Joe tells us, "My first loves are God, my mother and then Italy and its cuisines. I guess it's because I'm Italian." *Italian Family Cooking* makes you part of Father Joe's family. It may be the best thing that ever happened to you. As father Joe often says, "I wish you good food, warm friends, and a long life!"

—REGIS PHILBIN

Italian Family Cooking

Introduction

At the end of this second millennium, there are some who fear that the beginning of the third will find us unprepared for the future. I count myself in that number. It is my firm conviction that unless we have been securely anchored in the values and belief systems generated by our ancestors, we will wander adrift into the future like unfortunate astronauts floating off into the darkness of infinite space, directionless and lost, because the tethers to the mother ship have been irreparably cut.

I originally titled this book *Nourishment for the Body and the Spirit: Italian Recipes and Reflections*. This is not an ordinary generic cookbook and should not be treated as such. Yes, the recipes are uniquely good, but unless the meals prepared from them are shared as vehicles of communication with significant others, the food simply feeds the Body and ignores the needs of the soul. Without food, the Body suffers. In the same way, if the *implied purpose* of food as an occasion for sharing sustenance and bolstering community is ignored, then the soul suffers. Both the Body and the Spirit need nourishment so we can accomplish our goal as members of the human family. That objective or purpose has been clearly described by all of the world's philosophies and religions: to acknowledge one another as brothers and sisters striving together to create an open and tolerant society despite our cultural, ethnic, religious, philosophical, and political differences.

Claude Levy-Strauss, a famous French anthropologist, wrote that eating habits are the most abiding characteristic traits of a culture. Italian emigrants frequently forget the Italian language, but they never forget how to cook Italian foods. Since I have not included any recipes for bread in this book, I highly recommend Carol Field's book, *The Italian Baker* (New York: Harper & Row, 1985.) Carol's book has become my bread baking bible. But I must say something about bread because it has great significance in all cultures and religions. Italians still use the expression "as good as bread," to describe a person who leads an exemplary life. As I celebrate Mass each day, the simple unleavened bread becomes the very Body of Jesus Christ.

In England, where they still use the titles "Lord" and "Lady," the aristocrats would be surprised to know the origins of their titles. "Lord" comes from *loaf-ward,* which meant "bread guardian" while "Lady" comes from *load-dyghe,* which meant "she who bakes the bread." This is noble recognition of those of our ancestors who gave us bread.

None of us should be too impressed with our various titles because true nobility is evidenced in how we treat one another. The material food we share with others becomes food for the Spirit when we prepare and serve it with love and respect.

In this book I have attempted to share my personal experiences and reflections of the Italian family and food and to make them as delicious and memorable as my recipes. During the years I have shared good food and fellowship with my Italian and American family and friends, I have discovered an important cultural phenomenon: the kitchen is the focal point for the creation of community and for the strengthening of family bonds.

Bountiful and good, food is the essence of fond and enduring memories. "This smells and tastes just like what Grandma and Mamma used to make! Wow, it makes me remember the time when we were crowded around the kitchen table and Uncle Tony fell off his chair. His wig came flying off and landed right on top of the pasta! We didn't want to laugh and make Uncle Tony feel bad, but when he retrieved the wig and plopped it on his head with sauce running down his white shirt, we all lost it! Even Uncle Tony said, 'My wig never smelled better.'"

Yes, our ethnic foods help us remember who we are and from whence we originated. Certain foods remind us of meager times, such as polenta (cornmeal mush) when money was scarce, or sumptuous lasagna when Papa got a raise. Whatever the economic conditions of the time and the food we could afford, that strong sense of family love, loyalty, and strength was ever present.

In the Italian tradition, families are noted for their conspicuous allegiance to their immediate and extended members. Even in the modern Italian-American family there exists a strict order of the family. This "order of the family" views the family unit as central to the life of each individual and is characterized by a complex structure of rules regarding the roles of each member. Also involved in this concept of family life are traditional ideas of family honor, pragmatic attitudes toward sex and religion, and special respect for food as the host of life.

When I was a child, food was symbolic in a concrete way of the love my family had for me. It was the product of the hard hours of labor of my father and brothers, and it was prepared for us with care by my mother assisted by my sister. It was, in a very emotional sense, a connection with my parents and symbolized their outreach to their children. In a very poignant way, meals were a holy communion of the family, and food was sacred because it was a means of that communion. I believe that this attitude toward food and meals is characteristically shared by most Italians and is one of the reasons why many consider the practice of saying a short prayer before meals to be superfluous. Since the food comes from God, it is already blessed; why bless it again?

True, these values had their origins in times that were far less rushed and hectic than ours. But they are values well worth reestablishing since they represent a positive and stabilizing influence in our rapidly changing world.

This book is full of Italian family treasures; recipes handed down from generation to generation. I welcome you into the treasury and invite you to partake of the priceless jewels and gold of these valuable recipes. Mothers and grandmothers are repositories of wisdom gained through experience. This book was written to ensure that their cooking expertise would be captured in a written record. No one could cook like Mamma and Grandma, they had a special touch; but these recipes capture the essence of their cooking. That special touch will develop in your own kitchen with the passage of time, and your mom and grandmom will smile down upon you from the heights of paradise. They will whisper to your soul, "That's it, you've got it right. Now, you cook just like us!" Someday your grandchildren will taste your recipes and say, "You cook just like Mom and Grandma used to!"

A NOTE ABOUT FAT AND CHOLESTEROL

The medical community wisely warns us about our intake of fat and cholesterol. My dear friend Regis Philbin has been named spokesperson for The American Heart Association. When he consented to write the foreword to this book, he asked how my recipes could be adjusted to comply with the dietary recommendations of The Heart Association.

It is rather simple. When a recipe calls for butter, use olive oil instead; many nutritionists tell us that olive oil actually lowers cholesterol levels. Instead of cream, use evaporated skim milk. Instead of sour cream, use nonfat plain yogurt. They both have the tartness you want in your recipes. Always use cheeses that are naturally made because the natural enzymes neutralize the cholesterol.

Instead of whole eggs, use just the egg whites—and add a few drops of natural yellow food coloring if you like. Many manufacturers of egg substitutes do exactly the same thing and charge you exorbitantly for their products.

Armed with this knowledge, let us now venture into the world of Italian cooking and nourish our bodies and spirits.

Italian Cuisine After the Voyages of Columbus

The information contained in this chapter may astonish and enlighten the reader. Foods and their preparations are an integral part of any nation's history. Although most history books talk about wars, treaties, and political and socioeconomic factors that shape our world, I believe that food history is as fundamentally important to the story of the progress of humankind as is the record of our diversified evolution. Foods and the way they are consumed are clear indicators of the direction our societies are taking. For example, what does America's penchant for fast food emporiums really say about us? Is it not symptomatic of the disintegration of the nuclear family?

I don't intend to defend the Italian character of Christopher Columbus just because he was a native of Genoa, but facts are facts; he was the first Italian-American. People tend to forget this since he sailed under the sponsorship of Ferdinand and Isabella of Spain. At the end of the fifteenth century, Italy understood as a geographic and ethnological entity was excluded from the great power game of Europe and remained so for

centuries. It was relegated to the sidelines, an observer of events occurring around it. But a people with such a rich history and culture, that had developed over the many thousands of years the region had been a nexus of trade routes and communications, could not accept the passive role of spectator. Italy's art, architecture, music, and cuisines exerted a subtle but active role in the development of Western Civilization. It continues to give to the western world the ideals of family, stability, loyalty, honor, friendship, and rational gentility as the way to achieve our fullest potential.

When Columbus set out on his first voyage, he loaded his caravels with substantial quantities of extra-virgin olive oil. He allotted a daily ration of about one cup of oil for each member of the crew. When they reached the new world they combined olive oil with tomatoes, peppers, and green beans. This was a gastronomic event of universal magnitude; the crossing of a new frontier in nutrition comparable in its effects only to the 20th Century introduction of refrigeration in ordinary households.

Christopher Columbus returned to Europe from his epic voyage in 1493 with the ingredients of a new cuisine such as peppers and squashes that would revolutionize the Old World's eating habits and vastly improve the healthfulness of its diet. Columbus could have made his fortune in Italy had he been able to patent or register the culinary innovations he either introduced or opened the doors for others to introduce into his native country. The new American foods he brought back were rapidly fused with ancient culinary practices and traditions. They are still an essential part of the Italian diet and are now found all over the world.

When you examine the historical documents of the centuries following the first voyages to the New World, you discover that the Italians immediately integrated the new foods (except the tomato) into their dietary arsenal, while the other countries of Europe assigned the new foods an independent position in their cuisines. Such was the case with the potato, which entered Northern Italy in the knapsacks of Napoleon's troops and was immediately converted into gnocchi. In the same way, corn, which was introduced into the Kingdom of Naples by the Spanish and transplanted to the Veneto through the enterprise of Venetian merchants, was soon being ground up to produce polenta.

When it was finally accepted, the tomato quickly changed its appearance and color to become a sauce combined with other foods to create new dishes. The creative breakthrough was due to the encounter between the new foods and the existing Italian cuisine of that period.

Pasta, a culinary invention uniquely Italian and eaten for centuries since the time of the Etruscans (B.C.), seemed to be waiting for a catalyst to achieve its full potential. Until the first century, poor Italians ate pasta because of its long storage capacity and its outstanding nutritional value. It was customarily boiled and eaten plain or flavored with a bit of grated cheese. Vermicelli, thin strands of pasta, were clutched in the hand and lifted to the mouth. It was only when it became combined with tomato that pasta became a "dish" even the wealthy would eat.

The addition of tomato sauce made pasta a messy dish to eat with the hands so the Italians invented the pasta fork. The fork had been around for several centuries, but now it became an everyday utensil. The new fork had four curved tines, the length of which was not more than twice its combined width. Pasta joined with tomato sauce soon was combined with every available food product and the Italians entered into an orgy of innovation.

Although it might seem banal, the new Italy was fundamentally created in the field and gardens growing the New World foods, not by political revolution. Regional Italian cuisines derived from New World foods were symbols and syntheses of Italy's important contribution to the world's desire for peace, family stability, and healthy nutrition.

THE TOMATO

The tomato is perhaps the most emblematic of the foods characteristically associated with Italian cuisine. Anyone who has come into contact with Italy's gastronomy is convinced that the tomato is a fundamental and necessary element of it. In reality, the tomato's entry into the Italian kitchen occurred relatively recently, as did its "wedding" with pasta. The 150th anniversary of that marriage was celebrated only a few years ago, *in 1989.*

The path along which the tomato made its way to Italy was a long one that began in a vast area in South America, in what are now the countries of Peru, Ecuador, and Bolivia, where the original species grows wild. After its domestication, the tomato was cultivated in pre-Columbian times in an extensive area that included Mexico and Central America. The Spanish brought it to Sicily when they conquered and ruled the island.

The first written acknowledgment of the plant's existence was provided by Bernardine de Shagún, who mentioned it as an ingredient of a sauce that was sold in the huge market at Tenochtitlan (Mexico City) by women vendors who "usually blended it in the following manner: aji (hot red pepper), pepitas (pumpkin seed), tomatl (tomato), and chilies verdes (hot green peppers) and other things that make the juice highly savory."

From Shagún's mention it took more than a century and the ingenuity of Southern Italians, stimulated by chronic famine, to bring the tomato and pasta together. Who took the fateful step is impossible to say; but it seems that some teamsters in Trapani (Sicily) were the first to do so and were soon emulated by the poor of Western Sicily. They started the practice of adding a substantial amount of tomato slices to the water in which they cooked their pasta.

In the region of Campania, the adopted homeland of *pummarola,* or tomato sauce, cultivation of tomatoes on a large scale was late in getting started, despite the fact that the plant was grown there as early as 1596.

A botanist from Sienna, Pietro Andrea Mattioli (1500–1570), was the first in Italy to call the tomato by the name still used there today, *pomo d'oro* (golden apple). He was referring to the color that the tomato assumes during maturation. While the Italians refer to the fruit (yes, it is a fruit) as a *pomodoro,* the French, English, Spanish, and Germans continue to use terms directly derived from the name the Nahuatl Indians of Mexico gave it, *tomatl.*

In 1705, Francesco Gaudentio, in charge of buying provisions for the Jesuits in Rome, provided the first written Italian recipe for cooked tomatoes. Credit for being the first person in Italy to publish a recipe for the tomato goes to Vincenzo Corrado in the eighteenth century, in his republication of Aspicius' *De Re Coquinaria.* The first recorded recipe for pasta with tomato sauce was written by Ippolito Cavalcanti in 1839, in his book *Home Cooking in the Neapolitan Dialect.*

This brief history of the tomato in Italy shows how long it took for the fruit to become an ingredient in daily cooking. It became a common food only in the nineteenth century, when industrial canning of tomatoes began. However, we must note that the first mass production of bottled tomato sauce was by a North American, William Underwood of Boston in 1835.

Tomato sauce, now a standard addition to innumerable culinary preparations, is a fundamental element of Italian cooking, since it can be combined with almost any other food, including vegetable, fish, eggs, meat, and of course, pasta, as you will clearly see in a majority of recipes in this book. No other cuisine uses the tomato as much as Italian cooking. The tomato is the "king" of ingredients in all of Italy.

THE POTATO

The potato originated in the Andes Mountains and was domesticated by the native peoples, who were adept at growing crops at high altitudes, building terraces, and using irrigation as part of their farming techniques. The potato formed the dietary base of Peruvians and Chileans.

Once the potato crossed the Atlantic it assumed a European dimension and continues to play an important role in the cuisines of many countries. However, the Italians can claim to have introduced the tuber into their gastronomy in the most creative ways, all the while transforming the potato while integrating it with other ingredients to establish a family of extraordinary preparations, ranging from gnocchi (pasta dumplings) to crocchette (croquettes), tortini (thick, flat omelets), and sformati (molded dishes).

The potato was not one of the foods Columbus discovered and took back to Europe; he had encountered only the yam or sweet potato. The ordinary potato came to the attention of the Conquistadors in Peru and subsequently was taken to Mexico; it was later transported to North America to what became the colony and state of Virginia.

The first authentic scientific description of the potato has been credited to Dutch botanist Charles de Lecluse, who is better known by the name Clusius. While he resided in Vienna in 1588, he received two tubers from the governor of Mons in what is modern Belgium. The gift was accompanied by a watercolor, the first official drawing of the potato which is now part of the collection of the Plantin Museum Antwerp. Clusius tasted the tubers and found that they had an agreeable flavor that was close to the taste of turnips. His detailed description was published in the *Raziorum Plantorum Historia.*

In Ireland, although the potato resolved severe dietary problems, it also contributed to a substantial increase in the population leading many to believe the tuber to be some sort of fertility drug. In 1845, the potato crop in Ireland and other European countries failed because of blight and a severe famine ensued. Hundreds of thousands of people were forced to emigrate to the New World, North America in particular. Irish immigrants inundated New York City, which owed much of its growth in the nineteenth century to the potato famine.

In 1771, a contest aimed at identifying a food that could replace grains in the daily diet was announced in France. A military pharmacist and agronomist, Augustin Parmentier (1737–1813), won the prize by suggesting the *pomme de terre* (earth apple or potato). During the Seven Years' War (1756–1763), he had been held prisoner by the Prussians, which gave him an opportunity to test—the first Frenchman to do so—the dietary virtues of the potato. Frederick the Great of Prussia had succeeded in introducing *Kartoffeln* (potatoes) to the rations of his troops and his prisoners of war. (It was believed that the potato was a kind of truffle since it grew underground, hence the name *Kartoffeln*—truffle mushroom.)

Louis XVI of France enthusiastically supported Parmentier's experiments putting the Royal Botanical Gardens at his disposal. The king also began wearing a waistcoat decorated with the attractive bluish-white flower of the potato.

The French Revolution definitively established the potato as an important element of the daily diet. As Parmentier continued to play a leading role in that process, his services saved him from the guillotine; he went on to suggest how the potato could be used in soups and garnishes. He repeatedly urged that potato starch be substituted for wheat in bread making. His name has been inseparably linked to *soupe Parmentier,* made from potatoes, leeks, fresh cream, chervil, and seasonings.

The potato arrived in Italy around 1560. Its cultivation began to spread in Italy toward the end of the 18th century. Vincenzo Corrado, a Celestinian monk who was a well-known gourmet writer in the eighteenth century, wrote a "Treatise on Potatoes" in the fifth edition of his cookbook, *Il Cuoco Galante,* published in 1801, and included recipes for potato mush (similar to polenta), creamed potatoes, potatoes *in polpette* (balls) and *in bigne* (fritters), and potatoes roasted and stuffed with butter.

The region of Liguria can be described as the first and most enthusiastic Italian adoptive parent of the potato, but as usual each region of Italy adopted the potato into its own cuisine, creating recipes that reflect an uncommon gift of inventiveness.

The uses to which potatoes are put in Italian cuisine are so varied and special that close attention must be paid to the correct type of potato to use. Potatoes are divided into two principal groups on the basis of the color and texture of the pulp—yellow and white. Both are excellent and have the same nutritional value.

BEANS

The most common and widely consumed types of beans in Italian cuisine originated in tropical and subtropical America. They were introduced into Europe in the sixteenth century under the name *Phaseolus vulgaris* The ancient Greeks and Romans were acquainted with a phaseolus, but it belonged to a different species, the African *Vigna sinensis.* In Italy, *Vigna sinensis* is called the *fagiolo dall'occhio* or "bean with an eye," because of a black streak circling the hilum or point of attachment to the pod while in the United States, it is called the black-eyed pea or cowpea.

Numerous varieties of beans are cultivated today, because the plant constantly produces genetic variations, making it eminently suited to crossbreeding. The chemical composition of beans is extremely complex and closer to meat than any other plant. The bean is rich in protein, carbohydrates and mineral salts, and is almost fat free. From a dietary standpoint, a distinction must be made between the fresh green bean and the mature dry bean. The fresh bean is eaten along with the pod; the dry must be soaked in water overnight and then cooked.

The first Italian expert to provide information about the bean was the botanist Pietro Andrea Mattioli, who observed that "when eaten, they bloat the stomach but they generate virile seed and encourage sexual intercourse and even more if they are eaten with hot fresh or dried pepper."

An extensive account of the bean in a letter to the Duke of Mantova was written by Lodovico Castelvetro (1505–1574), who first described the botanical and gastronomical aspects of the legume, then added an amusing nonculinary use of the bean. "I have dealt fully with fresh and dried fava beans. Now I must deal with the beans from the New World. . . . Because the plant bears fine green leaves, the ladies in Italy and especially those of Venice, who like to tarry in the shade amid the greenery and who, even more enjoy watching passersby from their windows without being seen, are accustomed to putting on the windowsills of their bedrooms wooden flower boxes as long as the windows are wide. In them, they plant 10 or 12 of these beans. Then, using white sticks, they form a sort of grate to which the plants cling so that the window is well shaded."

Almost two centuries later, in 1781, Vincenzo Corrado wrote that "beans are of various colors and shapes," and added with a touch of humor, "if you want to know whether beans make tasty food, you should ask the people of Tuscany, since more than all others they make great use of them at all times and particularly the dried white types." Even in today's Italy, the people from Tuscany are called "mangiafagioli" (bean eaters).

Beans are no less popular in Italy today, which is confirmed by the existence of numerous regional recipes involving beans. Many of these dishes go back two centuries and are still prepared and eaten the same way they were two hundred years ago.

In Piedmont, for example, beans figure in the *paniscia novarese* (rice with salami, beans, and various vegetables), the *panissa vercellese* (beans and rice with pork), the *fagiolata con le cotiche* (beans with pork rind), the *tofeja canavesana* (a rich baked dish of beans, pork, and vegetables) and the *tajarin e fasoi* (noodles and beans). The people of Lombardy have *ris rosti* (rice, beans, Parmesan cheese, fatty bacon, chicken broth, and red wine). In the Veneto there is *faizioli sofegai* (beans with peverada [green bell pepper pesto] sauce in chicken broth). No less traditional are the *jota* (bean, cabbage, pork, and corn meal soup) of Trieste and the *fagioli col muset* (beans and fresh pork sausage) of Friuli.

Ligurians enjoy a *minestra di magro* (vegetarian bean soup), while the Emilians dote on *fagioli maritati* (a bean, tomato, and cheese soup), *pisarei e faso* (pasta with beans and tomato sauce), and *cazzagai* (beans cooked with tomatoes and served with polenta).

The Tuscans, as Corrado remarked, are extremely fond of beans. Among their dishes are *bordatino livornese* (a soup with pureed beans, black cabbage, and other vegetables thickened with cornmeal), beans *in fiasco* (beans cooked in the traditional round-bottomed, straw-wrapped Chianti wine bottle), and *all'uccelletto* (beans cooked with tomato). Lazio has its pasta and beans but also its *fagioli al corallo* (beans in tomato sauce). In Campania, beans are often combined with pasta or *alla maruzzara* (fresh beans cooked with tomatoes and poured over thick slices of oven-toasted bread). Basilicata is known for its *legane e fagioli* (wide noodles and beans), while Sardinia features *fagioli alla gallurese* (beans cooked with tomato paste, wild fennel, and black cabbage).

Vincenzo Corrado was, again, the first to give Italian recipes for beans, in his cookbook *Il Cuoco Galante.* Here follows one of his recipes, "Fagioli in Pottaggio da Grasso, 1781:

> Beans, whether large and white or small cowpeas, are cooked in fresh water, which should be changed after they have boiled for a time. The dish is finished with salt, pepper, slices of ham, chopped celery, parsley, whole hot peppers, and meat sauce. When the dish has cooked, remove the peppers and serve.

We should probably note that Italian recipe compilers both ancient and modern, make certain assumptions about their readers. They often do not explain basic procedures or specify an exact measurement for particular ingredients. They share with their readers an ancient culinary tradition. Prolonged acquaintance with that culture has made the preparation of numerous dishes so obvious that any detailed explanation is considered unnecessary and superfluous by both parties.

SQUASHES

The introduction of the New World's squashes caused less of a stir in Europe than the other unfamiliar vegetables from the Americas because some of their relatives had already been cultivated and consumed in Europe for centuries. However, the new squashes were more attractive and much tastier, among which were pumpkins and green and yellow summer squash.

Both the "old" and the "new" squashes belong to the gourd family (Cucurbitaceae). Most, if not all, of the Old World varieties belong to the genus *Lagenaria* and are true gourds. They originated in India and were brought to Europe in remote ages before the rise of the Roman Empire. Europeans ate the pulp of some species while they dried others and used them as containers. The new varieties of the genus *Cucurbita* brought to Europe from the New World are now grown and eaten throughout the continent.

The scientific nomenclature may be admirably precise, but there is much confusion in the vernacular. In Italian, for example, the word *zucca* usually means pumpkins and other squashes, although it can also mean gourds (inedible). However, just gourds are meant when the word *zucca* appears in documents that predate the New World. The diminutive *zucchini* refers specifically to green summer squash. In the United States, *squash* is the term widely used for members of the *Cucurbita* group, except for gourds and cucumbers. The word is derived from the Narraganset Indians' word for the vegetables, *askutasquash.* Americans use the Italian word *zucchini* to refer to green squash. In Britain, squashes, principally zucchini, are called marrows.

We must note that the exact origin of the pumpkin and some other so-called New World squashes is much disputed. Some experts say Europe acquired them thousands of years ago from Asia; others insist that they originated in the Americas. The ancient Romans were certainly familiar with the gourd. It was regarded as a food for the poor and the Latin poet Virgil observed that the "lowly gourd rested heavy on the stomach." Apicius, the writer of the first cookbook in Europe, who lived in ancient Rome, gave nine recipes for gourds.

Pumpkin and zucchini only entered Italian cooking after the seeds of Cucurbitaceae were brought to Europe from the New World and Italians planted them in their gardens. In the sixteenth century, botanist Pietro Andrea Mattioli observed in reference to pumpkin that "it is the practice to eat it either boiled or fried in the pan or roasted. Boiled, it is almost tasteless. When roasted or fried it releases a great deal of moisture. Nonetheless, because of its natural water, it should be eaten with oregano."

In his *Economia del Cittadino in Villa,* published in 1644, Vincenzo Tanara talks about "white or long squashes, called cucuzze in Rome," which because they require "a lot of sun and a great deal of water, are not much consumed in our area [Emilia-Romagna]. In Rome, these white *cucuzze* are forced to grow to an unusual length and to remain thin by having pots of water placed under them. They are attracted by the water and grow toward it, stretching out in the process. Once they have been peeled, the cucuzze are cut in slices, fried in oil and served with lemon juice." Tanara notes there are two New World types of squashes, those with yellow and those with white rinds.

In virtually the same period, Lodovico Castelvetro gave numerous recipes for the use of New World squashes in Italian cooking. A century later, in the 1700s, zucchini was praised by Vincenzo Corrado in his treatise *Cibo Pitagorico.* "Italians not only use the fruit of the Plants, but also use their flowers (fiori di zucca) by stuffing

them with mozzarella cheese; dipping them in batter and frying them."

CORN

Corn or maize was domesticated and cultivated in two primary areas of the New World, one to the north of the equator, which included Mexico, Central America, Colombia, and Venezuela, and the second to the south, including Ecuador, Peru, Bolivia, Chile, and Brazil.

Corn was already extensively grown by the natives of the New World when Christopher Columbus first reached its shores. The cultivation of corn was of primary importance to the daily diet of the Native Americans, of both North and South America who used it primarily as a sort of bread, the *tortilla,* made exclusively by the women of the tribes. The Spanish encountered corn as they penetrated every part of Central America and especially Mexico, where it was made into tortillas, flavored with meat sauce or honey, and sold in the market of the capital.

Columbus took the seeds back to Spain at the conclusion of his first voyage in 1493. It took many decades for the plant to become widely diffused in Europe. The cultivation of corn was begun in Europe around 1520. Initially the plant was grown in the Spanish regions of Andalusia, Galicia, and Catalonia, then it was brought into southwestern France. Soon farmers throughout the Mediterranean Basin grew it, and with the growth of trade it spread to Africa and Asia, introduced by the Portuguese through their colonies and trading posts. Corn adapted rapidly in all these places because of the ease with which it spontaneously develops hybrids, and its pronounced genetic variability.

In Italy, corn was brought into the region of the Veneto around 1530. It was highly successful there and by the beginning of the seventeenth century it was also grown in the Friuli region and the delta of the Po River. It also reached Naples, a possession of Spain at the time.

The first to record the appearance of corn in Italy was sixteenth-century botanist Pietro Andrea Mattioli, who firmly insisted that corn did not originate in Asia. In 1580, Costanzo Felici of Romagna told his readers that "this Indian cereal, which is improperly called *granoturco* [Turkish wheat], is appreciated in our lands, and used to make a rather white and sweet bread."

Corn became a culinary fixture, along with rice and potatoes, in the north of Italy. Extensively consumed by the peasants since they were poor and primarily concerned with avoiding starvation, corn became the mainstay of their diet.

Although less appreciated than wheat, corn steadily spread to new agricultural areas on the Italian peninsula and acquired different names from place to place. The most popular name remained *granoturco,* but the Turks, who knew very well that they had nothing to do with the domestication of this grain, called corn *grano di Rum* (Roman wheat).

In the United States, the grain is always called corn. Britain calls it maize. Maize is the grain's proper name in all European languages. In Italian this is *mais.* The word is derived from the Spanish *maíz,* taken from the *mahiz* of the Taino Indians of the Caribbean.

Beans, another plant native to the Americas, and corn spread throughout Italy at the same time. When the Council of Trent (1545–1563) emphasized strict observance of abstinence from meat on Fridays and during Lent, beans and corn supplied the vital proteins contained in the forbidden meat.

In Northern Italy corn was ground into meal and revolutionized the ancient Italian preparation of polenta. Polenta, or grain mush, goes as far back in history as the Roman Republic, when it was the diet of the poor, who made the mush out of other grains such as millet, sorghum barley, and buckwheat. *Polenta di mais,* cornmeal mush, replaced all other grains and fed generations of poor working people. It was used as a substitute for bread and pasta, because bread and pasta were too expensive for the poor. But polenta was not a real blessing for the poor. It is deficient in certain vitamins and so the health of the poor deteriorated. The disease pellagra became common in Northern Italy.

Meanwhile, in southern Italy, from Naples on down, pasta—or "macaroni," as they say in Naples—had become the most important dish by the end of the eighteenth century.

Nevertheless, almost every region of Italy invented interesting polenta recipes. The Neapolitans created *polenta pasticciata* (baked layered cornmeal mush with meat sauce, olive oil, and cheese) and *polenta cunscia* (boiled mush enriched with garlic and butter). The Lombardy region invented *pasticcio di polenta* (cornmeal tart filled with pigeon, veal, or chicken, cooked ham, Parmesan cheese, and porcini mushrooms). The Veneto came up with *polenta e osei* (small birds served atop cornmeal mush). Calabria invented *polenta di carne di maiale salata* (cornmeal mush with salted pork).

Following a period of decline, polenta has once again returned to tables all over Italy and gained snob appeal. This has also happened in Italian restaurants in the United States—suddenly polenta is chic and trendy. But please don't pay premium prices for good ordinary and inexpensive food.

The traditional method of cooking polenta is time-consuming and hard work for it must be constantly stirred for almost an hour. Today, Italian companies like Beretta export to the United States instant polenta, which cooks in 5 to 6 minutes. Although of finer consistency than traditional polenta, I find it very satisfactory.

SWEET AND HOT PEPPERS

Chili peppers and capsicum are believed to have originated in the tropical regions of Central or South America, most probably in what is now Brazil. Uncertainty on that point is due to the fact that both have been widely consumed for thousands of years in extensive areas of the New World. Pepper seeds have been found in ancient Peruvian tombs, particularly in the vicinity of Lima. Other discoveries, along Mexico's Gulf coast, as well as historical sources further confirm that peppers were a common food of the Olmec Indians, whose civilization reached its zenith between the fifth and first centuries B.C.

The discovery of peppers and their subsequent introduction into Europe was, in fact, closely linked to one of the principal objectives of the expedition led by Christopher Columbus: obtaining direct access to spices. As a consequence, Columbus had hardly set foot on the soil of the New World when he diligently made inquiries about every thing he saw that appeared suitable to be a condiment. On Haiti Columbus concluded that he had found a new type of pepper. "Theirs [the Indians'] is of finer quality than ours; no one eats a dish without seasoning it with this spice, which is believed to be beneficial to health," he wrote. "On this island alone, 50 caravels of this article could be loaded every year."

The peppers that were brought to Europe, like other solenaceous plants, including the tomato and the potato (all in the nightshade family), were fully domesticated and had been cultivated for centuries. They readily adapted to conditions in European countries as on other continents, including North America.

The ease with which they could be grown promoted their rapid diffusion. By the end of the nineteenth century and the beginning of the twentieth, botanists were listing nearly three hundred varieties. For new varieties, growers relied on spontaneous development of hybrids. Later, when genetic selection was done scientifically, the result was a substantial improvement of quality.

Vincenzo Corrado notes in the 1781 edition of his *Il Cuoco Galante* that "Although peppers are a rustic food of the poor masses, there are many who like them. . . . They are eaten when they are green, fried and salted or roasted over coals and flavored with salt and oil." Corrado's comment is virtually the only known reference to peppers between the fifteenth and eighteenth centuries.

It was the writer Giovanni Gherardini (1778–1861), annoyed at the lack of mention in the dictionaries, who first described the pepper: "A tube or conical berry, with a tough skin that is fine red or yellow in its maturity and bright green when it is immature." In respect to its culinary qualities, he said, "it has a piquant flavor almost like black pepper. But these are eaten raw, basted with oil, but, in addition, they are preserved in vinegar and are called *pepperoni acconciatti.*"

In traditional Italian cooking, peppers are more popular in the south where hot peppers are frequently used as a spice, and sweet peppers of various shapes and sizes are used in hundreds of recipes.

TURKEY

The turkey is a member of the Meleagridae family of birds and originated in the New World. It was found throughout North America as well as on the central plateau of Mexico, in the Yucatan Peninsula, and as far south as Guatemala. Two species existed at the time the Europeans first reached the Americas, the common turkey and the ocellated turkey (which has eye-shaped spots on its feathers.)

The Native Americans were well acquainted with the bird. They ate its meat and used its feathers as ornaments. There is documentary evidence that the Aztecs raised them and it is probable that other Indians did so as well.

Christopher Columbus made fleeting contact with the turkey along the coast of Honduras on his fourth voyage (1502–1504). However, the bird was only officially discovered by Europeans during the conquest of Mexico by Hernan Cortes. "They [the Indians] raise many hens that are like those of the mainland [Europe] and they are as big as peacocks," Cortes wrote in his *Cartas y Relaciones,* which was sent to Charles V, Holy Roman Emperor and King of Spain, and published at Zaragosa in 1522. But Cortes provides no information about *mole,* a dish made with turkey and powdered cocoa that is characteristically a feature of Central American cuisine.

The Spanish immediately learned to appreciate the turkey and imported it to Europe, although it is impossible to determine the exact date. The first turkeys known to the English appear to have been offered to Henry VII of England at the beginning of the sixteenth century. The "chicken of India" was being raised and eaten in England by at least 1525, brought by English merchants who traded with the Turkish Empire and India. The Italians were eating "rooster of India" by the middle of the sixteenth century. The first birds raised in continental Europe were served at the marriage of Charles IX of France in 1570. It seems probable that the birds reached the table of the French king by way of the Jesuit Residence in Bourges, where turkeys were first raised on a large scale in Europe. The Jesuits were largely responsible for establishing the bird's reputation in Europe. Their *coq d'Inde* (rooster of India) was widely referred to as *Jesuite* before it became known as *dindon* or *dinde.* The turkey made what seems to have been its debut in the art world in a still-life painting by the Dutch artist Joachim Beuckelaer (1530–1574), which is now owned by the Rijksmuseum in Amsterdam.

The original European names for the turkey are an example of the enduring fallout from the erroneous conclusion that the lands Columbus "discovered" were part of India. Columbus himself believed he had reached the Far East. In Germany, the bird is still known as *Calecutischberban* (Calcutta hen). However, the people of India, who knew very well that the bird was not native to their country, gave the turkey the name *mru*. The Spanish call the bird *pavo* (peacock) and the Italians now call it *tacchino,* which is believed to come from the French word *tache,* a stain or spot, because of the bird's mottled feathers.

It appears that the English were primarily responsible for launching the turkey on its extraordinary culinary career, for they soon adopted it as the traditional main course at Christmas dinner, a role it usurped from the goose. In the United States, of course, it is the main fare at Thanksgiving Day dinner as well.

In Italy, Bartolomeo Scappi included a recipe for "rooster of India" in the second volume of his recipe collection *Opera dell'Arte del Cucinare* published in 1570. Shortly afterward, Vincenzo Cervio, who was in the service of Cardinal Alessandro Farnese, described the turkey in his book *Il Trinciante* (The Carver), published in 1581, as "this bird of bone and meat and of the same goodness and prestige as the peacock, for which reason it should be carved in the same way."

In *L'Arte di Ben Cucinare,* published in 1662, Bartolomeo Stefani, cook to the Duke of Mantua, suggested a much speedier way of dealing with a turkey in the kitchen. "Cook those that are smaller and more tender on the spit, larded, so that they will satisfy every taste."

A couple of decades later, in 1684, Carlo Nascia, chief cook to Ranuccio II, Duke of Parma, Piacenza, and Castro, included about a dozen recipes for turkey in his *Li Quattro Banchetti Destinati per le Quattro Stagioni dell' Anno.* By that time, the turkey was called *tacchinotto* and held a firmly established place in Italian cooking.

CHOCOLATE

The cacao tree is tropical and originated in Central and South America. It is seldom found above the 20th parallel, and needs a hot and humid climate. By the time Columbus reached the New World, the cacao tree was flourishing throughout Central and South America.

A member of the Sterculiaceae family, the cacao tree grows to nineteen to twenty-six feet. The fruits are pods that weigh about seventeen to twenty-one ounces. Each contains about forty to fifty beans. There are two principal varieties, the highly valued Cacao Criollo of Venezuela and the bitter purple Cacao Calabacillo, found all over tropical South America.

The pre-Columbian peoples, especially the Mayans and the Aztecs, used the fruit of the tree as food and beverage. They also used the beans as money. In the reports that Cortes sent to Emperor Charles V, he wrote, "Cacao (cacap) is a fruit similar to the almond that the natives grind up to add to foods and make a beverage; they also use the beans as a means of exchange to buy necessities in their markets."

The Aztecs consumed cacao as a beverage by pounding the roasted beans in hot water. Sometimes they sweetened the drink with honey and thickened it with cornstarch. Cayenne pepper was often added to make the drink piquant. The beverage was called chocolate—a combination of two Aztec words: *choco* (cacao) and *latl* (water).

Columbus tasted chocolate on July 10, 1502, during his fourth voyage. This new and unusual food reached Europe in 1528, when Cortes sent some beans to Spain from Mexico. It was not immediately popular among the Spanish, even though Cortes wrote that "a cup of this precious beverage would put a man into condition to make a whole day's march without the need for other food."

The Catholic Church in Spain was suspicious of this new food and obstructed its diffusion, arguing that it was frivolous and could not be consumed during Lent and other days of fast. However, Cardinal Brancatio, who was a gourmet as well as a nonsuperstitious man, pronounced chocolate an essentially good beverage. With his endorsement, chocolate became the national drink of Spain.

Soon the product was used in other parts of Europe and as the demand for it rose, it became increasingly rare and costly, arousing the interest of Dutch and English smugglers. They soon engaged in a brisk trade of cacao and made substantial profits. Within two hundred years, all of Europe had acquired a taste for chocolate but it was very expensive; only the rich could afford it. It was used as a breakfast beverage.

It was not a good idea to indulge too heavily in chocolate in those days, because it was hard on the digestive system. Fifty percent of the cacao bean is fat and it took a long time for processors to find a way of separating the cocoa butter from the powdered chocolate. It was only in 1828 that a Dutchman, Van Hauten, was authorized to use a press to separate cocoa butter from powdered chocolate. Now it was possible to sell solid chocolate on a large scale.

Italy learned about cacao in 1600 in a report by the Florentine Francesco Carletti, who wrote: "We made port at San Jonat, 1,600 miles from Lima . . . a place where houses are occupied by Spaniards and where cacao grows, a widely celebrated fruit of great importance . . . its principal use is as a beverage."

Carletti may have been responsible for the fact that the Florentines were the first producers of chocolate in Italy. But it is clear that cacao arrived first to the Italian Peninsula in those regions under Spanish rule. However, Piedmont is the true homeland of Italian chocolate. Emanuele Filiberto, Duke of Savoy, built the first facilities for processing chocolate in Turin. Its production became Turin's leading industry. It was eventually decided to make this production a monopoly and on October 9, 1679, confectioner Giovanni Antonio Ari obtained exclusive authorization to sell chocolate beverages.

In the nineteenth century, Turin's chocolate was regarded as the best in Europe and the first modern chocolates were made at that time. A native of Turin invented a hydraulic device to refine and blend chocolate paste. In a further triumph, Turinese chocolate makers combined chocolate with hazelnuts, roasted and ground to powder, and *giandoujotto* was invented.

In Italy today, chocolates are works of art as well as popular candies exported all over the world.

Hints for the Italian Kitchen

In Italy, cooking is an art. The essence of food is the perfect blending of ingredients. Sauces, spices, and herbs play important roles. Olive oil must be of the highest quality and not overpower any recipe. The Italians are known for their use of pasta, rice, beans, and, of course, veal.

In Italy, shopping for food is a daily routine. The food is chosen with great care. Cooking is very important, but so is the serving of the meal. In an Italian meal, the portions are small, but they are expected to be done to perfection.

In the typical ordinary Italian meal, pasta, rice, or soup is served as a first course. Meat or fish will follow, accompanied by vegetables, and then a very simple salad is served with an olive oil and vinegar or lemon juice dressing. Fruit or dessert is then served and this is usually followed by a regional cheese, which ends the meal. Wine, of course, is the ordinary accompaniment to the meal.

Espresso coffee is sipped as an aid to digestion.

I have found over the years while visiting Italy that there is less and less a distinction among regional cuisines. What other country has a telephone service you can call for a daily recipe? Travel and easy transportation facilities have also brought foreign ingredients into the national cuisine. A good example is salmon, once thought to be exclusively a northern European ingredient, but now almost an everyday item in Italian cooking. The world has indeed grown smaller, and ingredients once thought of as exotic and foreign have become "Italianized."

In the United States, there are "Little Italies" in our more important cities. If you live in proximity to one of these Italian communities, you will have no problem finding what you need to cook in the Italian manner. However, if you live far away from Italian markets and delicatessens, don't despair: Listed below are companies that will ship you whatever you need:

Some Mail-Order Suppliers of Italian Products

BALDUCCI'S
424 Sixth Avenue
New York, New York 10011
Tel: 212-673-2600
Fax: 212-995-5065

DEAN & DELUCA'S
121 Prince Street
New York, NY 10012
Tel: 212-514-7775
Fax: 212-514-8785

MANGANARO'S
488 Ninth Avenue
New York, NY 10018
Tel: 212-563-5331
Fax: 212-239-8355

TODARO BROTHERS
557 Second Avenue
New York, NY 10016
Tel: 212-532-0633
Fax: 212-689-1679

Tips for Cooking Pasta

- Choose a large pan (I always use a 6-quart pot) and allow plenty of water, about 4 pints for 12 ounces of pasta. Add 1 level teaspoon salt per pint water.
- Wait for a full rolling boil before putting the pasta in the water. Add the pasta gradually, stirring a few times. If using long spaghetti or macaroni, coil it around inside the pan as it softens. Keep the water boiling and cook without a lid.
- *Do not overcook.* Pasta should be tender but firm to the teeth (al dente). Cooking times vary according to the type and size of the pasta. Note label recommendations and use the "bite" test.
- When the pasta is cooked to your liking, immediately remove it from the heat, drain thoroughly in a colander, turn into a heated dish, and toss with a little butter or olive oil. Serve immediately, with a previously prepared sauce.

Quantities

- For main dishes, allow about 3 ounces uncooked pasta per person.
- For soups, use 4 ounces uncooked pasta to 1-1/2 to 2 pints soup.
- On average, expect pasta to double its volume when cooked.

Please bear in mind that many of these recipes have been passed down from generation to generation, many of them simply by word of mouth or by simple imitation. You will notice that in many of the recipes, seasoning quantities are to your own taste. Since this is the case, I encourage you to experiment with quantities that you think are too much or too little. Remember, it is easier to add oil or seasoning than to subtract it. So be adventurous and add your own personal touches. I've done it countless times and countless ways. Who knows? You may create your own recipe. Isn't that how it's been done for centuries?

ESSENTIAL INGREDIENTS: WHAT I USE

BEANS 🐟 If you have the patience to soak dried beans overnight in cold water, buy Goya brand dried beans. They are more flavorful and taste fresh. I often use good canned cannellini (white kidney beans), red kidney beans, and ceci (chick peas) produced and sold by the Progresso Company. They are the next best beans compared to Goya dried beans.

CANNED TOMATOES 🐟 My own company's brand, Father Orsini's Italian Specialties, of imported Italian peeled tomatoes are grown in the rich volcanic soil of Southern Italy. They are the meatiest and best-tasting tomatoes in the world. La Valle imported peeled plum tomatoes are also very good. All the Redpack tomato products are excellent even though grown and packed in the United States.

CHEESES 🐟 When recipes call for grated cheese, buy the Parmesan (Parmiggiano-Reggiano—so marked) or Pecorino (made from sheep's milk and imported from Italy) by the wedge. It's much less expensive that way. Grate it freshly yourself. The remaining wedge of cheese should be wrapped in plastic wrap, put into a plastic bag and refrigerated until needed again. Grated Parmesan or Pecorino in jars or cartons quickly lose their wonderful flavor. Don't buy them.

HERBS 🐟 I either grow my own or buy the freshest available (in season) at my Italian produce market. Basil is paramount. It must be fresh. The dried stuff just isn't worth it unless you're caught in a blizzard and you haven't stocked your freezer with a bag full of your fresh summer harvest. Oregano, marjoram, thyme, and rosemary are superb when they are fresh, but the dried varieties are an acceptable substitute.

OLIVE OIL 🐟 Try to imagine the Italian kitchen without olive oil. You will have no success, none whatsoever.

Olive oil is basic to all that goes on in an Italian kitchen, and this seems to have been true since times prior to the Roman Empire. Olive oil has remained the most basic ingredient of importance in Italian cooking. The others are wine, pasta, fresh herbs, bread, and cheese.

The current interest in the healthfulness of the "Mediterranean Diet" stems from the fact that olive oil seems to be helpful in the prevention of heart problems and high levels of cholesterol in the circulatory system. Use animal fats such as butter, lard, cream, and milk sparingly. Statistically, southern Italians who use animal fats in small amounts, simply to flavor some recipes, have fifty percent less incidence of heart disease than their northern counterparts. And please don't make the mistake of using margarine instead of butter, because margarine, although cholesterol free, still contains 2.5 grams of saturated fat and 100 calories from fat per tablespoon. One tablespoon of butter also contains 100 calories from fat and if unsalted has no sodium whatsoever, while the same amount of ordinary margarine has 104 grams of sodium. Margarine, no matter the claims of its manufacturers, cannot compare to butter's rich flavor.

One tablespoon of olive oil contains 120 calories from fat that is polyunsaturated and monounsaturated which most scientific studies demonstrate actually lowers cholesterol levels in the blood. Out of the 14 grams of fat in one tablespoon of olive oil, the total amount of saturated fat is only 2 grams. Obviously, olive oil is much healthier to use in your cooking than either butter or margarine.

Olive trees go back to prehistoric times, and by 2500 B.C. they were quite common in Syria, Palestine, and Crete. When I had the privilege of visiting the garden of Gethsemani in Jerusalem, I was overwhelmed by the fact that Jesus of Nazareth spent the night among its olive trees before his arrest and execution, and these were the same olive trees that I saw and touched almost 2,000 years later.

The Greeks were great producers of olive oil and shipped it around the Mediterranean, and certainly into Rome. The Greeks planted thousands of olive trees in southern Italy, especially in the plains of modern day Rosarno in the province of Reggio Calabria. Even today, the most massive production of olives for olive oil takes place in Calabria. The olives are then either pressed for their oil in Calabria and transported to olive oil canners in northern Italy who add their own small percent of northern Italian olive oils to obtain their finished product or they buy the Calabrian olives and press the oil themselves, adding their own locally grown olives to lighten the oil's taste and viscosity.

When you buy olive oil, its acidity content should be no more than one percent.

As I noted before, the Greeks sold great quantities of their olive oil to Rome. And, as the Romans have always done, they picked up on a great idea and improved it. They invented the screw press for the production of olive oil and we have been using their pressing methods in one way or another ever since.

Today olive oil is more widely used in Italy for cooking and dining than all other vegetable oils or animal fats put together. The reason is simple. Olive oil is outrageously delicious and a boon to healthy eating. At my dinner table, I always have a cruet of extra-virgin olive oil for my guests to dip their crusty Italian bread into and to add to my hearty bean and lentil soups.

I had a meal at an inn high in the hills of Tuscany outside of Florence. I had visited the olive groves that shared their space with grapevines and I tasted the Tuscan air. The perfumes, the aromas in the air, were rich and heavy in the warm fall sun. Just as I reached a point of near intoxication, I entered a small restaurant called Ristorante Stendahl (the famous German author Stendahl spent his last years in the inn that contained this restaurant).

This inn has always used the finest olive oil in almost every dish. Tall decanters of this flavorful olive oil were on every table and you were expected to use it liberally on almost every course. The antipasto was a platter of cooked white cannellini beans which I seasoned with the olive oil and salt and pepper. This was accompanied by charcoal grilled Tuscan bread slices rubbed with fresh garlic and drizzled with olive oil—bruschetta. I could have stopped there, but out came a fresh tomato soup made with garlic, stale Tuscan bread and olive oil—Pappa al Pomodoro. The main course was perfectly grilled, tender veal chops and roasted rosemary potatoes, all drizzled with olive oil. I can't remember the dessert, but the crisp pastry dough was made with olive oil.

Some Americans would say, "Oh my God, so much oil!" But these Italians were healthy, hearty, and beautiful.

I went into the olive grove to taste the ancient fruit. I was shocked by its bitterness. I was then informed that when the olives are pressed, using the great granite wheels invented by the ancient Romans, the liquid that comes from the pressing is a mixture of oil and olive juice. It is the juice that is bitter, not the oil. They then use a centrifuge to separate the juice from the oil.

There are many grades of olive oils, but for the normal American household cook, there are only five you need to know:

Extra-Virgin: This is the best. It is cold pressed and has a very low acid content. It is also the most expensive. Best used to dress salads, soups, and antipasta. It is not a cooking oil.

Virgin: Lower priced and a little more acidity. May be used as one uses the extra-virgin, but also excellent for cooking.

Pure: This is generally a third pressing done under heat. It is great for pan or deep frying and for cooking.

Light: A new category that is a pure oil, light in flavor, but contains the same caloric content as those above.

Pomace: This comes from the last pressing under extreme heat and crushes the pits of the olives also. The oil is bitter and cloudy. It's the cheapest you can buy, but I recommend you avoid it entirely.

STORAGE ⁓ You will get a much better price if you buy the oil in a gallon or three-liter tin. Spoilage is no problem as long as you keep the container in a cool dark pantry. If you pour some into a cruet, the unused oil can be refrigerated. It will become cloudy and thick. Simply allow it to come to room temperature and it will clear up for use at table or cooking.

BAKING WITH OLIVE OIL

Butter or Margarine	*Olive Oil*
1 teaspoon	3/4 teaspoon
1 tablespoon	2 1/4 teaspoons
2 tablespoons	1 1/2 tablespoons
1/4 cup	3 tablespoons
1/3 cup	1/4 cup
1/2 cup	1/4 cup + 2 tablespoons
2/3 cup	1/2 cup
3/4 cup	1/2 cup + 1 tablespoon
1 cup	3/4 cup

When you use olive oil instead of butter or margarine, your cookies and pastries will be lighter and crisper and your cakes fluffier and much moister.

PASTA ⁓ There are good dried pastas imported from Italy. In my opinion, Barilla brand is the best. There are also good pastas made in the United States. Look at the first ingredient. If it says "made from hard Durham wheat semolina," then it's a good domestic pasta. For frozen pasta products, such as ravioli, manicotti, conchiglione (stuffed shells), cavatelli, gnocchi, and fettuccine, I recommend Father

Orsini's Italian Specialties brand. These premier frozen pastas are manufactured by the D'Orazio company of Bellmawr, New Jersey. I haven't found any other frozen pastas that can compare in quality to ours.

RICE ⟋ For traditional Italian risotti, there is no substitute for Arborio Italian imported rice. For all other rice dishes, I use Uncle Ben's Converted Rice.

STOCKS ⟋ If you haven't the time to make your own chicken, beef, or vegetable stocks, do what the Italians do. They use Knorr's dried stocks and reconstitute them in hot water. Stay away from bouillon cubes because they are very salty. I only use them when a particular recipe requires their use.

VEGETABLES ⟋ Buy your vegetables when they are in season. They will be at the peak of their freshness and flavor. For good salads, try to buy romaine lettuce, escarole, arugula, and if you are splurging, radicchio. Make it simple. Use virgin olive oil, good red wine vinegar, and a generous grating of genuine Parmigiano-Reggiano cheese or the zesty Pecorino Romano.

Common Ingredients and Terms in Italian Cooking

Al Burro   Dressed with butter

Al Dente   Not overcooked;
firm-textured pasta

Al Forno   Cooked in the oven

All 'Aceto   In vinegar

Alla Casalinga   Home style

Alla Marinara   Seaman style

Arrosto   Roast meat

Asparagi   Asparagus

Baccala   Dried salt cod

Basilico   Sweet basil

Bel Paese   Semi-soft mild cheese

Biscotto   Biscuit

Bistecca   Beefsteak

Braciolo   Meat for rolling and stuffing

Brodo   Broth

Caffe Latte   Coffee with milk

Caffe Espresso   Black "espresso" coffee

Cannelloni   Large round pasta often
served stuffed

Capperi   Capers

Carciofo   Artichoke

Cassata   Rich cake

Cavolfiore   Cauliflower

Cavolo   Cabbage

Cipolla   Onion

Coppa   Cup

Costoletta   Cutlet

Crudo   Raw or uncooked

Ditali   Short tubular pasta

Ditallini   A small variety of the above

Dolce   General term for dessert

Fagioli   Dried beans

Fagiolini   Fresh beans

Farina Bianca   White wheat flour

Fegato   Liver

Fettucine   Homemade narrow ribbon pasta

Filetto   Thin fillet of meat or fish

Finocchio   Fennel

Formaggio   Cheese

Frittata   Omelet

Frittelle   Pancakes; term also used for fritters

Fritto Misto   Mixture of fried foods

Frutti di Mare   Small shellfish

Funghi   Mushrooms

Gamberi   Shrimp

Gelato   Frozen—usually ice cream

Imbottiti   Stuffed

Involtini   Slice of meat stuffed and rolled

Insalata   Salad

Lasagne   Wide flat noodles

Latte   Milk

Lesso   Boiled

Limone   Lemon

Maccheroni   Macaroni; a generic term for all types of pasta

Maiale   Pork

Manzo   Beef

Melanzane   Eggplant

Minestra   Soup; also generic term for pasta or rice course

Minestrone   Thick vegetable soup

Mozzarella   A soft white unsalted cheese

Olio   Oil

Oliva   Olive

Origano   Herb used for flavoring: Oregano

Pane   Bread

Pane Abbrustolito   Toasted bread

Panna   Cream

Parmigiano   Hard cheese much used in Italian cookery: Parmesan

Pasta   Dough; generic term for all macaroni products

Pasta Asciutta   Pasta served with butter or a meatless sauce

Pasta in Brodo   Pasta cooked in broth and served as soup

Pasta secca   Eggless pasta

Pasta all'uovo   Egg pasta

Pasta verde   Green (spinach) pasta

Pasticceria   General term for pastry

Pastini   Small pasta shapes used in soup

Pecorino   Strong sheep's milk cheese

Peperone   Sweet peppers

Peperoncini   Small hot peppers

Pesce   Fish

Pignoli   Pine nuts

Polenta   Cornmeal mush

Pollo   Chicken

Polpette   Small meat balls

Polpettone   Large meat loaf

Pomodoro   Tomato

Prezzemolo   Parsley

Prosciutto   Ham

Provolone   A hard yellow cheese

Ravioli   Stuffed squares of pasta

Ricotta   Soft curd cheese, "pot cheese"

Rigatoni   Large grooved macaroni

Ripieno   Stuffed or stuffing

Riso   Rice

Risotto   Rice dish

Salsa   Sauce

Salsiccia   Generic term for sausage

Scaloppine   Thin small slices of veal

Scampi   Large shrimp

Sedano   Celery

Spaghetti   Long, thin varieties of pasta

Spinaci   Spinach

Spumante   Sparkling wine

Sugo   Sauce

Tagliatelle   Homemade ribbon pasta

Tonno   Tuna fish

Torrone   A type of nougat candy

Torta   Generic term for cake

Tortellini   A stuffed pasta

Trippa   Tripe

Uovo   Egg

Uva   Grapes

Verdure   Vegetables

Vermicelli   Very thin spaghetti

Vino   Wine

Vitello   Veal

Vongole   Clams

Ziti   Tubular-shaped pasta

Zucchini   Squash

Zuppa   Soup

Antipasti (Appetizers)

Appetizers are not usually on my family's menu. When we sit down to eat, we're so hungry that we don't need anything to stimulate our appetites. But on holidays or for special dinners, we do go the extra step and prepare appetizers for our guests. Of course, we enjoy them too.

Antipasto means "before the meal" and can be the first course of an Italian main meal. If the meal is going to be a heavy one, you can substitute an antipasto for the usual pasta or soup. There is a wonderful choice of unusual flavors and colorful dishes from which to choose. An antipasto can be very simple or as elaborate as you like, anything from a crisp sliced tomato covered with slices of fresh mozzarella cheese garnished with olive oil and fresh basil leaves, to a dozen different ingredients artistically combined. The important point to remember is that the antipasto should complement the rest of the meal. A light dish would be best to precede a substantial meal. A platter of assorted salami, hard-boiled eggs, and olives would be more suitable before a main course of light fish.

The variety of Italian antipasti is practically unlimited. I bet that just by reading the following recipes your stomach is going to holler, "Feed me!"

Antipasto alla Casalinga
(HOME-STYLE ANTIPASTO)

SERVES 4

This is a typical mixed antipasto which can be varied at will to suit the availability of ingredients.

1 sweet green or yellow bell pepper, seeded and thinly sliced
4 medium firm tomatoes, sliced
4 ounces thinly sliced Italian salami
1 6½-ounce can tuna fish packed in oil, flaked
2 hard-boiled eggs, sliced
2 ounces black or green olives
Olive oil and red wine vinegar

(continued)

Serve the individual items on separate plates or arrange them on a large flat platter. Serve the vinegar and oil separately.

Tuscany has not only given us a superb cuisine, but in 1870 the Tuscany dialect was adopted as Italy's official national language. Other Italians disparagingly call the Tuscans mangiafagioli (bean eaters) because beans are such an important ingredient of their cuisine.

This recipe from Florence, Tuscany's capitol, I literally had to borrow from the kitchen of Enza AldoBrandini, my friend Father Aldo AldoBrandini's mom. I was invited to their home across the Ponte Vecchio near the Medici tombs. When Enza brought this antipasto from her kitchen and set it on the table I casually remarked, "Ah, so the Tuscans really are bean eaters." Enza pretended to me miffed by my comment and when I asked her for the recipe, this elegant lady said, "No, dear Father, figure it out for yourself." Father Aldo made an excuse to go into the kitchen. He came back and slipped a piece of paper into my hand. I had the recipe.

Fagioli con Tonno
(WHITE BEANS WITH TUNA)

SERVES 4

This is a dish from Tuscany made with delicious fresh cannellini beans locally grown, but a very pleasant dish can be made using canned beans (I use Progresso brand). The olive oil should be really "fruity" extra-virgin olive oil.

1 16-ounce can cannellini
1 8-ounce can tuna fish packed in oil, flaked
A few shreds raw onion
Salt and freshly ground black pepper to taste
Extra-virgin olive oil

Toss all the ingredients together. Allow to reach room temperature before serving. Simple yet terrific.

Mortadella con Insalata
(MORTADELLA WITH SALAD)

SERVES 4

Bologna is the capital of the region of Emilia-Romagna. It is a beautiful city with colonnaded streets and the oldest university in the western world. Its cuisine is so rich that it is called 'Bologna La Grassa' (Bologna the fat one). Mortadella di Bologna is a huge pork sausage laced with strips of white fat and pistachio nuts.

I was in the city visiting a Bolognese family who have relatives in Vineland, New Jersey from whom I purchase another Bolognese specialty, Tortellini (belly-button shaped fresh pasta pockets stuffed either with cheeses or spiced ground meats). Mrs. Tedesco started her feast with the above antipasto. I didn't have to borrow the recipe; it was easy to figure out.

4 slices paper-thin mortadella (no substitutions)
1/2 cucumber, thinly sliced
4 medium-firm tomatoes, sliced
12 green Spanish olives

Olive oil and vinegar

Place the mortadella flat on salad plates. Surround the edge with alternating slices of cucumber and tomato, and arrange the olives in the center. Serve oil and vinegar separately.

Crostini alla Fiorentina
(CHICKEN LIVER SAVORIES FROM FLORENCE)

SERVES 4

The Florence we're talking about here is the city that draws lovers of art from all over the world—not Florence the girl I dated in the ninth grade. The taste for liver of any kind, whether from chickens or other animals, is acquired. This antipasto is mild in flavor and does what it's supposed to do: stimulate the appetite.

> 8 ounces chicken livers
> 2 tablespoons butter
> 1/2 small onion, finely chopped
> 3 fresh sage leaves
> Freshly ground black pepper
> 8 1-inch slices Italian bread

Wash the livers under cold running water and remove any connective tissue or discolored pieces; chop very finely. Melt the butter in a small saucepan and over gentle heat cook the onion and sage leaves, covered, until the onion is soft and golden, about 10 minutes. Remove the sage. Add the livers and a few grindings of pepper and cook, stirring, for several minutes, until no pink color remains.

Meanwhile, lightly toast the slices of bread, or fry them in a little butter—either way the bread should remain soft enough to soak up the juices. Spread the chicken liver mixture on the bread and serve immediately, two slices of bread to each person.

Crostini alla Napoletana
(NAPLES-STYLE SAVORIES)

SERVES 4

Naples is the rather chaotic but gorgeous city that produces the best popular music and zestiest food of Italy. Although Neapolitans live in the shadow of Mount Vesuvius, they do not allow its ominous shadowy presence to blot out their sunny and bright dispositions. The Cathedral of Naples is the theater wherein an annual miracle takes place. The blood of St. Januarius (San Gennaro) has for centuries liquefied on his feast day. San Gennaro is the patron saint of Naples and Neapolitans love him fanatically. Throughout the Naples area, the most popular name given to boys is Gennaro. These appetizers capture some of the unique character of Naples; they are stimulating and very delicious.

> 4 slices Italian bread, 1/3 inch thick
> Olive oil
> 4 1-ounce slices Bel Paese or any other soft Italian cheese

(continued)

2 tomatoes, peeled (see Tip) and sliced

4 anchovies, cut in halves

Freshly ground black pepper

Pinch of dried oregano

Preheat the oven to 350°. Divide each slice of bread in half and place on a well-oiled baking tray. Cover each piece of bread with a thin slice of cheese and top with sliced tomato and half an anchovy. Sprinkle with pepper and oregano and finally drizzle a teaspoon of olive oil over each crostino. Bake for 12 to 15 minutes, until the bread is crisp and the cheese has melted. You can eat all four of these yourself for a snack that will beat potato chips any time.

TIP: To peel tomatoes, simply place them in a pot of boiling water for one minute. then place them under cold running water and the skins will peel off easily.

Crostini di Antonio
(ANTHONY'S SAVORIES)

S E R V E S   4

You will meet Anthony Oswald later on in this book. He is the fellow who cooks so well that he gets more proposals for marriage than Carter makes little pills. He made these for us one evening as we were cooking dinner together. These are so good that sometimes we make a batch of them and consume them accompanied with a bottle or two of quality dry red wine. We follow with a fresh escarole salad dressed with lemon juice and olive oil. It is a light dinner that leaves you smiling happily.

8 slices Italian bread, 1/4 inch thick

8 pats butter

8 tablespoons Gorgonzola or good-quality blue cheese

8 pieces jarred or canned roasted red peppers (we like Mancini or Progresso brand)

Butter each slice of bread and spread with Gorgonzola cheese. Top each slice with a piece of roasted red pepper. Place on an ungreased baking tray. Cook under the broiler until the bread is toasted and cheese begins to melt, about six minutes. Serve two to each person. They're going to love you and ask for more.

Uova Sode coi Spinaci
(SPINACH-STUFFED EGGS)

S E R V E S   4

Do you enjoy deviled eggs? I do, very much. This recipe and the one that follows are Italian versions that leave the devil behind and reach toward the heavenly gates. Yes, you can use either fresh or frozen spinach.

4 jumbo hard-boiled eggs, cut in half lengthwise

2 ounces cream cheese

2 level tablespoons squeezed dry and very finely chopped cooked spinach

2 level tablespoons freshly grated Parmesan cheese

Salt, freshly ground pepper, and grated nutmeg to taste.

1 or 2 tablespoons milk, if necessary

Scoop out the egg yolks and put in a bowl with the cream cheese, spinach, Parmesan cheese, salt, pepper, and nutmeg. Mix thoroughly; if necessary add milk to make a creamy consistency.

Pile the mixture into the egg whites and arrange on a flat serving dish. A platter of spinach-stuffed and tuna-stuffed (next recipe) eggs make an attractive and tasty antipasto.

Uova con Tonno
(TUNA-STUFFED EGGS)

SERVES 4

Canned tuna is the only fish that I can eat and enjoy. Tuna used in this recipe becomes gourmet fare. Give me a couple of these antipasti and I'm ready for the next course, unless there are one or two of these beauties left over. I'll eat them, no problem.

    4 extra-large hard-boiled eggs, cut in half
        lengthwise
    1 3¹/₂-ounce can tuna fish packed in oil
    1 teaspoon freshly squeezed lemon juice
    2 tablespoons good mayonnaise (I use
        Hellman's)
    1 tablespoon heavy cream
    Freshly ground black pepper to taste
    A few black olive halves for garnish

Scoop out the egg yolks and pound together with tuna fish and lemon juice. Mix to a smooth moist consistency with the mayonnaise and

cream. Season with pepper. Pile the filling into the egg whites and garnish with black olives. These are really yummy.

Peperoni alla Piemontese
(PEPPERS PIEDMONT STYLE)

SERVES 4

Piedmont is that region of Italy that lies at the feet of the Alps. Its name is descriptive of its location; Piedmont translates literally as "at the feet of mountains." These stuffed peppers are many steps above ordinary stuffed peppers and are wonderful appetizers.

    4 small bell peppers
    4 ripe tomatoes, peeled (see Tip, page 32), and
        quartered
    4 anchovy fillets
    2 cloves garlic, crushed
    4 tablespoons olive oil
    ¹/₄ cup chopped fresh Italian (flat-leafed)
        parsley, for garnish

Preheat the oven to 350°. Cut peppers in half lengthwise, discard the seeds and pith. Place them cut side up in shallow ovenproof dish, and in each put two tomato quarters. Mash the anchovies and garlic together, and mix with the oil. Pour a spoonful of the mixture into each pepper. Cook for 30 to 35 minutes.

The peppers should remain fairly firm. Serve cold, garnished with parsley. When you see how your family or guests scarf them up, you'll know that next time you had better double the recipe.

Funghi di Portobello in Aglio e Vino

(PORTOBELLO MUSHROOMS IN A GARLIC AND WINE SAUCE)

SERVES 4

My *sister-in-law Mary, married to my brother Dominick (Mimi) for fifty years, has become over the years my cooking buddy. She invented this recipe after becoming enamored of the exquisite taste and texture of Portobello mushrooms. They only cost $3.99 a pound at our local supermarket and they appear at our shared supper table at least once a week. They make a superb antipasto.*

¼ cup olive oil

1 large bulb (yes, bulb) garlic, peeled and
  chopped coarsely

4 large Portobello mushrooms

1 teaspoon freshly ground black pepper

¾ cup white cooking wine (we use Holland
  House). Cooking wine contains salt and
  that is why salt is missing from the list of
  ingredients.

In a 12-inch nonstick skillet, heat the olive oil on medium heat. Sauté the garlic until very brown, but not burned. Remove the garlic with a slotted spoon and set aside. Clean the mushrooms with a damp paper towel. Sauté the whole mushrooms slowly in the same skillet, turning once to cook both sides, about 10 minutes. Return the cooked garlic to the skillet. Add the black pepper. Add the wine, and adjust the heat to high for 5 minutes to reduce the wine. Immediately serve each person one mushroom covered with garlic-wine sauce. Always provide crusty Italian bread to soak up the great sauce. Yes, you will want more. But calm down, this is only the appetizer.

Minestre (Soups)

We can only imagine a dark, damp day as a small group of prehistoric men, women, and children sat huddled together before the warmth of a fire at the entrance to their cave in a valley of the Italian peninsula. They were hungry for something that would warm and comfort them. An enterprising and imaginative member of the clan glanced about the dwelling and saw that there were bones of animals that they had killed and cooked. There were stones of the fire pit glowing with heat. There were all kinds of roots and leaves of plants that they had gathered, and there was a supply of water nearby.

The would-be chef got up from the circle, and picked up a basket woven so tightly that it would hold water. The chef filled the basket with water and brought it to the fire, then carefully extracted some hot rocks from the fire and dropped them into the water-filled container. The water began to steam and simmer. In went some bones, roots, and vegetation. Soon a delicious aroma filled the cave. Some brave soul picked up a hollowed-out gourd, dipped it into the aromatic water, hesitated, and then bravely tasted the contents. Wow! It was mm-mm good! Thus the first soup was invented. Maybe.

Since that day in prehistoric times, soup has become the comfort food of all nations and peoples. There is no food like soup, good hot soup, to warm one's body and lift one's drooping spirits. Some scientists say that the old time-honored remedy for a cold, delicious hot chicken soup, really works. They really don't know how it works, but it does. I say who cares? Even if it doesn't help to cure my cold, it's still a wonderfully delicious food that always makes me feel good.

I must confess that one of the reasons that I love to cook soup is that I only (most of the time) have to use one pot. I am a fanatic when it comes to cooking but hate cleaning up. Of course I clean up as I go along, but it's not one of my favorite chores.

In my book *Father Orsini's Italian Kitchen*, (New York: St. Martin's Press, 1991), I recount the biblical story of Esau and Jacob. Now Esau was nuts about lentil soup; so much so that he handed over his birthright to his clever brother Jacob for a bowl of steaming delicious lentil soup. I doubt if I would go that far, but I make my mother's recipe for lentil soup at least once a week. Soup is marvelous food. It is delicious, nutritious, and satisfying. It can be the centerpiece of a whole meal or an appetizing opening to a formal dinner. I am sure that the Frugal Gourmet would agree with me that soup is probably the most economical way to feed a hungry crowd.

My predilection for or attraction to soup began when I was a four-year-old toddler. It was the first time I could reach my mother's kitchen stove. My mother was preparing Pastina al Burro (tiny macaroni boiled in salted water and seasoned with butter, a typical dish prepared by Italian mothers for their tots) and as she looked away for just a second, I reached up to see what was in the pot. Thus my first encounter with a stove became a disaster. I spilled the contents all over me and suffered burns on my left arm. But that didn't stop me or turn me away from soup.

The Italians are great soup eaters, and "eaters" is often the operative word, as many of their traditional soups already thick with a variety of vegetables are further thickened with rice or pasta until "the spoon will stand up." Such a soup is served instead of and almost never at the same meal with, a rice or pasta dish. At our house when we're having soup for supper, that's it. We have two bowls of soup each, and that's enough for a full meal.

In Italy, the family cook is essentially practi-cal—he or she uses vegetables in season for his or her soups and invariably makes enough for two meals. On the second day the addition of rice or pasta conveniently varies and extends the soup. The basis of a family supper is often a nourishing soup, followed by cheese and fresh fruit.

Although the minestrone-type soup (thick, rich vegetable soup) has gained international fame, there is, in fact, a surprising variety of interesting and unusual soups to be found in Italy. All around the coasts colorful "zuppe di pesce" (fish soups) vary from place to place according to the local catch of the day. These soups are difficult to reproduce as most of them require fish or seafood found only in the Mediterranean and Adriatic seas. Dried pea, bean, or lentil soups are popular and so are consommés and cream of vegetable soups. There are soups thickened with egg or stale bread.

Some of the most practical soups are the "pasta in brodo," which are clear chicken or meat broth to which is added one of the following: any type of pastina (soup pasta shapes), pastina and vegetables, stuffed pasta such as tortellini, or slices of thin rolled omelet, and miniature meatballs. Similarly, "riso in brodo" soups combine broth, rice, and vegetables. Although traditionally the broth was made at home, today it is often purchased from special shops or restaurants or made from stock cubes marketed by well-known firms (such as Knorr). These stock cubes do make a very quick and useful substitute.

With Italian soups, freshly grated Parmesan or pecorino cheeses and sometimes croutons as well are offered, so be sure to serve the soup in wide, deep bowls which allows for stirring without messing up your tablecloth.

Mamma's Chicken Broth

SERVES 6

- 3–4 pound whole chicken
- 1 cup chopped fresh Italian (flat-leafed) parsley
- 1 tablespoon salt
- 1 teaspoon freshly ground black pepper
- 3 quarts cold water
- add one cup cooked rice or pasta for each serving
- Freshly grated Parmesan or Romano cheese

Wash the chicken well, discarding the giblets and trimming any excess yellow fat. In a 4-quart pot, place the chicken, parsley, salt, and pepper. Cover with 3 quarts (or more if necessary) cold water. Bring to boil and skim any froth that may form. Lower the heat to a simmer. Cook at simmer for 1-1/2 hours, covered. Check periodically and skim any more froth. When the meat is falling off the bones, the soup is ready.

Remove the chicken and discard all skin and bones when cool enough to handle. Dice the chicken meat and return it to the broth.

Serve very hot, over cooked rice or cooked soup macaroni. Sprinkle with grated Parmesan or Romano cheese. Boy, is this good!

VARIATION: For a supply of useful chicken stock, strain the broth and use the meat for a tasty salad.

BEEF STOCK

For a satisfactory and aromatic beef stock, please turn to page 97 and use the recipe for Pasta Daniele. Simply omit the pasta in the recipe. Strain the broth through a sieve, and use the meat, vegetables, and condiments as a hearty main course; the remaining beef broth will provide you the homemade stock you need for other recipes.

MINESTRONE

Minestrone translates as "big soup" and so it is. There is no such thing as "a" recipe for minestrone because it is a soup that varies from district to district and according to the vegetables in season. The essential elements of a true minestrone are a variety of vegetables, some aromatic herbs, and a small quantity of fat, usually in the form of bacon (pancetta) or olive oil. It is sometimes made by simmering the diced vegetables in water or stock, starting with those that take longest to cook and adding the other ingredients according to the time they need. Other recipes begin by gently sautéing the vegetables in oil. In either case, some short-cut pasta or rice, or both, is added toward the end of the cooking time and the result is a colorful soup, thick with tender vegetables. Owing to the time required for preparation, minestrone is usually made in large quantities. A little grated cheese, Parmesan or pecorino, is usually stirred into the soup just before serving. The two recipes that follow are typical of Genoa and Milan.

No, I'm sorry, but canned minestrone, even if it has an Italian brand name, just won't do it. Please, use your imagination and experiment with minestrone. I assure you, your minestrone will be better than the canned variety can ever be.

Minestrone alla Genovese
(GENOVESE-STYLE MINESTRONE)

SERVES 8

Genoa's most famous son is the often maligned Christopher Columbus. Its most famous sauce is pesto. Let's leave all that aside and get into the following recipe. It tastes as fresh and delicious as its ingredients.

- ¹/₂ cup dried navy, pea, or white kidney beans, stones removed, washed, covered with cold water, and soaked overnight (I use the same six-quart saucepan in which I'm going to cook the soup. Don't drain the beans the next day. Trust me.)
- 10 cups hot water or chicken stock
- 3 tablespoons olive oil
- 1 large onion, chopped
- 1 leek, sliced and washed carefully under cold running water
- 2 carrots, sliced
- 2 potatoes, diced
- 1 turnip (not a rutabaga—a small turnip), diced
- 1 cup green peas or chopped green beans
- 8 ounces spinach, finely chopped
- 4 ounces soup macaroni (ditallini or tubettini)
- Salt and freshly ground black pepper to taste
- Pinch of sugar
- 4 tablespoons Salsa di Pesto Semplice (page 53)
- Freshly grated Parmesan or pecorino cheese

Add 2-1/2 cups of the water or stock to the soaked beans and cook for 1 hour. Meanwhile, heat the oil in a large, deep skillet and sauté the onion, leek, carrots, potatoes, and turnip on gentle heat for 10 minutes.

Add the remaining 7-1/2 cups of hot water or stock to the bean saucepan. Add the contents of the skillet, bring to a boil, cover, and simmer for 1 hour. Add the peas or green beans, spinach, pasta, and seasonings to taste and simmer another 20 minutes. Stir in the pesto just before serving. Allow your guests to add grated cheese at the table.

Minestrone alla Milanese
(MILAN-STYLE MINESTRONE)

SERVES 6

Rome may be the political capital of Italy, but Milan is the business and cultural center of the country. A comparison can be made between Washington, D.C., and New York City in the United States. All roads may lead to Rome, but it is in Milan that styles and trends are set. It is a great city that draws people from all over Italy like a magnet. As in the song "New York, New York," if they can make it there, they can make it anywhere. This delectable minestrone is reflective of Milan; it has a little bit of everything, yet it harmonizes different entities creating a masterpiece.

- 1 ounce butter
- 2 ounces unsmoked bacon or pancetta, diced
- 1 onion, diced
- 4 ribs celery, diced
- 1 large carrot, diced
- 4 ounces white beans (navy, Northern, or

cannelini), cooked as in Minestrone alla
Genovese (page 38)

8 ounces potatoes, peeled and diced

4 ounces unpeeled baby zucchini, diced

7 1/2 cups chicken or beef stock or water

8 ounces cabbage, shredded

2 large tomatoes, peeled (see Tip, page 32) and
chopped

4 ounces rice

Salt and freshly ground black pepper

2 fresh sage leaves, finely chopped, or 1/4
teaspoon dried

1 tablespoon fresh Italian (flat-leaf) parsley,
finely chopped

2 tablespoons freshly grated Parmesan or
pecorino cheese, and lots more for the table

Into a large saucepan put the butter, bacon,
onion, celery, and carrot. Cook on gentle heat,
stirring now and then, for 10 minutes. Stir in the
beans, potato, zucchini, and stock or water, cover,
and simmer for 1-1/2 hours. Add the cabbage,
tomatoes, rice, sage, and salt and pepper and simmer for 20 minutes. Finally, stir in the parsley and
the 2 tablespoons grated cheese. Pass more grated
cheese at table. In summer, this Minestrone alla
Milanese is served at room temperature.

Minestra di Fagioli d'Anna
(ANNA'S BEAN SOUP)

SERVES 4

You will meet my dear friend Anna Conti in the
Pasta section of this book. She invented an outrageous

Pasta Pizza and is an accomplished cook. Her bean
soup is a hearty and delicious combination of simple
ingredients.

1 pound dried white navy pea beans, stones
removed, washed, covered with cold water,
and soaked overnight (use the same 6-quart
saucepan in which you will cook the soup;
do not drain the beans)

1 1/2 quarts water

1/4 cup olive oil

1 28-ounce can whole or stewed tomatoes

1 tablespoon dried oregano

1 large onion, chopped

1 large carrot, diced

2 ribs celery, sliced

Salt and freshly ground black pepper

Freshly grated Parmesan or pecorino cheese

Add 1-1/2 quarts cold water, to the soaked
beans and heat to boiling on medium heat. Turn
the heat to simmer. Add the oil, tomatoes,
oregano, onion, carrot, and celery. Simmer on
lowest heat for 3 hours, covered. Add salt and
pepper to taste. Pass the grated cheese separately
at the table. This is good eating.

Minestrina per I Bambini
(SOUP FOR TODDLERS)

SERVES 4

Italians are crazy when it comes to their children.
Especially when the kids are toddlers. They are crazy
about their kids no matter how old they are. Period.

My mamma had me when she was forty-four years old and I remained her bambino until the day she died, even though I was forty-seven by then. She was crazy about me, my sister, and my brothers. Italian mammas prepare this nutritious tasty dish for their little ones. In fact, the first solid food for Italian kids is usually a pastina cooked in the following manner. Try it with your toddlers. They'll love you even more.

1 small onion
1 rib celery
1 large carrot
1 large potato
1 cup fresh or canned peas
4 cups chicken stock or water
1 tablespoon butter
Salt and freshly ground black pepper
3 ounces alphabet egg pastina
Freshly grated Parmesan cheese

Prepare and slice the onion, celery, carrot, and potato. Put the vegetables into a saucepan with the fresh peas and water or stock, bring to a boil, and simmer until tender, about 30 minutes. If using canned peas, add them after 25 minutes. Pass the soup through a food mill or place in food processor fitted with the steel blade and process until liquefied or creamed. Return to the saucepan, and add the butter and the seasoning to taste. Add the pastina and cook for another 5 minutes. Serve sprinkled with grated Parmesan cheese.

Minestra di Frittata
(OMELET SOUP)

SERVES 4

I learned this uniquely enjoyable recipe from a witty and warm Sicilian grandmother, Nonna Lena, who has since passed on into the heavenly kingdom. It is the easiest way I have learned to make egg noodles. Lena called them "scapelli." They add a lot of digestible protein to a dish of marvelous soup.

2 pints (5 cups) good chicken or meat
  stock
2 eggs
1 level teaspoon all-purpose flour
4 tablespoons milk (you may use skim)
1/4 teaspoon salt
2 tablespoons olive oil, for frying
2 tablespoons freshly grated Parmesan or
  pecorino cheese, plus more for the
  table

Heat the stock in a saucepan. Meanwhile, beat the eggs with the flour, milk, and salt. Grease the bottom of a large skillet with the oil and when hot, pour in the batter. Cook over brisk heat until set and golden, about one minute. (You should have a very thin omelet.) Turn out onto paper towels, roll up like a jelly-roll, and cut across into thin strips about 1/4 inch wide. Throw the noodles into the boiling stock with the 2 tablespoons grated Parmesan. Serve immediately, and hand around more cheese separately.

Minestra Primaverile
(SOUP FOR SPRING TIME)

SERVES 4

This uncomplicated soup is as pleasing to the eye as it is to the palate. It takes about 10 minutes to prepare and another 15 minutes to cook. It allows you to serve a dainty soup and still go out to enjoy the enchanting days of spring.

1 tablespoon butter
1 medium-sized onion, finely chopped
1 small rib celery, finely sliced
5 cups good chicken or beef stock
2 tomatoes, peeled (see Tip, page 32) and
  chopped
10 ounces green peas, frozen or fresh
1/2 cup soup pastina or noodles
Freshly grated Parmesan or pecorino cheese

Heat the butter in a medium saucepan and on gentle heat sauté the onion and celery until soft, about 5 minutes. Add the stock and bring to a boil. Add the tomatoes, peas, and pastina; cook for 10 minutes. Hand the grated cheese at the table.

Minestra con Carciofi
(ARTICHOKE AND PASTA SOUP)

SERVES 4

When I first made this soup I used fresh artichokes that cost $1.00 each. I cut away the stalk and one third off the top, and discarded the choke and outside leaves so that only the heart was left. I cut the heart into thin strips and to prevent discoloring, threw them into cold water with a tablespoon of lemon juice. When I finished that process and saw what I had left, I almost wept at the waste. Now I buy a 14-ounce can of artichoke hearts packed in water, use what is required in this recipe, and use the rest to make artichoke fritters. This is a dainty soup that will please your family and friends.

1 tablespoon butter
1 tablespoon olive oil
1 small onion, finely chopped
4 canned artichoke hearts, cut into thin strips
  (I like Pope brand—no, not because they
  call me the Pope of Pasta, it's just an excellent brand)
Salt and freshly ground black pepper
4 cups good chicken or beef stock
1/2 cup ditalini or other small pasta for soup
2 eggs
2 tablespoons freshly grated Parmesan cheese,
  plus more for the table

Heat the butter and oil in a large saucepan and cook the onion until soft on low heat, about 5 minutes. Stir in the artichoke strips and salt and pepper to taste, then add the stock. Bring to boil and simmer another 5 minutes. Add the pasta and cook al dente, about 5 to 8 minutes.

Meanwhile, in a soup tureen beat together the eggs and the 2 tablespoons grated Parmesan cheese; stir the boiling soup into the egg mixture, and check the seasoning. Serve immediately, with more cheese handed separately.

Zuppa Crema di Piselli
(CREAM OF FRESH PEA SOUP)

SERVES 4

I *really enjoy the standard split pea soup on a frosty winter's evening. But after I tasted this soup in Venice, I came to the conclusion that there is pea soup and then there is Pea Soup. I know you catch my meaning. I also know that this is going to go on your list of special dishes.*

I sampled this refreshing and satisfying pea soup as a first course when I was the houseguest of the Cardinal-Patriarch of Venice, Albino Luciani. He later was elected Pope and took the name of John Paul I. Unfortunately, this "smiling Pope" only lived thirty-three days after his possession of the throne of St. Peter.

3 tablespoons butter (not margarine, please)
1 small onion, chopped
1 rib celery
2 slices boiled ham
1 pound green peas, frozen or fresh
2¹/₂ cups water
¹/₄ cup half and half or whole milk
Croutons

Melt the butter in a saucepan and on gentle heat sauté the onion until soft, about 5 minutes. Meanwhile, chop the celery and ham, and sauté with the onions for another 6 minutes. Stir in the peas and when thoroughly mixed with the butter, add the water and simmer until soft, about 20 minutes.

Pass the soup through a food mill or grind in a food processor fitted with the steel blade until pureed. Return the soup to the rinsed saucepan and heat through. Just before serving, stir in the half and half or milk to thin the consistency. Top with croutons, homemade preferably and serve.

Minestra di Pasta Reale
(CONSUME WITH SOUP BALLS)

SERVES 4

T*his soup looks and tastes dramatic, but it should take only about 30 minutes to make (including baking the soup balls). If you want to impress someone, this soup will help you along the way. If you want to impress someone that you really care for, this soup says "I love you." Isn't it great when soup can speak for you?*

1 tablespoon butter
⁵/₈ cup water
¹/₈ teaspoon salt
2¹/₂ ounces all-purpose flour (I can't work without an accurate kitchen scale. Come on, they are not expensive)
2 medium eggs
5 cups good beef broth or canned consommé, very hot
Freshly grated Parmesan or pecorino cheese

Preheat the oven to 375°. To make the soup balls, put the butter, water, and salt into a small saucepan and bring to boil. Add the flour all at once, stirring with a wooden spoon until smooth.

Cook gently until the mixture leaves the sides of the pan, about ¹/₂ to 1 minute. Allow to cool before adding the eggs one at a time, beating until smooth after each addition. Turn into a pastry bag fitted with a ¹/₄-inch plain pipe and pipe small hazelnut-sized balls onto a nonstick baking sheet. Bake until well risen and completely dried out, about 10 minutes. Remove from oven and leave to cool.

To serve, heat the broth or consommé to a boil, put 12 soup balls into each bowl, and ladle the boiling soup over the balls. Serve immediately, and hand the grated cheese separately.

Pappa al Pomodoro
(TOMATO AND BREAD SOUP)

SERVES 6

Leave it to the inventive Italians to find ways to use up stale Italian bread and make it the base of substantial soups. To be authentic and successful in making this soup and the one that follows, you must begin with good Italian bread. This recipe uses traditional Tuscan ingredients with a little more garlic (you know I reverence garlic).

1 cup olive oil

2 large cloves garlic, chopped

1 scant teaspoon tomato paste

2 pounds fresh ripe tomatoes, peeled (see Tip, page 32) and chopped

10 fresh basil leaves, chopped

6 cups chicken stock

Salt and freshly ground black pepper

1 1-pound loaf stale Italian bread, thinly sliced

Heat the oil in a 12-inch skillet on medium heat. Add the garlic and sauté for 5 minutes. Stir in the tomato paste, tomatoes, and basil and simmer on low heat for 5 minutes. Set aside. Heat the stock and add salt and pepper to taste in a large saucepan. Bring to a boil. Stir in the bread and the tomato mixture and cook on medium heat for 3 minutes. Remove from heat and let stand uncovered for 1 hour. Just before serving, stir thoroughly. Serve hot, at room temperature, or cold. Drizzle a little olive oil over the top of each bowl. Surprise! No grated cheese.

Zuppa di Verdure Agliata
(GARLICKY VEGETABLE SOUP)

SERVES 4

Just this year, after a humdrum cruise to the Greek islands on the Italian cruise line, Costa, I spent two great days in Genoa, the capitol city of Liguria. Genoa is a gorgeous city, the jewel of Liguria. I had this soup that was prepared by owner-chef, Elenora Raggio, for her kitchen staff. Elenora owns a pizzeria/restaurant not far from Genoa's aquarium in the harbor. I struck up a conversation with her and when she found out I was a priest who writes cookbooks she graciously invited me to her kitchen table and served this soup. Both the soup and Elenora were unforgettable. Incidentally, her kitchen staff was made up of her two sons, Cristoforo and Lorenzo, and their wives. This was truly a family affair.

The Liguria region is known for its vegetables, garlic, and basil. Its olive oil is terrific. The soup is genuinely Ligurian and won't stand up to reheating. It is chockful of beautiful and nutritious vegetables and it is simply awesome.

1/4 cup olive oil, plus more for sautéing the bread

1 large yellow onion, very finely sliced

1/2 pound fresh kale leaves, finely chopped

2 medium zucchini, finely chopped

2 ribs celery, finely chopped

2 large carrots, finely chopped

1 large potato, peeled and diced small

2 tomatoes, peeled (see Tip, page 32) and chopped

Salt and freshly ground black pepper

4 1/2 cups good chicken stock

10 ounces frozen peas, thawed

3 large cloves garlic, crushed

3 tablespoons finely chopped fresh Italian (flat-leafed) parsley

6 1-inch slices good day-old Italian bread

Olive oil, for the bread

Freshly grated pecorino cheese

Heat the 1/4 cup olive oil in a six-quart saucepan on medium heat. Add the onion and sauté until golden, about 8 minutes. Stir in the kale, zucchini, celery, carrots, potato, and tomatoes and salt and pepper to taste. Sauté about 10 minutes. Pour the stock over the vegetables and cook, uncovered, on medium heat for 20 min-utes. Add the peas, garlic, and parsley, and cook briefly for 8 more minutes.

Sauté the slices of bread in a large skillet in olive oil on medium heat until toasty-brown on both sides. Place 1 slice in the bottom of each bowl. Ladle the hot soup over the toast and serve immediately. Pass the grated pecorino cheese at the table. This one is fantabulous!

Aunt Madeline's Escarole Soup

SERVES 6-8

DOM DELUISE,

CALIFORNIA

Dom DeLuise gave me permission to use this wonderful recipe from his delightful book Eat This . . . It'll Make You Feel Better (New York: Simon and Schuster, 1988). He says: "When I was in Italy visiting my mother's hometown of Spinoza, I had lunch at my Aunt Madeline's farm. This wonderful, tiny woman (she's five foot nothing) insisted that the simple soup she was going to serve was a peasant dish. She kept apologizing for it! Of course it was extraordinary, just like the escarole soup my mother makes, but this was extra-delicious served with the hot bread that came out of her stone oven."

2 tablespoons olive oil

2 garlic cloves, minced

1 onion, chopped

2 carrots, sliced

1 potato, peeled and diced (optional)

2 cups chicken broth
2 heads escarole, well washed and coarsely cut
grated cheese for garnish

In a large saucepan, heat the olive oil and gently brown the garlic. Add the onion, carrots, and, if using, the potato (this helps thicken the soup), and then after 1 minute, add the broth. Add the escarole, cover, and let come to a boil. Lower the heat and simmer for 1 hour. For a soupier soup, add a little broth or water. Serve in soup bowls and sprinkle with grated cheese. Have lots of hot Italian bread on the table.

VARIATION: You can add spareribs and/or a couple of Italian sausages at the same time as the garlic and brown the meat well. Then add everything else.

Salse (Sauces)

In this section I want to introduce you to the magical qualities of Italian sauces. Each one has its own character and taste. Most have the ability to transform plain foods like pasta into epicurean celebrations.

Mamma Orsini's Tomato Sauce

YIELD 10 CUPS

The most important feature of Italian-American cooking is the indispensable tomato sauce. Without a tomato sauce that is correctly spiced, most Italian recipes will taste like gruel prepared for patients with severe digestive problems. The secret is in the sauce. In my haphazard career as an amateur cook, I've found that if you've spoiled the sauce, it's better to throw the whole thing away and start all over again.

During the years before my retirement for medical reasons, I lived in many "Homes for Unwed Fathers," more commonly known as rectories. With one or two

exceptions, the meals served in those rectories were nothing to write home about. Usually it was meat and potatoes; sometimes, for variety, it was potatoes and meat. But there always came a point when I just couldn't stand it anymore and would invade the rectory kitchen (almost always to the delight of the housekeeper) to prepare a huge pot of tomato sauce. Well, from then on I was caught; making sauce became a weekly assignment—unofficial, of course, but a duty nonetheless. Now we can share, dear reader, the magic and mystery of my mamma's famous tomato sauce.

Before you start, let me share some helpful information with you. This recipe yields about 10 cups of sauce, enough to dress about 4 pounds of pasta. Unless you are feeding a large crowd, 10 cups is a bit much. Don't you agree? However, since you have to do almost the same work for 2 cups that you do for 10 cups, you might as well do it all at once and freeze what is left over.

Sauce freezes well in plastic containers as well as plain old zippered plastic freezer bags and is easy enough to defrost to enjoy a delicious, quick dish some other time. I usually freeze mine in about 2 1/2 half cup portions which is enough for 1 pound of pasta. If you like your pasta heavily sauced, use your own judgment about portion size.

Want less sauce? You can just halve the recipe.

2 no. 3 (2 pound, 3 ounce) cans Italian plum
  tomatoes (5 pounds total)
1/3 cup olive oil
2 large onions, peeled and thinly sliced
5 garlic cloves, finely minced, or 1 tablespoon
  garlic powder
1 1/2 tablespoons salt
1 teaspoon freshly ground black pepper
1 teaspoon dried oregano
1 teaspoon fresh basil, if not available do not
  use dried, ever!
1 tablespoon sugar

Run the tomatoes through a food mill or chop
them in a blender for a few seconds, and reserve.
In a large sauce pan, sauté in olive oil the onions
and garlic until soft. Add the salt, pepper,
oregano, and basil; stir. Add the reserved tomatoes and sugar. Slowly bring to a boil, then simmer, covered, over low heat for 2 1/2 to 3 hours,
stirring occasionally.

VARIATION: Add browned sausage, meatballs,
chunks of beef or pork, or chicken pieces in any
combination for the last hour of cooking the
tomato sauce. Serve along with pasta for a complete and hearty meal.

Salsa Pizzaiola
(NEAPOLITAN QUICK SAUCE)

YIELD: 4 CUPS

The recipe for this distinctive sauce is Neapolitan in origin, and may be used to make pizza, steak piz-zaiola, or spaghetti.

2 garlic cloves, peeled and crushed
2 tablespoons olive oil
1 pound fresh or canned tomatoes, peeled
1 teaspoon salt
1/2 teaspoon freshly ground black pepper
1 teaspoon dried oregano
1 teaspoon chopped fresh Italian (flat-leafed)
  parsley

In a saucepan over low heat, cook the garlic in
the olive oil for several minutes. Chop the tomatoes into fairly large pieces and add to the
saucepan with salt and pepper. Cook briskly for 5
minutes, or until the ingredients have softened.
Stir in the oregano and parsley.

Salsa ai Pomodori
(RED SAUCE)

YIELD: 1 1/2 QUARTS

This Sicilian sauce is ruby-red in color, thick and pulpy in texture, and sweet in taste. It's excellent over fresh or commercially made pastas, fish dishes, and poultry.

I owe thanks to Enza La Bozzetta, the wife of my

'compare' Franco. They have lived in Catania, Sicily for almost forty years. She gave me the recipes for the next four sauces.

Franco is my agent in Italy who oversees the importation of olive oils, peeled plum tomatoes, and other specialties that are sold in the United States for my company, Father Orsini's Italian Specialties.

- 2 tablespoons olive oil
- 1 medium onion, chopped
- 2 garlic cloves, halved
- 1 2½-pound can plum or whole tomatoes
- 1 6-ounce can tomato paste
- 3 sprigs fresh basil, or 1 tablespoon dried
- 5 sprigs fresh Italian (flat-leafed) parsley
- 1 teaspoon salt
- ¼ teaspoon freshly ground black pepper

Heat the oil in a saucepan and sauté the onion and garlic until golden, about 3 minutes. Add the tomatoes, tomato paste, basil, parsley, salt, and pepper. Bring to a boil, cover, and simmer slowly for 1 hour. Correct the seasoning if necessary. Discard garlic and parsley before serving.

Salsa di Conserva Pomodori
(QUICK TOMATO SAUCE)

YIELD: ABOUT 1 1/2 QUARTS

Quick Tomato Sauce is economical during the winter months, when fresh tomatoes are expensive, but actually it is an ideal sauce all year around. It's so simple to prepare, and basic enough to be served with meat or fish dishes and over pasta, rice, and pizza.

- 3 tablespoons olive oil
- 1 large onion, finely chopped
- 3 garlic cloves, cut in half
- 2 7-ounce cans tomato paste
- 3 cups water
- 3 sprigs fresh basil
- 1 teaspoon salt
- ¼ teaspoon freshly ground black pepper

In a large saucepan, heat the oil and sauté the onion and garlic until the onion is soft. Add the tomato paste and sauté for 3 minutes. Pour in the water, and season with basil, salt, and pepper. Bring to a boil; cover and simmer slowly for 30 minutes. Discard the garlic and correct seasoning if necessary.

Salsa di Funghi e Pomodori
(MUSHROOM AND TOMATO SAUCE)

YIELD: ABOUT 2 QUARTS

This sauce may be teamed with fish, poultry, spaghetti, and rice dishes.

- 2 tablespoons olive oil
- 1 medium onion, chopped
- 2 garlic cloves, cut in half
- 1 no. 3 (2 pound, 3 ounce) can plum tomatoes in puree, or 2 pounds fresh plum tomatoes, cored, peeled (see Tip, page 32) and diced

(continued)

¼ cup chopped fresh Italian (flat-leafed) parsley

1 teaspoon salt

¼ teaspoon freshly ground black pepper

½ pound fresh mushrooms, sliced lengthwise

In a large saucepan, heat the oil and sauté the onion and garlic until golden, about 3 minutes. Add the tomatoes, parsley, salt, and pepper and bring to a boil. Cover, lower the heat, and simmer slowly for 30 minutes. Add the mushrooms and simmer 10 minutes longer. Correct the seasoning if necessary and discard garlic before serving.

Salsa Marinara
(SAILOR-STYLE SAUCE)

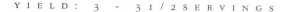

YIELD: 3 - 3 1/2 SERVINGS

"**Q**uick and easy" superlatively describes Salsa Marinara. Its fresh flavor adds a touch of spring and summer to pasta, fish, and poultry dishes.

2 tablespoons olive oil

1 bunch scallions, chopped fine or 1 medium onion chopped fine

4 cloves garlic, peeled and coarsely minced

1 no. 3 (2 pound, 3 ounce) can whole tomatoes or 2 pounds fresh, cored, peeled (see Tip, page 32) and diced

4 sprigs fresh basil or Italian flat leafed parsley left whole

1 teaspoon oregano

2 teaspoons salt

1 teaspoon freshly ground pepper

1½ teaspoons sugar

In a large saucepan, heat the oil and sauté the scallions for 3 to 5 minutes. Add garlic. Cook 3 minutes. Stir in tomatoes, basil or parsley, oregano, salt, pepper, and sugar. Bring to boil, cover and simmer slowly for 30 minutes.

Sugo Di Vitello Genovese
(VEAL SAUCE GENOA STYLE)

YIELD: 4 - 5 SERVINGS

This is more in the category of soupy stews than thick sauces. It can be used as a stew if you desire, but it is fantastic when tossed and served with spaghetti cooked al dente. That is the way my mamma used to make it. Whoever heard of pasta with brown sauce? You did, right now. And I'm telling you, it's scrumptious.

In my mother's home we had the following dish once in a while as a pleasant change from macaroni with tomato sauce. This one, I'm pretty sure, was taught to my Mom by my sister's godmother, Comare Raggio. Comare Raggio was a wonderful woman who was born in Sardinia, married her husband Carlo who had come from Genoa, and settled in New York. My parents were befriended by them when they arrived in New York from Italy, and when my sister Evelyn was born, Comare and Compare Raggio became her godparents. It is in their memory that I have included this recipe.

2 pounds stewing veal, cut into bite-size chunks

1/4 cup olive oil

3 large potatoes, peeled and quartered

1 large onion, thinly sliced

1 tablespoon salt

1 teaspoon freshly ground black pepper

1/4 cup chopped fresh Italian (flat-leafed) parsley

4 cups water

In a large saucepan, brown the veal well in olive oil. Remove the veal and add the potatoes, browning them and adding more oil if needed. Remove the potatoes. Sauté the onion until well browned in the same pan, and add salt, pepper, and parsley. Then return the cooked meat and potatoes to the pan. Simmer for 5 minutes, add the water, bring to a boil over medium heat, then simmer over low heat for 1 hour.

Ragu Bolognese Officiale
(OFFICIAL RAGU BOLOGNESE)

YIELD: 4-6 SERVINGS

A *Ragu is a thick meat sauce. This sauce starts by cooking vegetables and browning meat in them. (In Italian cooking, an uncooked vegetable mix, battuto, serves as the base for many dishes. Once it is sautéed, it is known as soffrito.) How brown the meat should be is strictly an individual taste. Then the liquids are added and reduced. Finally the sauce is simmered.*

One general point of agreement is how to serve Ragu Bolognese—over tagliatelle, a handcut pasta that's a little wider than fettuccine. But let's not get fanatical about this. My preference is fettucine; you may use your favorite cut of pasta. If nobody squeals, you won't get into trouble with the pasta police.

1/2 cup heavy cream

10 ounces fresh unsalted fatback or bacon, diced

1 cup diced carrot

2/3 cup diced celery

1/2 diced onion

1 1/4 pounds beef skirt steak or boneless chuck blade roast, coarsely ground

1/2 cup dry Italian white wine

2 tablespoons tomato paste diluted in 10 tablespoons meat or poultry stock

1 cup whole milk

Salt and freshly ground black pepper

Simmer the cream in a small saucepan until reduced by one-third. There should be about 6 tablespoons. Set aside. Sauté the fatback in a 3- to 4-quart heavy saucepan over medium-low heat until almost all the fat is rendered, about 8 minutes. Stir in the carrot, celery, and onion, and sauté over medium-low heat until the onion is translucent, about 3 minutes. This is the soffrito.

Raise the heat to medium and stir in the ground beef. Brown until the meat is medium-brown in color and not quite crisp, about 5 minutes. Stir in the wine and diluted tomato paste. Reduce heat to very low—it is critical that the mixture reduce as slowly as possible. Cook partially covered for 2 hours. Periodically stir in a tablespoon or so of the milk. By the end of 2 hours, all the milk should be used up and the ragu should be only slightly liquid. Stir in the reduced cream. Season to taste with salt and pepper. Toss the hot ragu with 1 1/2 pounds freshly cooked and drained pasta.

NOTE: For a lower-fat version, substitute milk for the cream, and add it with the rest of the milk during simmering. Instead of fatback, sauté 1 ounce pancetta in 3 tablespoons extra-virgin olive oil.

Salsa Besciamela (Bechamel)
(WHITE SAUCE)

YIELD: 2 CUPS

Either the Italians borrowed this smooth white sauce from the French, or the French borrowed it from the Italians. There are arguments for both sides. I couldn't care less. It is a very useful sauce for many recipes and will keep well in the refrigerator for 4 or 5 days.

4 tablespoons butter
1/4 cup all-purpose flour
2 1/2 cups milk (boiling hot)
Salt and freshly ground black pepper
Nutmeg (optional)

In a small saucepan melt the butter over gentle heat. Add the flour, and, using a wooden spoon, stir and cook without browning for several minutes. Remove from the heat, and stir in the milk, little by little, mixing to a smooth sauce. Return to the heat and stir until boiling, then simmer for 10 minutes. Season to taste with salt and pepper; a little nutmeg wouldn't hurt either.

Salsa di Carciofi
(ARTICHOKE SAUCE)

YIELD: 2 CUPS
(6 SERVINGS)

Artichokes provide both an interesting texture and a subtle flavor to this sauce. Of course, it's a natural over pasta, but it can also be used over grilled meats, poultry, or fish.

6 fresh baby artichokes
1/3 cup virgin olive oil
4 garlic cloves, peeled and crushed
1 tablespoon chopped fresh Italian
    (flat-leafed) parsley
4 fresh tomatoes, peeled, (see Tip, page 32)
    cored, and diced

Cut away the outer leaves of the artichokes. Cut the hearts into small pieces. Heat the oil in a saucepan and sauté the garlic for 2 minutes. Add the artichokes, parsley, and tomatoes, and cook 8 minutes, covered, stirring often. Serve hot artichoke sauce over 1 1/2 pounds cooked and drained rigatoni or penne pasta, and top with grated pecorino Romano cheese and freshly ground black pepper.

Salsa di Pesto Semplice

(SIMPLE PESTO FOR PASTA, FISH, AND
EGGS)

YIELD: 1 CUP (5-6
3-TABLESPOON SERVINGS)

I *call this pesto sauce simple because it is simple. That's
right, cousin Maryann, it doesn't have the usual garlic
and toasted pine nuts. But it is nevertheless delicious. I
really don't want to go into the old story of its origins
and how it got its name from the old-fashioned mortar
and pestle (pesto in Italian); how it was developed in
the Liguria region of Italy where basil grows luxuri-
antly and has a distinctive flavor; how the Ligurian
olive oil is prized for its aroma and delicacy; no, I don't
want to repeat that story—but I guess I just did. No
matter. Make it and enjoy it.*

> 2 cups large fresh basil leaves
> 3 tablespoons freshly grated pecorino Romano
>   cheese
> 3 tablespoons olive oil
> 1/4 cup chopped fresh Italian (flat-leafed)
>   parsley

Wash the basil thoroughly in cold water, then
dry it. Place it in a blender with the cheese, oil,
and parsley. Blend for 5 seconds, or until smooth
and creamy. Serve with 1 lb. hot or cold pasta.
You may store the pesto sauce in the refrigerator
for a week.

Salsa di Caperi

(CAPER SAUCE)

YIELD: 1 1/2 CUPS (8
3-TABLESPOON SERVINGS)

T*his is more a dressing than a sauce. But the piquancy
of the capers makes it very special. It doesn't matter
whether it's a dressing or a sauce. Make it, use it,
you'll love it (if you like capers, that is). It's wonderful
over salads, fish, veal, cold vegetables, and pasta
salads.*

> 2 hard-boiled eggs
> 1/4 cup red wine vinegar
> 3 tablespoons extra-virgin olive oil
> 2 tablespoons drained chopped capers
> 1 garlic clove, peeled and crushed
> Pinch of cayenne pepper

Mash the eggs and place them in a blender
with remaining ingredients. Blend for 2 seconds, or until well mixed and smooth. Cover
and chill.

Salsa di Porcini

(PORCINI MUSHROOM SAUCE)

YIELD: 1 1/2 CUPS

D*ried porcini mushrooms are outrageously expensive.
Some cooks suggest substituting dried mushrooms from
Poland or South America; I do not. There are times
when expense shouldn't matter. Especially in this case.*

If you want to have an exquisite and authentic sauce, use the porcini. You won't be sorry.

1 cup water
1 cup dried porcini mushrooms
2 tablespoons olive oil
$^1/_2$ cup chopped onions
1 tablespoon chopped pancetta or bacon
1 tablespoon butter
1 tablespoon tomato sauce

In a saucepan, boil the water. Add the mushrooms and simmer until soft. Set aside. In a skillet, heat the oil and brown the onions and pancetta. Drain the oil from the skillet. Add the softened mushrooms with their water (strained through a fine wire mesh sieve lined with cheesecloth to remove any grit), the butter, and the tomato sauce; simmer until the sauce thickens. Serve with your choice of pasta.

Salsa di Ricotta e Ghergigli
(WALNUT-RICOTTA SAUCE)

YIELD: ABOUT 1 1/3 CUPS

Cheese combined with nuts is a natural. They were made for each other. And this recipe doesn't require any cooking! We're talking easy and delicious here. Try this on your favorite pasta. Applause, Applause! Thank you.

1 cup shelled walnuts
$^1/_2$ cup fresh ricotta
$^1/_3$ cup toasted pignoli (pine nuts)

$^1/_4$ cup olive oil
2 tablespoons fresh Italian (flat-leafed) parsley, minced
$^1/_2$ garlic clove, minced
1 tablespoon fresh basil, minced
Salt and freshly ground black pepper to taste

Process all the ingredients in a food processor fitted with the steel blade for 3 seconds. Toss with any kind of pasta cooked al dente and drained, and serve.

Salsa di Peperoni
(ROASTED PEPPER SAUCE)

YIELD: 8 SERVINGS

Fooled you, didn't I? When you read "peperoni" you had visions of that tasty, salty, and fatty dried concoction that is sliced and used as a topping on pizza. I didn't mean to mislead you. Peperoni in Italian means large bell peppers. Besides, what we know as pepperoni in this country is so full of preservatives that its half-life is about as lengthy as nuclear waste. When I desire the real thing—dried Italian sausage—I go to my favorite Italian deli and buy the handmade genuine version. Anyway, this sauce takes a little more time to make, but it is well worth the effort.

2 large red bell peppers
2 large green bell peppers
1 pound ripe fresh plum tomatoes
1 onion
2 tablespoons olive oil
1 garlic clove, peeled

$^{1}/_{3}$ cup chopped fresh Italian (flat-leafed)
  parsley

Cayenne pepper

6 marinated artichoke hearts, drained and
  diced (optional)

$^{1}/_{2}$ cup crumbled Asiago cheese (optional)

Roast the peppers over direct heat or under a broiler until the skin is browned. When they are cool enough to handle, peel off the skins but do not wash the peppers. (If some blackened specks of peel remain on the pepper, it doesn't matter.) Discard the pepper ribs and seeds and then dice. Wash and core tomatoes, then chop. Place the tomatoes and peppers in a blender and reduce to a puree. Peel and mince the onion.

Heat the olive oil in a deep saucepan and push the garlic through a press into the oil. Add the onion and sauté until translucent. Add the pepper-tomato puree, parsley, and cayenne pepper to taste, and cook for 5 to 6 minutes. Toss with 1 pound of any pasta cooked al dente and drained. If desired, garnish with artichoke hearts and Asiago cheese.

Salsa di Melanzane
(EGGPLANT SAUCE)

YIELD: 6 SERVINGS

Eggplant is often used as a meat substitute; no other food product can match its uses. In this sauce it travels to the summit of the culinary mountain. This recipe originated in Sicily and was probably introduced by the Arabs of North Africa during their domination of the island. Hey Martha! We have to try this one.

5 small eggplants, or 1 medium eggplant
  (about 1 pound)

2 tablespoons olive oil

2 garlic cloves, crushed

3 shallots or $^{1}/_{4}$ cup diced yellow onion,
  minced

$^{1}/_{4}$ teaspoon crushed red pepper flakes

2 cups canned Italian plum tomatoes with
  juice, coarsely chopped

$^{1}/_{4}$ cup chopped fresh Italian (flat-leafed)
  parsley

Peel and dice the eggplant, then soak in salted cold water for 15 minutes. Rinse and pat dry. Place the oil, garlic, shallots, red pepper flakes, and eggplant in a large frying pan. Sauté, stirring often, for 8 to 10 minutes. Add the tomatoes and parsley and cook for another 10 to 15 minutes. Toss with any long pasta cooked al dente and drained.

VARIATION: Add 1/2 cup sliced fresh mushrooms and sauté with the shallots. This version can be made without the tomatoes, using just the eggplant, shallots, garlic, and mushroom mixture with lots of parsley.

Salsa Gorgonzola
(BLUE CHEESE SAUCE)

YIELD: ABOUT 2 CUPS

This is a stupendous sauce to use with cavatelli or fusilli.

   2 tablespoons butter
   2 tablespoons all-purpose flour
   1 cup milk
   ¹/₂ pound Gorgonzola cheese,
      crumbled

Mix the butter and flour and cook in a heavy saucepan for 3 minutes on medium heat. Add the milk and whisk. Bring to a simmer, add the Gorgonzola, and stir.

Salsa di Tonno e Pomodori
(TUNA AND TOMATO SAUCE FOR PASTA)

YIELD: 2 1/2 CUPS
(10 1/4-CUP SERVINGS)

Freshly grated lemon rind pleasantly masks the tuna if it happens to be strong in flavor, and enhances the entire sauce. Yes, you may substitute a medium chopped yellow onion for the shallots, but the fresh Italian parsley is essential.

   1 7-ounce can water-packed tuna
   3 tablespoons freshly grated lemon rind
   ¹/₂ pound fresh plum tomatoes
   2 tablespoons olive oil

   6 large shallots, peeled
   ¹/₄ cup chopped fresh Italian (flat-leafed)
      parsley
   1 medium avocado, sliced (optional)

Drain the tuna and mash it in a bowl. Sprinkle with the lemon rind. Wash and core the tomatoes, then chop (there should be about 1 cup). Heat the oil in a frying pan and slice the shallots directly into the pan. Sauté until the shallots are translucent. Add the tomatoes and parsley and cook for 5 minutes, stirring. Add the tuna and cook for 2 minutes. Serve over green or white fettucine cooked al dente and drained. If desired, garnish with sliced avocado.

Salsa di Filetto di Pomodoro
("BEEFSTEAK" TOMATO SAUCE)

YIELD: 4-6 SERVINGS

Plum tomatoes are referred to as small "beefsteaks" in Italian. Their plump, plum-shaped bodies yield a sweet, light, and savory sauce.

   ¹/₄ cup butter
   1 small onion, chopped fine
   ¹/₂ pound boiled ham or prosciutto,
      diced
   2¹/₂ pounds fresh plum tomatoes, or
      1 no. 3 (2 pound, 3 ounce) can, sliced
      into strips, juices reserved
   6 sprigs fresh basil
   1 teaspoon salt
   ¹/₄ teaspoon freshly ground black pepper

If using fresh tomatoes, plunge in boiling water for 1 to 2 minutes. Then remove the stems and skins, slice, and discard seeds. Set aside. In a large saucepan, melt the butter and sauté the onion until golden. Add the ham and sauté 3 minutes longer. Stir in the tomatoes and reserved juice, basil, salt, and pepper. Simmer slowly until the excess water from the tomatoes has been reduced, 20 to 30 minutes. Toss some of the sauce with fettuccine cooked al dente, drained and transferred to a warm serving bowl. Sprinkle with grated cheese. Serve with additional sauce and grated cheese.

Sugo "Agghiota" per il Pesce
(CALABRIAN TOMATO SAUCE FOR FISH)

YIELD: 4 CUPS

This sauce is used in Calabria to cook with fish or with 1 lb of pasta. I had it with pasta in my cousin's house in Reggio. It was wonderful.

6 tablespoons olive oil

1 medium onion, diced

4 cloves garlic, minced

1 no. 3 (2 pound, 6 ounce) can Italian peeled plum tomatoes, chopped

1/2 cup raisins, plumped in warm water for 1/2 hour, then drained

1/4 cup pignoli (pine nuts), lightly browned in a dry skillet on the stove

2 tablespoons capers, washed under cold running water and drained

4 tablespoons pitted green olives, chopped coarsely

1/2 cup washed and chopped Italian (flat-leafed) parsley

1 teaspoon salt

1 1/2 teaspoons freshly ground black pepper

In a large saucepan, heat the oil over moderate heat. Add the onion and garlic and cook 5 minutes. Add the tomatoes, raisins, pignoli nuts, capers, olives, parsley, salt, and pepper. Bring to a boil, lower the heat to simmer, cover and simmer for 30 minutes.

NOTE: This sauce may be cooked with swordfish or fresh tuna steaks. Wash the fish under cold running water, and pat dry with a clean dish towel. Salt and pepper both sides lightly. Place fish in an oven-proof glass dish greased with 1 tablespoon olive oil, cover with the sauce, and cook in a 350° oven for 15 minutes. Turn the fish over after 7 1/2 minutes and continue to cook for remaining 7 1/2 minutes. Serve over angel hair pasta, cooked al dente, or cooked rice, orzo, or couscous.

Sugo di Pomodori Insaporito con Maiale
(PORK-FLAVORED TOMATO SAUCE)

YIELD: 4 CUPS

I tasted this sauce while on my last trip to Italy. My relatives took me to a rustic farmhouse on Aspromonte, the highest mountain in Reggio Calabria. The lady of the house served this delicious sauce on her homemade

(continued)

fusilli pasta. From the window in the kitchen, I saw Mount Etna in Sicily, glowing with molten lava. My spirit was transported by the view of God's splendor and brought down to earth as I ate my bowl of pasta. Both my spirit and body were richly nourished.

6 tablespoons olive oil

1 boneless pork chop

4 cloves garlic, chopped

1 16-ounce can peeled Italian plum tomatoes, coarsely chopped

1 teaspoon dried oregano

2 teaspoons salt

1 teaspoon sugar

1 teaspoon freshly ground black pepper

2 tablespoons capers, washed and drained

In a large saucepan, heat the olive oil over moderate heat. Brown the pork chop lightly on both sides, remove, cool, and shred. Cook the garlic in the same pan for 5 minutes. Add the tomatoes, oregano, salt, sugar, black pepper, and capers and cook covered for 20 minutes. Add the shredded pork and cook 5 more minutes. Cook the pasta of your choice al dente, drain well, and toss into the sauce. Blend gently, then cook 2 more minutes. Serve with grated pecorino cheese.

Sugo di Pomodori alla Calabrisella

(THE PRETTY CALABRIAN GIRL'S TOMATO SAUCE)

YIELD: 2 CUPS

The legend of this sauce is that when a Calabrian girl wants to marry the boy she loves, she makes this sauce for his parents. When they taste it, it's so good that they give their son their approval to marry the girl.

3 tablespoons olive oil

3 cloves garlic, minced

1 medium onion, diced small

1 16-ounce can peeled Italian plum tomatoes, crushed with a fork

1 teaspoon salt

1 teaspoon sugar

1 teaspoon crushed red pepper flakes

6 whole leaves fresh basil

1/4 cup marinated mushrooms, chopped

1/4 cup marinated artichokes, chopped

In a large saucepan, heat the oil over moderate heat. Add the garlic and onion and cook until lightly browned. Add the tomatoes, salt, sugar, red pepper flakes, basil leaves, mushrooms, and artichokes and bring to a boil. Lower the heat to simmer, cover, and cook 30 minutes on simmer. Toss with pasta of your choice cooked al dente and drained.

Sugo alla Moda d'Irpinia

(LAMB AND RICOTTA SAUCE IRPINIA STYLE)

YIELD: 1 1/2 CUPS

Irpinia is a quaint, small village in the mountains near Naples. Its people are engaged in raising sheep. The shepherd families hardly ever see tourists and when I visited, I was first viewed with suspicion. I engaged an old shepherd in conversation. His gnarled hands gripped his shepherd's staff tightly until he realized I was a priest (the priests in Irpinia still wear the long black cassock; I was dressed in a suit and wore the Roman collar). Old Gennaro smiled his toothless smile and explained, "I thought you were a minister who would try to convert me." We laughed together, prayed together, and finally entered his tiny home to eat together.

Gennaro was a widower, his sons and daughter had left Irpinia to find work in Germany. The house missed a woman's touch, but could he cook! We shared this meal together and he said, "Tonight we eat Adelina (referring to the lamb) and Pasqualina's ricotta (referring to the ewe from whose milk he made ricotta)". Now I share Gennaro's recipe with you. Share it with your loved ones; perhaps someday it will evince beautiful memories.

5 tablespoons olive oil

1 large onion, minced

1 rib celery, minced

1 medium carrot (don't peel it!), minced

1/4 pound pancetta or prosciutto, minced

1/4 pound hot salami (sopressata piccante), diced

1/2 pound ground lean lamb

1/2 cup dry white vermouth

3 tablespoons tomato paste, diluted in 1/2 cup warm water

1/2 cup ricotta cheese

1/2 teaspoon salt

1/2 teaspoon crushed red pepper flakes (yes! you may use black pepper instead)

In a large saucepan, heat the oil over moderate heat. Add the onion, celery, carrot, pancetta, lamb, and salami and cook 10 minutes. Add the vermouth and cook until it evaporates. Add the diluted tomato paste and cook, covered, on simmer for 1 hour. Remove from the heat. Stir in the ricotta, salt, and pepper. Toss with pasta cooked al dente and drained. Sprinkle with pecorino (sheep's milk) cheese.

Salsa di Pesto Siciliano

(SICILIAN PESTO FOR PASTA, SOUPS OR AS A DIP)

FRANCA PAVONE

MISILMERI (PALERMO) SICILY

YIELD: 2 CUPS

When I was in Italy recently doing more research for this book, I was the house guest of Franca and her son Maurizio.

He told me that his Mom made a "knock-your-socks-off" pesto sauce. I smiled and thought, 'every kid thinks that his mom is the best cook in the world.' Well, I tasted Franca's pesto, and if my shoes were not tightly laced, it would have knocked my socks off.

2 cups fresh basil leaves packed down

2 cloves fresh peeled garlic

$^1/_2$ cup pignoli (pine nuts) toasted in fry pan
  until lightly browned

$^1/_2$ cup grated Parmigiano Reggiano cheese

$^1/_2$ cup grated pecorino cheese

1 small jalapeno or other hot fresh pepper, stem
  removed, de-seeded and cut into chunks

$1^1/_2$ cups extra-virgin olive oil

Put all ingredients in food processor fitted with steel blade. Process by pulsing for about one (1) minute. Sauce should have a grainy consistency. Do not over process. Serve with hot or cold pasta, place a dollop in your minestrone soup or serve as a dip for toasted Italian bread. Enough sauce for 1 lb of pasta.

No kidding! This pesto will knock your socks off.

Pasta

This book contains an abundance of pasta recipes—and we haven't even scratched the surface. Pasta is one of the first forms of convenience food and provides an excellent variety of culinary opportunities. Please stay away from the instant forms, ready-made meals, and quick-cook mixtures. Use fresh pasta—either homemade, with the help of a pasta machine, or store-bought—or good-quality dried pastas imported from Italy.

The exciting aspect of pasta is that it can provide whatever you need—be it a really tasty, satisfying family meal, a romantic dinner for two, or a stunning dinner-party dish. It is all things to all people, from interesting shapes for toddlers to a gourmet topic of conversation for connoisseurs.

For the Southern Italian, pasta, rather than bread, is the staff of life. It is healthful, hearty, and surprisingly low in calories—and probably the most thoroughly adaptable of foods. It goes with just about anything—meat, fish, or vegetables. All by itself it's a good source of carbohydrates. Pasta is to the Italian what the potato is to the Irishman.

Many civilizations claim to have originated it. Once simple peasant fare, it's now a must on the most elegant menus.

Pasta is considered by many to be a meal fit for a king. Some "authorities" even go so far as to claim that it began at the court of Frederico II, the Holy Roman Emperor and King of Sicily, in 1220—a contradiction to the more popular notion that spaghetti found its way to Italy from China thanks to Marco Polo in 1279. Some maintain it first took shape with the Etruscans, others say it started with the Arabs, and then there are those who claim that it was introduced into Europe during the Mongol invasions of the thirteenth century. Although pasta may have had its beginnings in many different countries, and its dates of origin are hard to pinpoint, it is, of course, most often associated with Italy.

Not too long ago, people ate spaghetti mainly because they were unable to afford anything else. But through the years, the low-priced staple has won over the most sophisticated diners; many now select fettuccine over filet mignon. In fact, it has acquired such snob appeal that many restaurants can and do charge too much for just a sampling of these al-dente delicacies.

In the sports community, pasta has been called the food of champions. Because of the complex carbohydrates it contains, it is a high-energy food, whereas sugar and candy, which contain simple carbohydrates, give quick, short-lived boosts. Today, many athletes fill up on pasta before going into competition in order to build up the level of carbohydrates that will be burned off during the event. Low in protein, pasta is easier to digest than foods such as red meat and enables the body to concentrate on breaking records rather than on breaking down protein.

Pasta also contains eight vitamins, riboflavin, niacin, and iron, and is—contrary to popular belief—low in calories. An average serving (5 ounces) has only 210 to 220 calories, and some pastas in today's market are even lower in calories. The sauce that tops the dish is what adds on the pounds. Pasta is also low in cholesterol. One study showed that Southern Italians, who eat more pasta than their Northern counterparts, had lower levels of cholesterol in their blood and suffered from fewer coronary diseases.

Although pasta is not usually a part of most weight-reduction diets, it can be worked in as a substitute depending on the quantity and the manner in which it is served. Think of it this way: The word *diet* originated from the Greek word *diaita,* which was originally defined as "a way of living well," and later came to mean "health-giving nourishment." Perhaps the Italians understand the first definition better. According to the National Pasta Association, Italians consume about sixty pounds of pasta per capita per year. Yet Italy does not suffer from an obesity problem because pasta is a low-fat, low-sodium, easily digested food. The conclusion is that a diet rich in carbohydrates and low in protein develops more energy within the body, burning off more calories.

Perhaps the best thing about pasta is that it can be found in over one hundred shapes and sizes. There is *pasta lunga,* long pasta, which includes spaghetti, spaghettini, cappellini, bucatini, mezzanelle, ziti, linguine, and fresine. And *pasta corta,* or short pasta, which includes such fun shapes as rigatoni, ditalini, tortiglioni, gemelli, penne, tofette—and the list goes on and on. There is even a special category of the pale yellow delectable called *paste speciali,* which includes lasagne, mafaldine, tripoline, and farfalle, as well as farfalline, fusilli lunghi, and tagliatelle. Remember, each region in Italy has its own special varieties; this listing is only a sampling.

The next best thing about pasta is the sauce with which it is served. The preparation can be as easy as adding butter and cheese. You can eat just about anything with pasta. If you have a craving for fish, there are sauces made with tuna or salmon; a desire for meat can be satisfied with a Bolognese sauce; while vegetarians can get their fill with any number of sauces—the most popular being salsa primavera, made with broccoli, artichokes, eggplant, mushrooms, peas, and even cauliflower.

To obtain the tastiest results, remember that certain pasta shapes best accompany certain sauces. Spaghetti is the most adaptable to the greatest variety of sauces, and spaghettini is best served with seafood sauces or olive oil based sauces. Meat sauces and other chunky sauces go with stubby pasta, such as rigatoni and shells, which trap bits of the sauce in their openings and ridges. A creamy sauce goes great with fusilli since it can cling to the twists.

In Italy, pasta is eaten as a primo piatto (first course) and never as a side dish as is sometimes done in America. So take your choice from the many shapes—fresh or dry—pick a sauce, pour a glass of wine, and mangia!

PASTA RECIPES FROM ITALIAN-AMERICAN FAMILY AND FRIENDS

When my last cookbook, *Father Orsini's Pasta Perfetta* (New York: Hearst Books, 1995), was published, it received a very favorable review in *Publishers Weekly.* The reviewer said, "Father Orsini worships pasta." Well, I don't worship pasta; I worship the Creator who gave the human race the genius to invent pasta. I must admit, however, that I reverence pasta. That's not worship, is it?

When I was hard at work writing my last book, I asked my family members and some dear friends to share their favorite pasta recipes with me. I also asked them to write an introductory paragraph explaining their relationship to me. I had hoped that their recipes and comments would become part of *Pasta Perfetta.* However, my diplomatic editor at Hearst, a division of William Morrow Publishing, Megan Newman, very wisely and delicately advised me to drop that chapter from the book. It just didn't fit in with the rest of the book. When I began to read the recipes again, I knew they were terrific. So I decided to use them in this book. Since the personal comments regarding me

were like reading testimonials of witnesses in the formal process of declaring a person a saint, I knew that my family and friends were being extremely kind; I deleted their comments because God isn't finished with me yet.

Most cookbooks are collections of recipes, and a good cookbook must have, I believe, clear, easy-to-follow recipes. I am also convinced that if the author of a cookbook is candidly revealed in the book—if he or she becomes real to the reader—then the cookbook advances to a higher level. It functions as a medium through which real human contact can be made and even friendship can blossom. For that reason, I replaced the testimonials with commentary of my own.

Fedelini con Sugo di Mare
(PASTA WITH SEAFOOD SAUCE)

LEO AND INEZ ORSINI
BAYONNE, NEW JERSEY

My sister-in-law Inez is a terrific cook; she consistently pleased the infamously finicky palate of my oldest brother Leo. During the sixty-one years of their marriage, I was often a guest at their table and was never disappointed. In fact, oftentimes when I was a young boy living down the street from their home, I would eat supper at my mother's table and run over to Inez's to have another tasty meal. That's how I became a fat kid who had to be taken to Barney's "Husky Boys Department" for mom to buy my clothes.

SERVES 4

(continued)

This is as near to perfection as you can get if you are a lover of seafood. You will almost be able to smell the refreshing salt air blowing in from the sea and taste the heat of the sun-drenched beach. You will want to have fresh, crunchy Italian bread to soak up the tantalizing sauce. My oldest brother, Leo, who passed from this valley of tears into eternal life on March 14, 1999, loved this dish. I know you will too.

1 teaspoon crushed red pepper flakes

2 large cloves garlic, peeled and chopped

2 tablespoons olive oil

1 pound fresh tomatoes, peeled (see Tip, page 32) and chopped

Salt and freshly ground black pepper

³/₄ cup fresh shrimp, peeled and deveined

1 dozen small clams, scrubbed

¹/₄ cup chopped fresh parsley and basil

1 pound fedelini or spaghettini

¹/₂ pound lump crabmeat

Sauté the red pepper flakes and garlic in half the olive oil. Add the tomatoes and cook for 15 minutes. Add salt and pepper to taste. Set aside. This is your tomato sauce.

In another pan, sauté the shrimp and clams in the remaining oil. Cook until tender (about 5 minutes), then add the tomato sauce and fresh herbs. Remove from the heat.

Cook the pasta al dente. Drain well, pour into a warm serving bowl, and toss with the sauce. Add the crabmeat, stir to warm, and serve immediately.

Pasta con Finocchio
(PASTA WITH FENNEL)

CARMEL AND CARMEN FERRANTE

TOTOWA, NEW JERSEY

My niece Carmel is my brother Leo's first daughter. We are close in age and for an extended period of time, practically grew up together. Ironically, I met her husband Carmen when I was a freshman and he was a senior at Seton Hall University. He had been my friend before he met my niece on a blind date. Go figure!

They are both accomplished cooks, and Carmel is not too shabby in the baking department either.

SERVES 4

Fennel is an ambrosial and palate-cleansing vegetable that when eaten raw tastes like anise or licorice. The Italians often serve it sliced after dinner because they believe it helps your digestion. It is great when it's served crisp and cold, and it acts as a breath-freshener.

In this recipe, fennel climbs to new heights of gustatory pleasure. What I'm trying to say is that it tastes wonderful. Make this dish and you will join me in singing fennel's praises.

3 tablespoons olive oil

1 medium onion, chopped

3 cloves garlic, minced

1 small fennel bulb, cut into strips 1¹/₂-2 inches long

1 16-ounce can crushed tomatoes

1 pound fresh plum tomatoes, chopped

³/₄ cup vegetable stock (available in bouillon or powdered form)

1 teaspoon fennel seeds, crushed

Salt and freshly ground black pepper to taste

1 pound farfalle (bowties) or your favorite
   pasta

Heat the oil in a saucepan. Add the chopped onion, garlic, and fennel. Cover and simmer for 15 minutes. Add the remaining ingredients and simmer uncovered for 1 hour. Cook the pasta al dente and drain well. Turn into a warm serving bowl. Pour the sauce over the pasta, toss, and serve.

Rigatoni con Fagiolini e Patate
(MACARONI WITH GREEN BEANS AND POTATOES)

INEZ C. ORSINI, A.K.A. NEZZIE

TITUSVILLE, FLORIDA

SERVES 4

Now we're talking simple yet outrageously delicious, flavorsome, and gratifying. My Mamma used to make this recipe sometimes on Friday nights for supper when she got tired of the usual pasta e fagioli ("pasta fazool"—you know, pasta and pinto beans). When she did, it was delightful change. My niece Nezzie, fell in love with it. It reminds her of Grandma. That is what some recipes do, they remind us of loved ones.

1/4 cup olive oil

4 large cloves garlic, peeled and minced

1 pound fresh green beans, washed, ends
   snapped off

3 medium potatoes, peeled, washed, and
   diced

Salt and freshly ground black pepper

1 1/2 cups water

1 pound rigatoni

Freshly grated Parmesan or Pecorino Romano
   cheese to pass at table

In a large saucepan, heat the oil over medium heat. Add the garlic and sauté until golden. Add the beans and potatoes and sauté until fork–tender. Add salt and pepper to taste. Add the water and bring to a boil. Lower to a simmer and cook, covered for 15 minutes.

Cook the pasta al dente. Drain. Pour the pasta into the beans and toss well. Pour into a warm serving bowl and bring to the table. Provide grated Pecorino Romano or Parmesan cheese for each person to sprinkle on their serving.

Pasta e Lenticchie con Polpettinni di Salsiccia
(LENTILS WITH SAUSAGE AND PASTA)

JO-ANNE ORSINI MARTIN

BAYONNE, NEW JERSEY

SERVES 6

With the aid of my trustworthy calculator, I just figured out how much it costs to prepare this recipe. Would you believe under ten dollars? Oh, I'm sorry, I forgot to add in the cost of a huge loaf of Italian bread. This is another $1.55. So its still inexpensive for a meal that is fit for a king. And it serves six people. Mamma mia!

What a bargain! This stuff is goluptious (I looked that one up in my thesaurus; it means delicious).

- 4 stalks celery, cut into chunks
- 5 leaves fresh basil
- 5 cloves garlic, peeled
- 2 cups warm water
- 1 pound lentils, picked over, washed, soaked for 1/2 hour, and drained
- 1/4 cup olive oil
- Salt and freshly ground black pepper
- 1/4 teaspoon crushed red pepper flakes (optional)
- 1 pound sweet Italian sausage, skinned, formed into tiny balls, and fried until very brown
- 1 pound dittalini pasta or any soup pasta

In a food processor, place the celery, basil, and garlic. Add the warm water and liquefy. Add to drained lentils in a large saucepan and slowly bring to a boil. Lower to a simmer. Add the oil, salt and pepper to taste, and pepper flakes. Cook for 45 minutes. If mixture becomes too thick, add up to 3 cups water. Add the sausage balls for the last 15 minutes of cooking. Cook the pasta al dente. Drain well. Add the pasta to the cooked lentils and stir well. Pour into a warm bowl and then serve.

Linguine con Cozze alla Calabrese
(LINGUINE WITH MUSSELS CALABRIAN STYLE)

DIANE ORSINI

GLENDALE, CALIFORNIA

SERVES 4

Diane is my brother Leo's youngest daughter. Her recipe reflects the cooking expertise of her mother Inez.

- 1/3 cup finely minced onion
- 1/2 cup dry white wine
- 1 teaspoon dried thyme
- 4 pounds small fresh mussels, well scrubbed
- 6 tablespoons olive oil
- 2 large cloves garlic, peeled and crushed
- 1/4 cup finely minced Italian (flat-leafed) parsley
- 4 large ripe tomatoes, peeled (see Tip, page 32) and chopped
- 1 tablespoon finely minced fresh oregano, or 1 teaspoon dried
- Freshly ground black pepper
- 1 tablespoon tiny capers, drained
- 1 pound linguine

Combine the onion, wine, and thyme in a large 6-quart pot and simmer for 1 minute. Add the mussels and steam, covered, until they open; discard any that do not. Remove with a slotted spoon and set aside. Reduce the cooking liquid to 1 cup, strain, and reserve. Add the oil to the pot and sauté the garlic and parsley for 1 minute. Add chopped tomatoes and cook on high for 10 minutes. Add the reserved mussel liquid and simmer 5 minutes. Season with ground pepper to taste, add the capers, and keep warm. Cook the linguine al dente, drain well, and return to the pot. Add the mussels and sauce. Toss gently, transfer to a warm pasta bowl, and serve.

Pasta con Salsiccia
(PASTA WITH SAUSAGE)

MARIE AND JOHN ORSINI
BRICKTOWN, NEW JERSEY

SERVES 4

In 1993, when I received this recipe, I had no idea that just one year later I would have had the sad obligation of officiating at the funerals of my brother and sister-in-law. It is with fond memories of them that I share this special recipe. If you are monitoring your intake of fat and cholesterol, stay away from it. If not, then you will really enjoy this lip-smacker. It is right up there among the top ten. Of course I'm not going to tell you my top ten. I don't want you to photocopy them and not read the rest of the book.

1 pound penne or rigatoni
3 cups Mamma Orsini's Tomato Sauce (page 47)
2 tablespoons olive oil
1 large clove garlic, peeled and minced
Salt and freshly ground black pepper
$^{1}/_{4}$ teaspoon fresh basil
$^{1}/_{4}$ teaspoon dried sage
4 ounces heavy cream

$^{1}/_{4}$ pound **Italian sausage, skinned, crumbled, and fried until crisp**
2 ounces each **fontina, mozzarella, and pro-volone cheeses, freshly grated**

Cook the pasta al dente, drain well, and set aside. Warm the tomato sauce on moderate heat in half the olive oil. Add the rest of the oil and the garlic and cook until an aroma develops, about 10 minutes. Season the sauce with salt and pepper to taste, and the basil and sage. Simmer 2 minutes. Remove from the heat.

Spoon three-quarters of the sauce into a pasta bowl. Remove 2 tablespoons of the remaining sauce for garnish. To the remaining sauce add the cream and reduce for 3 minutes. Add the sausage, grated cheeses, and pasta and heat until the cheese melts. Pour over the sauce in the bowl, toss, and garnish with the reserved tomato sauce. Serve immediately.

Insalata di Tortellini
(TORTELLINI SALAD)

CARMEL AND GLENN GRIECO
BERKLEY HEIGHTS, NEW JERSEY

SERVES 6

Pasta salads are the rage today; even the salad bars at less expensive restaurants carry an old standby, macaroni salad dressed with mayonnaise. This recipe carries pasta salad to a new and sophisticated standard. Because it is so rich and satisfying, a generous helping is enough for a meal.

If you know people who are on a diet (who isn't?) and they tell you with a sad face, "I only had a salad for lunch," ask, "What was in the salad?" If they honestly describe this recipe, then don't feel sorry for them because they really ate better than you. Unless you've eaten the same salad. My niece Carmel, the daughter of my brother John and sister-in-law Marie, says that her six children are nuts about this pasta salad. I'm sure that you will be nuts about it too.

1 1-pound package frozen meat tortellini

1 tablespoon olive oil

¼ pound sliced pepperoni or Italian salami, cut into small wedges

1 6-ounce jar marinated artichoke hearts with liquid

1 9-ounce jar Tuscan peppers, drained

1 6-ounce can black pitted olives, drained

1 10-ounce jar green olive salad (Goya Alca-parrado with pimientos and capers), drained

½ pound fresh mozzarella, cubed

Italian salad dressing

Cook the tortellini, drain, and toss with the olive oil to prevent sticking. Let cool, then add the remaining salad ingredients. Toss with your favorite Italian salad dressing and refrigerate for several hours. Toss again before serving.

Pasta alla Carbonara
(SPAGHETTI WITH BUTTER, PARMESAN, AND BROWNED BACON)

ANN AND SANDY DAVIDSON
CLEMENTON, NEW JERSEY

SERVES 4

Hold on folks, this is another delicious artery-plugger! Why is it that the best-tasting foods are the ones that the medical people tell you to avoid? Hey, once in a while you have to treat yourself and enjoy, right? Just don't tell your physician . . . he'll be jealous. My niece Annie swears by this recipe. Now we're not supposed to swear, but in this case we'll make an exception. By the way, Annie is my brother John's youngest daughter.

4 strips bacon, cut into ½-inch pieces

1 pound spaghetti

4 tablespoons butter

½ cup freshly grated Parmesan cheese

2 tablespoons chopped fresh Italian (flat-leafed) parsley, or other fresh herbs to taste

Sauté the bacon until browned. Drain on paper toweling and discard the fat. Cook the spaghetti in plenty of boiling water (salted) until al dente, or firm to the bite, about 8 minutes. Ladle out ¼ cup of the pasta-cooking liquid and reserve it. Drain the pasta.

Melt the butter in the pasta-cooking pan until just creamy; add the pasta, the reserved cooking liquid, and the cheese, and toss. Sprinkle with the bacon and the parsley. Toss once again and serve.

Spaghetti Agli'e Olio

(SPAGHETTI WITH GARLIC AND OIL SAUCE)

MARY AND DOMINICK ORSINI
BAYONNE, NEW JERSEY

SERVES 4

Garlic, glorious garlic! This pungent, tasty bulb of pearly white cloves is related to the gorgeous lily. Almost every dish I cook has garlic as its most essential ingredient . . . beautiful garlic. There is nothing that can match its flavor. As soon as I smell it sautéing in olive oil, I begin to salivate.

This simple recipe is, I must confess, my favorite pasta dish. It is so light and easy to digest that I always have two generous servings.

Be sure to cook the garlic until golden brown, but be careful not to burn it. The flavor will be unbelievably nutty and sweet at the same time. I urge you to try it; you won't be sorry. My brother Dominick and sister-in-law Mary and I eat together almost every day. We live next door to one another. We have this dish often; once you try it, you will too.

1/2 cup olive oil, less 1 tablespoon reserved
    for toasting bread crumbs
1 whole bulb garlic, peeled and minced
Salt and pepper to taste
6 quarts water
1 tablespoon salt
1 pound spaghetti
1/4 cup chopped fresh Italian parsley
1/2 cup bread crumbs seasoned with 1 clove
    garlic, chopped, 2 tablespoons grated
cheese, and 1 teaspoon freshly ground
    black pepper and toasted in a skillet
Freshly grated Parmesan cheese

Heat the oil in a large skillet over moderate heat. Add the chopped garlic, adjust the heat to a simmer, and cook until golden brown. Season with salt and pepper to taste. Set aside.

Bring the water to a boil, add the salt, and cook the pasta al dente. Reserve 1 cup of the cooking water, then drain the pasta completely. Sauté the bread crumbs until toasty brown in the reserved 1 tablespoon of olive oil.

Empty the cooked pasta into a serving bowl. Stir the reserved pasta-cooking water into the oil and garlic, pour it over the pasta, and toss. Sprinkle with the parsley. Bring to the table. Serve the toasted bread crumbs and grated cheese separately.

Pasta Vegetaria

(VEGETABLE PASTA)

MARY E. ORSINI
BAYONNE, NEW JERSEY

SERVES 3-4

What a terrific way to enjoy guiltless pasta! The fresh vegetables and herbs brighten the wonderful taste and you will not feel the need to go to confession afterward. My niece Mary doesn't cook often, but when she does, she comes up with winners.

I have a physician who is also a close friend. He was getting a little chunky, but then I noticed he was starting to shed pounds. I asked him what was going on. He told me, "Simple, Father Joe. I eat one meal a day, in the afternoon. A big plate of pasta with a fresh vegetable and tomato sauce, a crisp green salad, and a glass of red wine. The pounds just roll off." Thanks Dr. Simone, this is a diet program we could all follow easily, especially with Mary's Pasta Vegetaria.

2 tablespoons olive oil

3 garlic cloves, minced

1/4 cup chopped onions

1 pint cherry tomatoes, halved

2 cups chopped broccoli

1 tablespoon chopped fresh basil

1/2 teaspoon crushed red pepper flakes or to taste

Salt and freshly ground black pepper to taste

1/2 pound fettucine

Freshly grated Parmesan cheese

Heat the oil in a large skillet over medium-high heat. Add the garlic and onion and sauté until tender, about 5 to 10 minutes. Add the tomatoes and cook until softened, about 10 minutes. Blend in the seasonings.

While preparing sauce, start to boil water for the fettuccine; 4 or 5 minutes *before* the pasta is done, add the chopped broccoli. Continue to boil until the pasta is al dente, about another 8 minutes. Drain the fettuccine and broccoli in a colander.

Add the fettuccine and broccoli to the mixture in the skillet. Sprinkle lightly with Parmesan cheese and toss again. Serve immediately.

Linguine con Vongole di Leo
(CLAM SAUCE AND LINGUINE)

LEO ORSINI

OKEMOS, MICHIGAN

SERVES 4

Some people, like my nephew Leo, are crazy about clams. I'm not. In fact, although I will cook seafood and fish dishes for guests, they never pass my lips. I have a strong aversion to any creature that lives in the water—salt or fresh. When I was four years old, I was forced to eat a fish dish that my dear Mamma had prepared for the family. I promptly got sick all over the place, and was severely reprimanded for ruining everyone's appetite. Since that day, although I've tried, I simply pass when seafood or fish is served. Thank God there is always plenty of Italian bread and salad!

6 cloves garlic, chopped

3 tablespoons olive oil

1 28-ounce can whole tomatoes (or 2 16-ounce cans)

1 teaspoon salt

1/4 teaspoon pepper

1 tablespoon dried oregano

1 6 1/2-ounce can chopped clams

1 pound linguine

In a large skillet, brown the garlic in the oil; do not burn. Add the tomatoes, salt, pepper, and oregano. Crush the tomatoes with a fork. Simmer for 30 minutes. Add the clams and their juices, and simmer 5 more minutes. Cook the linguine al dente and drain well. Toss with the sauce and serve. If you eat this and you are allergic to clams, this will be your last meal. *Enjoy!*

Pasta e Fagioli
(MACARONI AND BEANS)

ANTHONY ORSINI

BAYONNE, NEW JERSEY

SERVES 4

Now we're talking about down-home, hearty, peasant, stick-to-the-ribs cooking! Who hasn't heard of "pasta fazool"? My brother Toto (Anthony) has to have this with us every Friday night. It's become a tradition—a delicious one. Beans combined with pasta or rice is what nutritionists call a complete protein source. If you are trying to avoid meat but know that your body needs protein, then here is a tasty alternative. You won't need to eat bread with this dish. Two servings will stave off your appetite for many hours. And if there is any left over, it tastes even better the next day.

1 pound pinto beans, washed and soaked
  overnight in cold water (Use the same pot
  that you are going to cook the beans in;
  don't drain the beans!)
5 large cloves garlic, peeled
5 large stalks celery, washed and cut into
  chunks
¼ cup olive oil
1½ teaspoons salt
1 teaspoon freshly ground black pepper
4 large potatoes, peeled, washed, and diced
1 pound ditali or elbow macaroni

Put the beans on medium heat in their soaking water. Meanwhile, put garlic cloves and celery chunks into a blender, fill with hot water, and blend until completely liquefied. Pour into the bean pot. Bring to a boil, then lower to simmer.

Add the oil, salt, pepper, and diced potatoes. Bring to a boil again. Lower to simmer and cook for 1 hour, stirring occasionally.

Cook the pasta al dente and drain well. Pour into the cooked beans, stir, and, if only family eating, put the pot right on the table. If you have company, pour into a serving bowl and bring to the table.

Pasta con Sugo di Carne
(PASTA WITH QUICK MEAT SAUCE)

DENISE ORSINI BERKERY

ABERDEEN, NEW JERSEY

SERVES 4

Unexpected guests arrive at your house around mealtime. You and your family had planned a supper of Chinese take-out. What to do? Look in your refrigerator; find the ground beef you were going to use for hamburgers. OK, now into the pantry. Good—everything you need for this recipe is on hand. Invite your friends to stay for dinner. In no time at all, you will bring this tasty dish to your table. No problem. Everyone is happy. (Except your kid, who was looking forward to hamburgers for lunch tomorrow.) Because my niece Denise is often in a hurry, this is her solution to making a great dinner in a jiffy.

2 large onions, peeled and cut in small dice

5 cloves garlic, sliced in halves

3/4 cup olive oil

2 pounds ground chuck beef

1 1/2 tablespoons salt

1 teaspoon freshly ground black pepper

2 1-pound cans Italian tomato puree

1 6-ounce can Italian tomato paste

1 cup water

1 pound pasta (spaghetti, rigatoni, whatever)

In a large saucepan, sauté the onions and garlic in olive oil until soft and golden, about 8 minutes on medium-high heat. Add the ground chuck, salt, and pepper. As meat is browning, stir frequently and mash the meat while stirring to keep it in very small pieces (avoid large chunks). When the meat is completely browned, add the tomato puree, tomato paste, and water (first use it to capture the residues of tomato in the cans). Bring to a slow boil, then simmer over low heat for 45 minutes, stirring occasionally.

Cook your favorite pasta al dente, and drain. Transfer to a warm serving bowl and toss with the sauce.

OPTION: Serve with Italian ricotta cheese, provided on the table in a separate bowl.

Linguine con Vitello Marengo
(VEAL MARENGO WITH LINGUINE)

JOSEPH AND MARY ORSINI
BAYONNE, NEW JERSEY

SERVES 8

There is a famous story that Napoleon Bonaparte's chef wanted to prepare a special dish for the General as the Battle of Marengo (Italy) was drawing to a close. He invented Chicken Marengo. The General was very pleased. Not only did his troops win the battle, but his cook was a culinary genius. Perhaps if veal had been available to the chef, and since this was Italy, the land of pasta, he would have invented the following stupendous recipe. This is a crowd-pleaser. Mary, my nephew Joey's wife, always gets applause when she serves it. Do you want applause? Then make this dish.

1/2 cup olive oil

4 pounds stewing veal, cut into 1-inch cubes

1 cup chopped onion

1 cup chopped celery

1 clove garlic, crushed

1 cup dry white wine

2 8-ounce cans tomato sauce

2 bay leaves

1 teaspoon dried oregano

1/2 teaspoon dried rosemary

2 teaspoons salt (optional)

1/2 teaspoon freshly ground black pepper

2 sprigs fresh Italian (flat-leafed) parsley, chopped

1 pound fresh mushrooms, sliced

2 tablespoons fresh lemon juice

1/2 cup butter

2 pounds linguine

1 tablespoon all-purpose flour dissolved in 2 tablespoons water

1/4 cup chopped fresh Italian (flat-leafed) parsley

Heat the oil in a large saucepan. Add half the veal cubes and sauté until browned all over, remove from the pan, then brown the other half and remove it from the pan.

In the same pan, cook the onion, celery, and garlic, stirring, until the onion is golden, about 5 minutes. Stir in 1/2 cup of the wine and the tomato sauce, bay leaves, oregano, rosemary, salt, pepper, parsley, and veal. Bring to a boil, reduce heat, and simmer, covered, 1 1/2 hours, until the veal is tender. Remove the bay leaves. Meanwhile, toss the mushrooms with the lemon juice in a medium skillet and sauté until tender, about 5 minutes.

Cook the linguine al dente, drain, and set aside. Add the reserved 1/2 cup wine and mushrooms to the veal mixture along with flour-water mixture, and simmer covered, about 15 minutes longer. Place the linguine into a serving dish, pour the veal over it, and sprinkle with parsley. Enjoy!

NOTE: Veal Marengo can be made a day ahead and refrigerated.

Penne alla Vodka
(PENNE MACARONI WITH VODKA SAUCE)

ORESTE ORSINI

BAYONNE, NEW JERSEY

SERVES 4

My brother Oreste got this recipe from a dear family friend, Madeline Santuoso. We liked it so much that we made it often for family and friends. Everyone except my sister-in-law Mary (who can't abide cold cuts) thought it was "the cat's meow." You know, really outstanding. My dear brother died suddenly on December 12, 1992. I am happy that "Rusti" had the opportunity to contribute his favorite recipe to the book before God called him home. Every time I make it now I see my loving brother's face smiling gleefully.

1/2 pound (2 sticks) butter
1/2 pound pancetta or prosciutto, diced
1 28-ounce can Italian plum tomatoes, pureed thoroughly in a blender or food processor
Salt and freshly ground black pepper to taste
1 cup vodka
1 quart half and half
1 pound penne
Freshly grated Parmesan or Pecorino Romano cheese to pass at table
Black pepper to grind at table if you prefer

In a large saucepan, melt the butter over medium heat. Sauté the pancetta or prosciutto until crisp. Add the tomatoes, stir, and bring to a boil. Add salt and pepper to taste. Add the vodka and cook for 5 minutes. Add the half and half and simmer for 20 minutes, stirring often.

Cook the pasta al dente. Drain well and add to the sauce. Stir and allow to rest for 5 minutes. Pour into a serving bowl and bring to table. Serve with grated cheese and have a pepper mill handy; lots of freshly ground black pepper enhances this dish.

Linguine con Pesce al Forno
(BAKED LINGUINE WITH FISH SAUCE)

JOSEPH AND EVELYN VARELA

BAYONNE, NEW JERSEY

SERVES 6

My sister Evelyn and her husband Joe love each other very much and share cooking together. I remember seeing billboard signs proclaiming, "The family that prays together, stays together." I believe that is true and I go a step further: The family that cooks together, sticks together. Evelyn and Joe practice both activities. This recipe combines the delicacy of white-fleshed fish fillet with the zestiness of spices and tomatoes. The wine helps too. I know you are going to enjoy this one.

2 pounds scrod or cod fillet

Cold water

6-8 ice cubes

3 tablespoons fresh lemon juice

3 tablespoons olive oil, plus 1 tablespoon for the baking dish

1 small onion, peeled and sliced thin

3 cloves garlic, peeled and sliced thin

1 28-ounce can crushed tomatoes

1 15-ounce can tomato sauce

1/2 teaspoon salt or to taste

1/4 teaspoon cayenne pepper

1/2 teaspoon dried basil

1 bay leaf

3 tablespoons medium salsa, thick and chunky (we use Ortega brand)

Dash of Louisiana hot sauce

1/4 cup clam juice

1/2 cup white wine

1 pound linguine

Preheat oven to 350°. Soak the fillet in a large bowl with cold water, ice cubes, and lemon juice until ready to bake, about 20-25 minutes.

Heat the oil in a large skillet, sauté the onion and garlic until transparent. Add the next ten ingredients, cover, and cook on medium heat for 1 1/2 hours, stirring occasionally.

Drain the fillet well. Grease a large baking dish with the 1 tablespoon oil, and arrange the fish in a single layer. Spoon 1 1/2 cups of the cooked tomato sauce entirely over the fish; reserve the rest of the sauce to use with the linguine. Bake uncovered for 25 to 35 minutes, or until the fish flakes easily. While the fish is baking, cook the linguine al dente and drain well. Toss with the tomato sauce and serve with the fish.

Linguine con Vongole di Francisco
(JERSEY SHORE CLAM SAUCE WITH LINGUINE)

FRANCISCO AND DEBBIE VARELA

SCOTCH PLAINS, NEW JERSEY

SERVES 4

It shouldn't surprise us that there are many variations on pasta with clam sauce. My nephew Frank, who gave me this version, says, "It doesn't matter how you cook, just cook, because it's a nice way of sharing some *of yourself with others." I agree entirely. Try not to be a slave to recipes. Use your imagination. Experiment— you may come up with a prize-winner. This recipe is certainly that, a prize-winner.*

2 cloves garlic, finely chopped

2 teaspoons olive oil

$^1/_3$ teaspoon dried rosemary

$^1/_4$ teaspoon dried marjoram

$^1/_4$ teaspoon dried thyme

$^1/_2$ teaspoon dried oregano, or 1 teaspoon
  Italian seasoning

1 8-ounce bottle clam juice

2 tablespoons red wine

1 6-ounce can tomato paste

Salt and freshly ground black pepper

2 $6^1/_2$-ounce cans chopped clams

1 pound linguine

Sauté the garlic in the olive oil until golden. Add the spices, clam juice, wine, and tomato paste, and stir well. Add salt and pepper to taste and bring the sauce to a boil. Add the clams, mix well, reduce heat, and simmer for 5 minutes. Cook the linguine al dente, and drain well. Turn into a warm serving bowl and toss with the clam sauce.

Capellini Degli Angeli con Pesce

(SEAFOOD AND ANGEL HAIR PASTA)

ORESTE AND KAREN VARELA

EVESHAM, NEW JERSEY

SERVES 8

You won't find this recipe in a reducing-diet cookbook. The seafood sings in a chorus of smooth cream sauce accented by the counterpoint of asparagus and mushrooms. This is an imaginative and delectable combination of ingredients, which will please the most sophisticated palate. My nephew Oreste is watching his cholesterol intake, so he and Karen make this dish only for festive occasions.

1 box frozen asparagus

$^1/_2$ pound fresh mushrooms

1 tablespoon butter

1 pound angel hair pasta cooked according to
  package directions

1 pound Sea Legs a.k.a. imitation crab meat

1 pound shrimp, boiled and peeled

$^1/_4$ pound (1 stick) butter

1 cup freshly grated Parmesan cheese

1 pint light cream

$^1/_4$ cup chopped fresh Italian (flat-leafed)
  parsley

Cook the asparagus and set aside. Slice the mushrooms and sauté in the butter; set aside. Cook the pasta al dente, drain, and set aside.

In a large pan, melt the stick of butter on a low flame. Add the cheese and stir, then slowly add the cream and stir until hot, being careful *not to boil.* Add the asparagus, Sea Legs, shrimp, and mushrooms. Cook on low until all is heated, about 8 minutes. Toss with the pasta. Sprinkle with the parsley and serve.

Ravioli di Gualtiere

(RAVIOLI ALLA WALTER)

KENNETH AND TRINIDAD WALTER

BAYONNE, NEW JERSEY

SERVES 4

It is easy to buy frozen ravioli today and cook them up in a jiffy. However, no commercial product can compare to the ravioli you can make in your own kitchen. For those of you who are adventurous, try this recipe, please! Once you have made your ravioli from scratch and taste their superior quality, I'm sure you will want to make them often. Trina is my sister Evelyn's daughter—yes, another niece. She and her husband Ken often cook together.

Ravioli Dough:

1 cup all-purpose flour

2 large eggs

Cold water as necessary

Filling:

1 cup ricotta cheese

1/2 cup freshly grated Pecorino Romano cheese

1 egg, beaten

3 tablespoons freshly chopped Italian (flat-leafed) parsley

Sauce:

1 recipe Salsa Marinara, page 50

Sift the flour into a mound on a working surface and make a well in the center. Crack the eggs into the well and use your fingertips to mix the egg yolks and whites. Draw the flour into the mix, a little at a time to form a firm but elastic dough. Add cold water if needed to achieve desired consistency.

Dust work surface with flour and knead dough for about 10 minutes or until dough is smooth and silky. Lightly dust dough ball if it becomes sticky as you knead.

Roll dough as thinly as possible into a square of about 24 inches by 24 inches; I like to be able to see my work surface through the dough. After rolling, allow dough to rest for about 30 minutes.

While dough rests, prepare filling by combining ingredients and mixing well. Refrigerate until ready to use.

After dough has rested for the allotted time, cut in half with a fluted pastry wheel or a sharp knife. On one square of dough, using a clean metal or wooden ruler, lightly impress the dough at 1 1/2 inch intervals both across and down creating a grid 8 rows across by 8 rows down creating 64 1 1/2 inch squares in all.

To fill the ravioli, spoon filling by teaspoonfuls in the center of each of the squares formed by scoring the dough. With a damp pastry brush, moisten the edges gently.

Lay second sheet of dough lightly over the first and seal by firmly depressing finger along the moistened perimeter and lines. Cut along lines with a fluted pastry wheel or sharp knife.

Cook or cover with a floured cloth for use within about an hour. If you plan to cook the pasta later in the day, refrigerate until ready to use or freeze for cooking at another time.

To cook the ravioli, bring water to a boil in a

large pot. Add the ravioli and allow water to return to a boil. Cook for an additional 10 minutes or until desired tenderness. Carefully remove the pasta with a slotted spoon and drain over pot. Place onto serving dish and cover with sauce and serve. Freshly grated cheese may be added at table.

Ravioli freezes wonderfully, uncovered on a cookie sheet or a tray. When fully frozen, they may be stored in a container or even a freezer bag. Freezing the ravioli in portions allows you to use only what you need.

When cooking frozen ravioli, do not defrost; add to the boiling water and allow water to return to boil. Cook an additional 12 minutes or until desired tenderness and serve as you would the fresh ravioli.

Cavatelli con Cavolo
(CAVATELLI WITH CABBAGE)

ROSE LETERA

TRENTON, NEW JERSEY

SERVES 6

Traditionally, Italians had large families and when money was scarce the mamma had to prepare meals that would fill everyone up without emptying the family's funds. This is one of those meals. It is uncomplicated yet appetizing. It is just good plain food, and ready in little time. Rose Letera is Anna Conti's deceased mom. Anna and her family have adopted me "unofficially." Now I am part of the extended Conti family.

1 pound cavatelli pasta

1 cabbage (about 3 pounds)

4 cloves garlic, peeled and crushed

$1/2$ cup olive oil

2 cups canned chicken stock

$1/2$ cup freshly grated Romano cheese

Cook the cavatelli al dente, drain, and set aside. Shred the cabbage as for coleslaw and sauté in a large saucepan with the garlic and oil. When the cabbage is soft, add the chicken broth. Then add the cooked cavetelli, mix, and heat through. Serve with the grated cheese.

Pizza con Pasta
(PASTA PIZZA)

ANNA CONTI

TRENTON, NEW JERSEY

SERVES 6

So you thought you've seen it all? Types of pizza, that is. Imagine pasta in conjunction with pizza. You don't have to imagine it because here it is. This recipe is so scrumptious and filling that one generous slice is a full meal. No kidding, it will knock your socks off!

Pizza Dough (makes 1 14 x 15-inch pizza):

1 package dry yeast

$1^1/2$ cups warm water (105-115°)

2 teaspoons salt

$4^1/2$ cups all-purpose flour

3 tablespoons olive oil

(continued)

Topping Ingredients:

>   2 cups cooked rotelle (circle pasta or wheels)
>
>   2 cups crushed Italian tomatoes
>
>   ½ cup ricotta cheese
>
>   ½ cup freshly grated mozzarella cheese
>
>   6 cloves garlic, crushed
>
>   2 tablespoons freshly grated Parmesan cheese
>
>   ½ teaspoon freshly ground black pepper
>
>   1 teaspoon dried oregano

Dissolve the yeast in warm water in a large bowl and let rest for 10 minutes. Add the salt and 2 cups of the flour to make a thick batter. Add the olive oil and beat for 1 minute. Gradually add the rest of the flour and mix until the dough pulls away from the sides of the bowl. Add more flour by tablespoons (if necessary). This can be done by hand or, as I do, with a Kitchen Aid Mixer.

Knead on a floured board for 10 minutes. Place the dough into a greased bowl, cover with plastic wrap, and allow to rise for 1 1/2 hours. Punch down the dough, cover again, and let rise 45 minutes.

Preheat the oven to 400°. On a floured surface, flatten the dough with your hands into a rough rectangle (14 x 15 inches). Let rest so it does not draw back. Place on a greased pan. Arrange all the topping ingredients on top in the order listed. Bake for 20 to 25 minutes.

Fettuccine Al Modo Mio
(FETTUCCINE "MY WAY")

RICHARD CONTI

TRENTON, NEW JERSEY

SERVES 4

I *was a twenty-two-year-old college kid when I first visited Rome. Of course I found the original Alfredo's restaurant and ordered the specialty, Fettuccine Alfredo. One forkful and I was hooked. It was magnificent. My tastebuds jumped for joy. Oh my God! I thought I'd died and gone directly to heaven. It was déjà vue all over again when, many, many years later, I tasted Richard Conti's (not the actor), Anna Conti's son's adaptation of the world-famous dish. Move over Alfredo. Richard's fettuccine is the apex.*

>   ¼ pound (1 stick) butter
>
>   ¼ pound prosciutto, chopped
>
>   1 cup sliced fresh mushrooms
>
>   ½ cup frozen green peas
>
>   1 pint heavy cream
>
>   ½ cup freshly grated cheese (Parmesan or pecorino, your choice) plus ¼ cup for sprinkling before serving
>
>   1 pound fettuccine

In a saucepan, melt the butter and sauté the prosciutto. Add the mushrooms and peas and simmer for 5 minutes. Add the heavy cream and bring to a boil, add the grated cheese, then simmer, stirring frequently, 5 more minutes until the sauce thickens.

Cook the fettucine, al dente, drain well, and

toss with the sauce. Add more grated cheese on top and serve.

Pasta con Basilico e Ricotta
(PASTA WITH BASIL AND RICOTTA)

CAROLINE NAPOLI

BAYONNE, NEW JERSEY

SERVES 6

Those of us who lived through hard times remember with fondness the economical meals our moms made to keep us happy and healthy. This recipe certainly falls into that category. It doesn't cost an arm and a leg, but it fills you up and strengthens you to face the labors of the next day. As a fringe benefit, it is totally satisfying to your sense of taste. My dear friend Caroline has passed from this life into the Heavenly Kingdom. If we can eat in Heaven, then Caroline will be in the kitchen singing her Neapolitan songs and cooking.

1/4 cup olive oil

1 large onion, peeled and diced

1 pound ricotta cheese

1 cup fresh basil, chopped

Salt and freshly ground black pepper to taste

1 pound fusili (spirals) or farfalle (bowties)

1/4 cup milk, if needed

Heat the oil in a large skillet over moderate heat. Sauté the onion until just wilted. Add the ricotta and mix thoroughly. Add the basil and salt and pepper and simmer for 5 minutes. Set aside.

Cook the pasta al dente and drain well. Pour into the sauce and toss well. If sauce is too thick, stir in the milk. Pour into a warm serving bowl and bring to the table.

Pasta con Salsiccia Italiana e Caperi
(PASTA WITH ITALIAN SAUSAGE AND CAPERS)

FRANK NAPOLI

WALNUT CREEK, CALIFORNIA

Frank and I went to high school together. An unforgettable character, Frank is also a good cook.

SERVES 6

Capers are the unopened blossoms of the caper plant that grows in wild profusion throughout the Mediterranean region. They have a distinct pungent flavor that adds character to many recipes. Capers work well in this recipe as they enhance the flavor of the sauce. When you buy the Italian sausage, make sure that it isn't too fatty and that it is seasoned with fennel seeds. This is an excellent dish.

1/4 cup olive oil

1 pound Italian sausage, skinned and chopped

1 28-ounce can peeled Italian style plum tomatoes

1/4 cup capers, well-drained

Salt and freshly ground black pepper

1 pound ziti, fusili (spirals), or farfalle (bowties)

(continued)

4 sprigs Italian (flat-leafed) parsley, finely
　　chopped
Freshly grated pecorino cheese to pass at table

Heat the oil in a large skillet on moderate heat.
Add the chopped sausage and brown well, 10 to 15
minutes. Add the tomatoes, pureeing in a blender
or processor prior to addition. Add the capers and
salt and pepper to taste. Mix thoroughly and maintain heat at high level for 10 minutes.

Cook the pasta al dente and drain well. Pour
into the sauce and toss well. Add the parsley
while tossing. Divide into portions and serve.
Pass the cheese separately so each may add as
much as desired.

Pasta con Cavolfiore e Cipolla
(PASTA WITH CAULIFLOWER AND ONION)

ROSE NAPOLI

BAYONNE, NEW JERSEY

*When I was a kid, Rose's husband Pete gave me my
first job, counting coins from his vending machines.
Rose is a conscientious cook and keeps Pete happily
husky and healthy.*

SERVES 4

The American Cancer Society urges us to eat more broc-
*coli, and broccoli is a first cousin to cauliflower. By
itself, cauliflower is almost tasteless, but in this recipe,
it absorbs the savory flavors of the other ingredients.
Most kids hate cauliflower, but they'll be asking for
more when you present it to them this way.*

¹/₄ cup olive oil
1 medium onion, peeled and diced
1 large head cauliflower, cut into bite-sized
　　florets
1 15-ounce can crushed tomatoes or peeled
　　Italian tomatoes
Pinch of oregano
1 cup water
Salt and freshly ground black pepper to taste
1 pound elbow macaroni
Freshly grated pecorino cheese to pass at table

Heat the oil in a large skillet and sauté the
onion to wilt. Add the cauliflower, tomatoes, and
oregano, bring to a slow boil and add the water.
Add salt and pepper to taste. Cook for 15 minutes on medium heat.

Cook the pasta, drain, retaining 1 cup of the
pasta-cooking water, and pour into the sauce. If
there is not enough sauce, add enough pasta
water to make the desired consistency. Pour into
a warm serving bowl and bring to table. Serve
the cheese separately so each may use as much as
desired.

Pasta Piselli alla Napolitana
(PASTA WITH PEAS NEAPOLITAN STYLE)

RACHEL NAPOLI BUDD

BAYONNE, NEW JERSEY

*Rachel is the only girl in the family. She is a retired
teacher, an environmental activist and a traditional
Italian cook.*

SERVES 6

This is another time-saving meal that your family won't tire of quickly. Serve accompanied with crusty Italian rolls and a huge green salad. You'll have it "made in the shade," as the saying goes.

1/4 cup olive oil

1 medium onion, peeled and diced

1 8-ounce can tomato sauce

2 medium potatoes, peeled and diced

Salt and freshly ground black pepper

1 cup water, if needed

2 7-ounce cans green peas with their liquid

1 pound elbow macaroni

Freshly grated Parmesan cheese

Heat the oil in a large saucepan and sauté the onion until just wilted. Add the tomato sauce and diced potato. Add enough of the water to barely cover the potatoes. Add salt and pepper to taste. Add the peas and cook for 20 minutes.

Cook the pasta al dente and drain well. Pour into the sauce and toss. Serve with the grated cheese.

Pasta con Gamberi e Broccoli
(SHRIMP AND BROCCOLI WITH PASTA)

HARRY DOMBROSKY

MOORESTOWN, NEW JERSEY

SERVES 6

It's five o'clock in the afternoon. You have just gotten in from work and guests are coming for dinner at 6:15 P.M. Not to worry! You have plenty of time to change your clothes, straighten up the house, and prepare this scrumptious meal. You can proudly bring this steaming delight to your table and smile while your guests throw you sincere compliments about your cooking skills. Harry, the originator of the recipe, is a good friend. His mom's parents come from Sicily.

1 pound linguine

4 tablespoons olive oil

5 cloves garlic, crushed

1 pound shrimp, shelled, cleaned, and deveined

Salt, freshly ground black pepper, and cayenne pepper to taste

3 tablespoons chopped fresh Italian (flat-leafed) parsley

2 cups canned chicken broth

1 head broccoli spears, steamed al dente

3 ounces freshly grated Parmesan cheese

Cook the linguine al dente, drain well, and set aside. Heat the oil in a large saucepan. Add the garlic and sauté until lightly brown. Add the shrimp, seasonings, and parsley. Sauté for 3 minutes. Add the chicken broth and broccoli spears and simmer on low heat for 5 minutes. Remove from heat. Pour shrimp mixture over the pasta. Sprinkle with the cheese and serve.

Pasta con Sarde

(PASTA WITH SARDINES)

THE BENANTI FAMILY:

CHARLIE, ANGELA, AND ROSALYN

BENANTI'S ITALIAN DELI

BAYONNE, NEW JERSEY

Charlie is the warm hearted owner of the busiest Italian deli in town. His non-Italian wife learned to cook from Charlie's Italian mom. Angela cooks so well, I asked her for two recipes, this and the one that follows.

SERVES 4

This is the quintessential pasta dish from the resplendent island of Sicily. It was most likely introduced to Sicily during its Arab domination. Note the exotic ingredients—pine nuts and raisins. Pasta con Sarde is synonymous with Western Sicily, Palermo, and the island's complicated history. This is a very popular dish that is prepared to celebrate many important religious holidays, especially Christmas Eve.

¹/₂ pound fresh sardines

2¹/₂ tablespoons olive oil

¹/₂ small onion, chopped

2 cloves garlic, chopped

1 quart plain home-made tomato sauce, heated to a simmer (for example, *Marinara* page 50)

¹/₂ cup plain bread crumbs

¹/₄ teaspoon salt

¹/₄ teaspoon freshly ground black pepper

¹/₄ pound fresh finocchio (fennel), whole

3 quarts water

1 pound linguine

1 cup pignoli (pine nuts), toasted in a 350° oven until light brown

¹/₃ cup raisins

Scrape the scales off the sardines. Cut the heads and tails off and debone them. Cut into small pieces. In a large skillet add 2 tablespoons of the olive oil and sauté the onion and garlic until golden. Add the sardines and cook about 3 to 5 minutes more. Bring the tomato sauce to a simmer, and add the sardine mixture to it.

In another skillet put the remaining 1/2 tablespoon olive oil. Add the bread crumbs, salt, and pepper, and brown until golden over a low flame. Set aside.

Cook the fennel in the water about 20 to 30 minutes. Keep them whole. Take fennel out; do not throw out the water. Now cut them into small pieces and add to the sauce. Cook the pasta in the fennel water until al dente, then drain. Put the pasta in a large warm serving bowl, add the toasted bread crumbs, sauce, pignoli, and raisins. Toss and serve.

Pasta al Forno Benanti

(BAKED MACARONI)

SERVES 4

There is no resemblance at all between this dish and the baked macaroni that comes in a box and tastes like its cardboard container. This is a real masterpiece that should cause a spontaneous celebration. I can almost hear the Sicilian tarantella played wildly on the friscalettu *(flute), organettu (accordion), tamburro (large tam-bourine), and castagnetti (castanets) when this superb work of culinary art is brought to the table. You will erupt with the Sicilian phrase "Sa benedica" (God bless you) when you dig in and savor this delight.*

1 teaspoon olive oil

1 small onion, chopped

³/₄ pound ground beef

1¹/₂–2 quarts homemade tomato sauce (6 to 8 cups)—for example, Salsa di Conserva Pomodori page (49)

1 teaspoon freshly ground black pepper

1 fresh basil leaf

¹/₂ package frozen green peas

2 eggs

1 pound farfalle (bowties) or fusili (spiral)

2 tablespoons butter

2 tablespoons plain bread crumbs

¹/₄ pound prosciutto, sliced thin

8 ounces mozzarella cheese, freshly grated

¹/₄ pound Romano cheese, freshly grated, 1 tablespoon reserved

Warm the sauce on moderate heat. Put the olive oil into a large skillet, add the chopped onion, and cook until glossy. Add the ground beef with a little pepper and brown it. When the meat is browned, take a pasta strainer, put 3 sheets of paper towel in it, put the meat in, and let the fat drain. Then put the meat back into the skillet. Add the basil leaf, frozen peas, and 1 or 2 ladles of tomato sauce. Simmer for 15 minutes.

In the meantime, preheat the oven to 350°. Hard-boil the eggs. Cook the pasta in a large pot until half done, then drain and put back into the pot. Add 2 cups of sauce and mix. Rub butter on

the bottom and sides of a baking dish. Sprinkle bread crumbs to coat the entire dish. Cut the prosciutto into small pieces (remove the fat, if you like). Mash the hard-boiled eggs with a fork.

Put 2 more cups tomato sauce and the eggs and prosciutto into the pot with half-cooked pasta and mix. Add the grated mozzarella and Romano. Add more sauce, about 2 cups. Remember, the pasta is only half-cooked. Mix again and put into the baking dish. Put a little more sauce on top and add the reserved grated cheese. Cover with foil and bake for about 30 to 45 minutes. When it starts to bubble, it is ready.

Pasta con Gamberi e Granchio
(FRESH TOMATO, SHRIMP, AND CRAB PASTA)

CHARLES AND OKSANA PESTRITTO

WILLIAMSTOWN, NEW JERSEY

I taught Charlie Latin thirty-five years ago. And we still keep our family friendship alive.

SERVES 4

F*rom what I have been told, "loving" and "gentle" are good adjectives to describe this recipe. "Fantabulous" is even better! You can eat this dish a couple of times a week and not mind at all.*

1 pound angel hair pasta

¹/₄ pound (1 stick) butter

¹/₂ pound medium shrimp, clean and deveined

3 ripe tomatoes, diced

(continued)

3 or 4 cloves garlic, diced

¹/₂ cup olive oil

3 large fresh basil leaves, left whole, no dried basil, if fresh unavailable, just drop the ingredient

¹/₂ pound fresh lump crabmeat

¹/₄ cup fresh Italian (flat-leafed) parsley, chopped

Freshly ground black pepper and dried oregano to taste

Cook the pasta al dente and drain well. As the pasta is cooking, melt the butter in a saucepan, add the shrimp, and cook and stir until pink—4 to 5 minutes.

In a large saucepan, mix the tomatoes, garlic, olive oil, and basil. Heat and stir about 5 minutes. Add the shrimp mixture to the tomatoes and stir in the crabmeat. Add the parsley, and pepper and oregano to taste. Simmer about 5 minutes for the flavors to blend. Serve over the drained pasta.

Pasta al Repice
(REPICE'S PASTA SPECIALTY)

ANTHONY REPICE

VINELAND, NEW JERSEY

SERVES 6

Sun-dried tomatoes and sautéed chicken breasts go together like beans and rice. They were made for each other. Talk about good eating! This takes the cake. But save the cake for dessert, with espresso coffee. Really, this is a terrific pasta dish. You must try it—

I insist. Anthony, the creator of this recipe, was my aide when I was the Catholic chaplain at Stockton University.

¹/₂ cup olive oil

2 boneless chicken breasts, cleaned of all skin, fat, tendons, then julienned (sliced into thin strips)

2 cloves garlic, peeled and crushed

2 teaspoons chopped fresh Italian (flat-leafed) parsley

1 teaspoon salt

¹/₂ teaspoon freshly ground black pepper

1 large head of fresh broccoli florets

¹/₂ pound marinated sun-dried tomatoes, julienned

1 pound spaghetti

Put the olive oil in a large saucepan and heat. Add julienned chicken breasts and brown. Add the garlic, parsley, salt, pepper, and broccoli. Cook until the broccoli is fork-tender and then add the sun-dried tomatoes. Simmer for 10 to 12 minutes. Meanwhile, cook the spaghetti al dente, and drain well. Toss the spaghetti with the sauce and enjoy.

Linguine con Pollo e Broccoli
(CHICKEN AND BROCCOLI WITH LINGUINE)

ANTHONY LA SCALA

PINE HILL, NEW JERSEY

SERVES 6

This is a simpler version of the previous recipe, *Pasta al Repice*. And it has an entirely different flavor. The increased amount of garlic permeates the rather bland chicken breasts. Broccoli and chicken seem to have a natural affinity. Together they become a symphony of interwoven textures and flavors. When pasta is the underlying theme, the dish moves dramatically into the last movement and stirs the spirit. Tony, who gave me this recipe, is a good friend whose folks came from Reggio Calabria; my parents' birthplace.

1/2 cup olive oil

12 cloves garlic (minced)

2 pounds boneless chicken breasts sliced in 2 inch strips

one large head fresh broccoli florets

1 pound linguine

Start boiling the water for the linguine in one pot, then in a separate 6-quart pot heat the olive oil. Once the oil is hot, add the garlic and brown. Do not burn. Add the chicken tenders to the oil, cover, and cook on simmer for approximately 20 minutes, stirring occasionally.

Cook the linguine al dente. Reserve 4 cups of the pasta-cooking water, then drain the linguine and set aside.

Add the broccoli to the chicken and continue to simmer everything, covered, for another 20 minutes. Add the reserved pasta water to the chicken and broccoli, stir, and serve over the linguine.

Penne Rigate con Broccoli di Rape

(PENNE RIGATONI WITH BROCCOLI RABE)

DR. SAL AND ROSEMARIE CERNIGLIA

MARGATE, NEW JERSEY

I met Sal fifty years ago when he and his family emigrated from Sicily; he's an "adopted" brother.

SERVES   4 - 5

The closest vegetable to broccoli rabe that I have tasted is Chinese broccoli. It has a certain bitterness that is hard to describe. It is one of those foods that you either hate or love.

Of course, you know that I love it. I use it as a vegetable side dish with roast pork or make a huge sandwich of it with Italian hot sausage on a warm Italian roll. In my opinion, broccoli rabe reaches its zenith when used in this recipe. Like they say in Brooklyn, "It's to die for."

6 quarts water, for broccoli rabe

1 tablespoon salt

3-3 1/2 lbs. broccoli rabe, stems trimmed and peeled

1/2 cup olive oil

4-5 large cloves garlic, minced

1/4 teaspoon crushed red pepper flakes (optional)

Salt and freshly ground black pepper

1 ounce imported pignoli (pine nuts)

1/2 cup oil-cured black Sicilian olives, pitted

6-7 quarts water, for pasta

Pinch of salt

(continued)

1 pound penne rigatoni

Freshly grated Pecorino Romano cheese to
pass at table

Bring the water and salt to a rolling boil and
add the broccoli rabe. Allow to return to a boil
and cook for 5 minutes. Drain in a colander and
set aside until cool. Chop into 1-inch pieces.

Heat the oil and sauté the garlic and red pepper flakes in a large skillet until lightly brown.
Add the broccoli rabe and sauté for 5 to 7 minutes over low heat. Add salt and pepper to taste.
Add the pignoli and black olives, and mix. Continue cooking for another 10 minutes.

Bring the water and salt to a boil for the
penne. Cook until al dente, then drain. Place the
pasta on a warm serving dish, top with the broccoli rabe, mix, and sprinkle some grated cheese.
Buon apetito!

Pasta Marinara alla Bruna
(SEAFOOD PASTA ALLA BRUNA)

THE DI MAURO FAMILY:

FRANK, BRUNA, LISA, AND FRANK JR.

LANDISVILLE, NEW JERSEY

SERVES 4

*B*runa hails from the Veneto region of Italy. Her husband, Frank, is from the Molise region. We are talking about North and South here. There is no love lost
between Northern and Southern Italians. They met in
the United States, fell in love, and married.

*As I have confessed earlier, I don't eat seafood. Period.
But when I observed Frank Jr. almost inhaling a huge
dish of this pasta, his eyes glazed over in ecstasy, I
knew that it must be superlative. Are you beginning to
see the pattern? Italians begin as friends and become
family.*

1 pound spaghetti

1 medium onion

4 cloves garlic, minced or crushed

1/4 cup olive oil

8 ounces beer or white wine

1 13 3/4-ounce can chicken broth

1/4 cup chopped fresh Italian (flat-leafed)
parsley

1 pound shrimp, cleaned and deveined

Salt and freshly ground black pepper

Cook the spaghetti al dente, drain well, and
set aside. In a large saucepan, sauté the chopped
onion and garlic in the olive oil. When lightly
golden, pour the beer or white wine into it. Simmer 1 minute. Add the chicken broth. Let boil
approximately 3 to 4 minutes. Add the chopped
parsley and shrimp. Boil an additional 3 minutes. Add salt and pepper to taste. Pour over the
cooked spaghetti and serve.

Rigatoni Vodka al Orazio
(ORAZIO'S PASTA IN VODKA SAUCE)

ORAZIO MARINELLA

HAWTHORNE, NEW JERSEY

SERVES 4

Listen, please! I am told that this recipe is dangerous. It is addictive, and can add inches to your girth from just one serving. I tried it without the shrimp (you already know why) and it was so stupendous that it brought tears of happiness to my eyes. Prepare yourself for a deeply moving spiritual experience. There is, I am told, a dangerous drug on the streets called Ecstasy. Well, folks, stay away from drugs. If it's ecstasy you want, it's ecstasy you'll get—from a plateful of Orazio's pasta. Orazio is a good friend of my nephew, Judge Carmen Ferrante.

1 pound rigatoni

4 tablespoons olive oil

1 pound shiitake mushrooms, cleaned and diced

10 jumbo shrimp, cleaned, deveined, and diced

4 tablespoons butter

1/2 pound green peas, fresh or frozen

3 plum tomatoes, chopped

4 ounces vodka

1 quart heavy cream

4 tablespoons freshly grated Parmesan cheese

Cook the rigatoni al dente, drain well, and set aside. Heat the olive oil in a large sauté pan. Sauté the mushrooms and shrimp until tender, about 10 minutes. Drain the oil. Return the mushrooms and shrimp to the pan. Add the butter to the same pan, then add the peas, tomatoes, vodka, and heavy cream and bring to a boil. Lower the heat to a simmer.

Add the cooked rigatoni and Parmesan cheese. Sauté about 5 minutes, until the liquid evaporates and the sauce becomes thick. Serve immediately.

Tagliatelle con Sugo Aromatico
(PASTA CAFE BELLO)
(NOODLES IN AN AROMATIC SAUCE)

CAFE BELLO: TOM PELLICCIO, RENATO DE MARCHI,
VINCENZO SITA, PHIL TREBOUR
BAYONNE, NEW JERSEY

SERVES 6

These wonderful guys, my friends, have created the finest gourmet restaurant in my home town, and this recipe gives you an idea of how they did it. You may have some difficulty finding arugula (roquette) in your local markets. If you live in proximity to a Little Italy, you will find arugula easily. If you can't find it, you may substitute the green outer leaves of escarole. But please make the effort. This recipe is so flavorsome and so easy to prepare that you will pencil in a star next to it to indicate it's a dish worth repeating.

1 large yellow onion, peeled and diced finely

2 leeks, washed, trimmed, and finely diced

8 tablespoons olive oil

15 fresh plum tomatoes, skinned (see Tip, page 32) and chopped coarsely

1/2 cup fresh basil leaves, torn in halves

Salt and freshly ground black pepper

1 pound long flat noodles—fettucine or tagliatelle

3/4 cup fresh arugula, cut into long strips

6 ounces freshly grated Pecorino Romano cheese

In a large deep skillet, sauté the onion and leeks in olive oil on moderate heat until transparent. Add the tomatoes and half the basil. Cook on high heat to reduce, about 5 minutes. Lower the heat and simmer for 10 minutes. Add salt and pepper to taste.

Cook the pasta al dente along with the arugula. Drain well. Pour into a warm serving bowl. Toss with the cheese and sauce, sprinkle with the remaining basil, and serve.

Penne alla Caponata
(PENNE MACARONI WITH EGGPLANT AND OLIVE SAUCE)

VINCENZO CALDERONE

VINCENZO'S BAKERY

BAYONNE, NEW JERSEY

SERVES 4

The beautiful shiny purple-skinned eggplant becomes an outstanding jewel in the treasury of Sicilian cooking. The caponata (eggplant relish) described in this recipe can be used as an appetizer when spread on a hefty chunk of toasted Italian bread or as a luscious accompaniment to omelets or grilled meats. Here it is used to sauce al dente pasta and becomes an exquisite main course. Vinnie, who contributed this recipe, is another Sicilian "compare." He supplies me with semolina flour and sesame seeds (at no cost) so I can bake my own Sicilian bread.

1 pound eggplant, trimmed, pared, and cut
  into $1/2$-inch chunks
6 tablespoons olive oil
1 cup chopped onion
$1/2$ cup chopped green bell pepper
$1/2$ cup chopped celery
1 cup chopped fresh tomatoes
$1/4$ cup chopped green olives
1 tablespoon rinsed small capers
1 tablespoon chopped fresh basil
1 tablespoon chopped fresh Italian (flat-leaf)
  parsley
2 tablespoons red wine vinegar
$1/2$ teaspoon salt
Freshly ground black pepper to taste
$1/16$ teaspoon sugar
1 pound penne or ziti

Salt the eggplant liberally, place in a colander, and drain for 1 hour. Rinse off the salt and dry with paper towels. Heat 4 tablespoons of the oil in a large nonstick skillet on high heat; add the eggplant. Sauté, stirring constantly, until the eggplant is tender and browned, about 10 minutes. Transfer to a plate lined with paper towels to drain.

Add the remaining 2 tablespoons oil to the skillet. Add the onion, green pepper, and celery; sauté until tender, about 5 minutes. Stir in the eggplant, tomatoes, olives, capers, basil, parsley, vinegar, salt, pepper, and sugar. Cover and simmer 5 minutes. Cook the pasta al dente, drain, toss with the sauce and serve.

Rigatoni Capriccio

(WHIMSICAL RIGATONI)

D. ANTHONY PULLELLA

OCEAN FRONT RESTAURANT

BRIGANTINE, NEW JERSEY

SERVES 6

Domenicantonio Pullella. That very Italian name jumped out at me as I read the roster of students for my freshman class at Camden Catholic High School in September of 1965. When "Tony" stood up to acknowledge his presence in class, he asked politely: "Can you please call me Tony, Father?" "Of course, Tony, no problem," I replied. I became a member of his extended family when I was sponsor to his brother Frank at his Confirmation and therefore compare (godfather) to the rest of this warm Italian immigrant family. Tony has become a restaurateur of distinction, and I am treated like a dignitary whenever I can get to his restaurant. I like it so much I've included four of his great recipes.

When I was chaplain at Stockton University in Pomona, New Jersey, Tony's restaurant was only a twenty-minute ride away. Once a week, we would have dinner together and invariably Tony would run into the kitchen and come out with a huge bowl of this rigatoni. This is serious and delightful eating here, so don't fool around. Make it for your family and friends and be ready for the bear hugs of appreciation.

> 1¹/₂ pounds rigatoni
> 4 cloves garlic, sliced
> 2 tablespoons olive oil
> 6 ounces hot Italian sausage, diced
> 2 ounces imported porcini mushrooms
> 1 shallot, chopped
> 1 ounce Chianti wine
> 2-3 medium size ripe tomatoes (peeled {see Tip, page 32}, seeded, and diced)
> 3 tablespoons unsalted butter
> ¹/₄ cup freshly grated pecorino cheese

Cook the rigatoni al dente, drain well, and set aside. Sauté the garlic in the olive oil until golden brown. Add the sausage and brown. Add the mushrooms, shallot, and wine, and simmer 2 to 3 minutes. Add the tomatoes and cook for 4 minutes over low heat. Finish with the butter and pecorino cheese. Toss the sauce with the hot rigatoni. Serve immediately.

Linguine Puttanesca

(LINGUINE WITH SPICY SAUCE)

TONY PULLELLA

SERVES 8

As I commented in my introduction to this book, Italians take a pragmatic and realistic attitude toward sex. Morality aside, according to Italian legend, this tasty spicy sauce is credited to the "working girls" of the world's oldest profession. No matter, whoever invented this recipe knew what she was doing. It is savory and makes you stand up and take notice.

> 3 tablespoons olive oil
> 4 tablespoons butter
> 5 cloves garlic, chopped
> 8 anchovy fillets, minced

(continued)

2¹/₂ cups imported canned Italian peeled
   tomatoes, drained and chopped
Freshly ground black pepper
¹/₄ cup capers, drained
³/₄ cup pitted green olives (or oil-cured olives;
   regular black olives will not work here)
1 tablespoon chopped fresh Italian (flat-
   leafed) parsley
Pinch of dried oregano
2 fresh basil leaves, chopped
2 pounds linguine
¹/₂ cup freshly grated pecorino cheese
Freshly ground black pepper

Heat the oil and 4 teaspoons of the butter in a
saucepan. Add the garlic and cook quickly, without browning, about 3 minutes. Add the
anchovies and cook for 3 minutes. Add the tomatoes and pepper to taste and cook for 10 minutes.
Stir in the capers, olives, parsley, oregano, and
basil. Cook for 4 minutes. Set aside; keep warm.

Cook the linguine al dente. Drain well. Spoon
some sauce (a ladle full or 1 cup) into a skillet
over low heat. Add the pasta, toss well, and
transfer to a serving dish. Add the remaining
sauce, and top with pecorino cheese and freshly
ground black pepper.

Capellini Caprese
(ANGEL HAIR PASTA WITH FRESH
MOZZARELLA)

TONY PULLELLA
*Although Anthony was born in Calabria, he has this
authentic Neapolitan dish down to perfection.*

Melting stringy mozzarella cheese and a quick tomato
sauce deserve a heavenly pasta. So we use angel hair
pasta in this nirvana of a recipe. Close your eyes as you
eat this ambrosial dish and you will be in paradise.
Hallelujah!

   4 teaspoons extra-virgin olive oil
   6-8 cloves garlic, sliced
   3¹/₂ cups canned Italian plum tomatoes, diced
   Freshly ground black pepper to taste
   ¹/₄ cup chopped fresh basil leaves
   Pinch of salt
   1 gallon water, salted
   1 pound angel hair pasta (capellini)
   3 balls (about ¹/₂ pound) fresh buffalo moz-
      zarella, diced—yes, you may substitute
      ordinary mozzarella cheese
   Freshly grated Pecorino Romano cheese to
      pass at table

Heat the oil in a saucepan, add the garlic, and
cook until browned. Add the diced tomato,
ground pepper, basil, and salt. Cook for 8 miutes
on low heat.

Bring the salted water to a boil and cook the
capellini for 2 minutes. Drain quickly. Spoon a
little sauce into the frying pan over low heat.
Add the pasta and toss well. Transfer to a serving
dish. Toss with the mozzarella cheese and the
remaining sauce. Serve with grated pecorino.

Fettuccine Nina
(FETTUCCINE WITH CHICKEN)

TONY PULLELLA

SERVES 6

Tony named this dish in honor of his irrepressible mamma. Sometimes recipes can capture the character of a human person. This is one of them. Anthony's mamma is a strong, no-nonsense, yet compassionate and generous person. This recipe captures her complexity and genuineness. If you could meet her, you would love her. I am sure you are going to love this dish named after her.

- 4 ounces butter
- 8 ounces chicken breast, skinned, diced, and dredged in flour
- 1 teaspoon minced shallot (onion may be substituted)
- 4 teaspoons white wine
- 1 grinding black pepper
- 4 ounces mortadella, diced (boiled ham may be substituted)
- 3 cups heavy cream
- 2 ounces roasted red pepper, diced
- 4 fresh basil leaves
- 3 teaspoons green peas (fresh or frozen)
- 2 teaspoons freshly grated pecorino cheese
- 1 pound fettuccine

Melt the butter in a saucepan, add the chicken, and cook until golden brown. Add the shallot, white wine, black pepper, and mortadella, and cook for 3 minutes. Add the heavy cream and reduce for 2 minutes. Add the roasted red peppers, basil, peas, and cheese. Cook for 1 minute. Cook the pasta al dente, drain well, and toss with the sauce. Serve immediately.

Linguine con Salsa Cruda
(PASTA WITH RAW TOMATO SAUCE)

FATHER ORSINI

SERVES 4

I make this recipe only in the middle of summer when the tomatoes in my side yard are at their best. Talk about refreshingly good eating! This is awesome. It brings back memories of happy summer days, Mamma singing in the kitchen, when all was right with the world.

- 4 pounds very red firm ripe tomatoes, peeled (see Tip, page 32), cooled, seeded, and diced
- 6 garlic cloves, peeled and minced (If, like me, you find raw garlic hard to digest, substitute a diced medium onion)
- 3/4 cup chopped fresh basil leaves
- 1 cup olive oil
- Salt and freshly ground black pepper to taste
- 1 pound linguine

Combine the tomatoes with the garlic, basil, and oil in a pasta bowl. Add salt and pepper to taste. Cook the pasta al dente and drain quickly, leaving some water in the pasta. Pour into the bowl with the raw sauce. Toss and serve.

Pasta con Carciofi
(PASTA WITH ARTICHOKES)

JO-ANNE GAGLIOTI

MAYWOOD, NEW JERSEY

I first tasted this dish when I visited Jo-Anne's sister-in-law, Pina, at her home in Rosarno, Calabria, in Italy. I have never forgotten how delighted I was with its fragrance and taste. Make some memories of your own. Serve it to your loved ones and someday when they make it themselves, they will say, "I remember when . . ."

SERVES 4

Artichoke hearts are wonderfully delicate in texture and taste. They arrive nearly to perfection in this easy pasta recipe. Jo-Anne, who gave me the recipe, is the wife of one of my closest friends. Antonio and I speak the same Calabrian dialect and share the same ideals.

8 cloves garlic, minced

1 cup olive oil

2 12-ounce cans artichoke hearts packed in water, drained (reserve 1 can artichoke water) and cut into quarters

1/3 cup chopped fresh Italian (flat-leafed) parsley

1/2 teaspoon freshly ground black pepper

1 pound linguine or spaghetti

Freshly grated Pecorino Romano cheese to pass at table

Sauté the garlic in the olive oil in a large skillet until lightly golden. Sauté the artichokes in the same skillet for 5 minutes. Add the can of artichoke water, and the parsley and pepper, and bring to a boil. Cover and simmer for 30 minutes.

While the sauce is cooking, cook the pasta al dente and drain well. Pour the artichoke sauce over the hot pasta and serve with freshly grated cheese.

Penne alla Boscaiola
(PENNE WITH BOSCAIOLA SAUCE)

NICK AND DEE SESTITO

INTERLAKEN, NEW JERSEY

SERVES 4

Boscaiola means a woodsman's wife. The woodsman's wife would hunt the forest for a fresh crop of wild mushrooms in order to make this dish. Mushrooms have an earthy, woodsy flavor that permeates the dish and rewards the eater with complete satisfaction. This kind of fungus you won't want to get rid of. Nick and I go way back. When we were in university, we often spent hours discussing philosophy.

1 pound penne or rigatoni

1 ounce olive oil

1/2 onion, finely chopped

3 1/2 ounces parma ham or prosciutto, julienned

8 ounces mushrooms, julienned

3 ounces dry white wine

Freshly grated black pepper to taste

1 cup heavy cream

1 cup tomato sauce (homemade or canned)

Freshly grated Parmesan or pecorino cheese to pass at table

Cook the pasta al dente, drain well, and set aside. Heat the oil in a deep skillet over moderately high heat and sauté the onion until golden. Add the ham and cook for about 2 minutes, then add the mushrooms. Cook until water has evaporated. Moisten with the wine and reduce by half. Lower the heat and add the pepper, heavy cream, and tomato sauce. Simmer for a few minutes to thicken. Serve over the hot pasta. Sprinkle with grated cheese.

Pasta con Zucchini
(PASTA WITH FRESH ZUCCHINI)

VALERIE AND JOSEPH CASSANO

AURORA, ILLINOIS

SERVES 4

When zucchini are ready to harvest in your garden, they are so abundant that you go searching in your cookbooks for recipes to use them up. They even wind up in moist and sweet zucchini bread. Here is a recipe that will help. I know, I know! It's not that much help— the dish only uses two small zucchini. But it's a delicious way to use them. Joe and I were in university together. You're right, now he and his family are my family too.

3 tablespoons olive oil

3 tablespoons butter

2 large cloves garlic, crushed

½ small onion, chopped

Freshly ground black pepper to taste

2 small young zucchini, sliced with skin on

2 small carrots, sliced thin

1 8-ounce can stewed tomatoes

4 ounces white or rosé wine

Pinch of dried oregano

1 pound ziti or spaghetti

Salt to taste

Freshly grated Parmesan or Pecorino Romano
cheese to pass at table

In a large deep skillet melt the butter in the olive oil. Add the garlic, onion, pepper, zucchini, carrots, tomatoes, wine, oregano, and salt. Cook on low heat, covered, for 20 to 30 minutes, stirring often.

Cook the pasta al dente, and drain. Mix the hot pasta gently into the zucchini mixture. Top with the grated parmesan cheese, and serve. Enjoy!

Spaghetti con Gamberi e Carciofi
(SPAGHETTI WITH SEAFOOD AND ARTICHOKES)

NICK AND RITA GIORDANO

OAK PARK, ILLINOIS

SERVES 4

By now, I am definitely convinced that I am a member of a minority. And I don't mean priests . . . although that is true too. I mean the minority of the human race who don't or won't eat seafood.

During a visit to Chicago I was a guest in Nick's home. Nick was one of my high school students. He's one of those people who never ages and is a constant friend. He, his wife Rita, daughter Gina and son Nick are my Chicago area family. Rita gave me two recipes, this and the next. I chose to use them both. He prepared this recipe to the rave reviews of Rita, his lovely wife, Gina, his vivacious daughter, and Nicky, his lively son. They almost worshiped the dish. Me? I ate stuffed peppers that I had prepared for the next day's supper. You can guess what happened. These four skinny friends couldn't resist. They finished off the rest of the peppers.

3 medium artichokes (1 12-ounce can artichokes hearts with their water may be substituted)
$^1/_4$ cup olive oil
$^1/_3$ cup water (eliminate if using canned artichoke hearts)
Salt and freshly ground black pepper
$^1/_2$ pound shrimp, shelled and deveined
$^1/_2$ pound scallops
$^3/_4$ pound spaghettini
2 tablespoons chopped fresh Italian (flat-leafed) parsley

Clean the artichokes and use only the heart and the very inner leaves. Heat the artichokes in the olive oil and water in a skillet. Add salt and pepper to taste, cover, and simmer for 7 minutes. Add the shrimp and scallops, cover, and cook for 5 minutes. Cook the spaghettini in salted water al dente. Drain. Add the hot spaghettini to the skillet and mix over high heat for about 1 minute. Add parsley. Serve.

Pasta con Erbe Aromatiche
(PASTA WITH HERBS)

SERVES 4

You have just gotten in from a stressful day at work. You open the refrigerator door and look at the bunches of fresh herbs in the vegetable bin. At this very moment, your husband and children walk into the kitchen and hungrily ask: "What's for dinner?" You calm down, smile, tell them to go wash up, and in two shakes of a lamb's tail (really quick), you use your imagination and throw this recipe together. You're happy, they're happy, everybody's happy. And it tastes great too.

1 cup fresh herbs, a combination of thyme, rosemary, parsley, mint, basil, tarragon, and marjoram. (Don't substitute dried—it won't work with dried herbs.)
1 pound spaghettini
1 cup vegetable broth (they use Knorr's)
$^1/_4$ cup olive oil
Salt and freshly ground black pepper
$^1/_4$ cup freshly grated Pecorino Romano cheese

Chop the herbs. Cook the pasta in salted water until al dente, then drain. Combine the herbs, vegetable broth, olive oil, and salt and pepper to taste. Mix with the hot pasta and serve. Pass the cheese.

Pasta con Sugo di Tre Carni Bolognese

(THREE-MEAT BOLOGNESE)

ANTHONY OSWALD

CHERRY HILL, NEW JERSEY

SERVES 4

Here's Anthony again! Yes, he's now become my adopted son and his family is also mine. Wow! I have a big family, don't I?

Bolognese has become a generic term for meat sauce. I included the official version sanctioned by L'Accademia Italiana della Cucina (The Italian Academy of Cooking) in my section on sauces (page 51). Nevertheless, one evening when Anthony joined me in the kitchen, we experimented and invented this sauce. Ordinarily it would serve four, but not when Anthony and I are around. So if you invite us over for dinner, just double the recipe.

1 pound ground meat, a mixture of beef, pork, and veal
1 tablespoon olive oil
6 cloves garlic, finely minced
2 tablespoons finely minced onion
3 pounds fresh tomatoes (or 2 28-ounce cans plum tomatoes), coarsely chopped
2 tablespoons tomato paste
½ cup chopped fresh Italian (flat-leafed) parsley
1 tablespoon chopped fresh basil
Crushed red pepper flakes to taste
½ cup dry red wine
1 pound thin pasta, preferably homemade (packaged spaghettini also works well)
Freshly grated Pecorino Romano cheese to pass at table

In a saucepan brown the meat in the olive oil. Add the garlic and onion halfway through the browning and stir repeatedly. When meat is browned, add the remaining sauce ingredients and simmer on low heat for 30 minutes. While the sauce is cooking, cook the pasta al dente and drain well. Pour most of the sauce on the pasta, mix lightly, and allow to sit covered for 10 minutes before serving. Serve with freshly grated Pecorino Romano cheese and pass the extra sauce.

Pasta con Gamberi in Salsa Rosa

(SHRIMP IN A FRESH TOMATO BLUSH SAUCE)

ANTHONY OSWALD

SERVES 4

Anthony told me a story regarding this recipe. He cooked it for a dinner party for eight married couples. Of course he multiplied the ingredients by four. After dinner sixteen people, both women and men, asked Anthony to marry them. Now you know that this dish is dynamite . . . can you imagine?

1 tablespoon minced garlic
2 tablespoons olive oil

(continued)

2¹/₂ pounds ripe plum tomatoes, coarsely
chopped

3 tablespoons chopped fresh Italian (flat-
leafed) parsley

1 tablespoon chopped fresh basil

2 ounces dry red wine

Crushed red pepper flakes to taste

1 pound raw shrimp, cleaned and deveined

4 ounces light cream or half and half

1 pound spaghetti

Freshly grated Romano cheese to pass at table

In a large saucepan, cook the garlic in the olive
oil over low heat until soft; do not brown. Add the
tomatoes, parsley, basil, wine, and red pepper
flakes and simmer approximately 15 minutes.
Add the shrimp and continue to simmer until the
shrimp are pink and cooked through (approximately 10 minutes). Add the cream and stir while
simmering over low heat for 5 minutes.

While the sauce is cooking, cook the pasta al
dente, and drain well. Pour the sauce over the hot
pasta and serve with freshly grated Romano
cheese.

Linguine con Saccoccie di Vitello

(LINGUINE WITH VEAL POCKETS IN
WINE SAUCE)

CUONO CHIRICOLO

BAYONNE, NEW JERSEY

FONTANA PIZZERIA RESTAURANT

SERVES 6

*I agree with you completely. This is a complicated
recipe and you're going to spend a lot of time in the
kitchen preparing it. Is it really worth all the time?
The work? The expense? Yes!*

*I met Cuono fresh from Italy when he was fourteen.
He is now my grandnephew Eugene's father-in-law.
Go figure! When I observed Cuono cooking this royal
feast, I scrunched myself into a corner and stayed out of
his way. He literally flew around that kitchen. When
we all sat down to eat, he studied everyone's face for a
reaction. We all smiled with delight—it was superb.
Cuono was proud and had every right to be.*

12 milk-fed (white) veal cutlets

Salt

Garlic powder

Freshly ground black pepper

1 cup chopped fresh Italian (flat-leafed)
parsley

1 cup freshly grated Parmesan cheese

6 slices prosciutto or boiled ham

6 slices mozzarella cheese

6 ¹/₄-inch-thick slices peeled eggplant,
browned in olive oil

1 cup freshly grated Pecorino Romano cheese

1 cup all-purpose flour

1 cup olive oil

Freshly grated Parmesan cheese to pass at
table

Egg Wash:

6 large eggs

¹/₂ cup chopped fresh Italian (flat-leafed)
parsley

1 teaspoon salt

1 teaspoon freshly ground black pepper

¹/₂ cup freshly grated Pecorino Romano cheese

Sauce:

1 large red onion, peeled and chopped

1 large Spanish yellow onion, peeled and
  chopped

2 pounds fresh mushrooms, sliced

1 cup dry white wine

2 cups beef stock or bouillon

1½ pounds linguine or spaghetti

Place the veal cutlets between sheets of heavy plastic and pound with a kitchen mallet to 1/8 inch thick. Season 6 of the cutlets with a pinch of salt, a sprinkle of garlic powder, a dash of black pepper, a sprinkle of chopped parsley, and 1 teaspoon of grated cheese each. Cover each seasoned cutlet with 1 slice apiece of prosciutto, mozzarella, and cooked eggplant. Top each with one of the remaining cutlets and pound the edges with the mallet to seal the pockets.

Beat together the egg wash ingredients. Dredge the veal pockets in flour. Dip each pocket in the egg wash. Lightly brown the pockets in the olive oil in a large skillet on high heat, at least 3 minutes on each side. Remove with a slotted spoon and drain on paper towels.

In the same skillet, prepare the sauce. Sauté the onions and mushrooms until golden brown. Add the wine and adjust to high heat to evaporate the wine (about 3 minutes). Add the stock, reduce the heat, and simmer for 10 minutes. Replace the veal pockets into the sauce, cover, and simmer for 5 minutes. Remove the pockets and set aside while you cook the pasta al dente. Drain the pasta quickly and toss with the sauce.

On each dinner plate, place a veal pocket accompanied with a generous serving of pasta.

Bring to table and serve. Pass the grated cheese and pepper mill.

Pasta Daniele
(DANNY'S PASTA)

DANIEL HUGHES, JR.

PINE HILL, NEW JERSEY

SERVES 4

No, not all my friends are Italian. Dan's daughters, Rachelle and Nicole, call me "Pop-Pop." His wife, Nancy, treats me like a beloved father-in-law. And you're right, this recipe is not Italian—it's Irish. In fact, Danny got it from his dad, Dan Sr., and Danny's mom was Polish. When Danny's parents were still living, we often shared this meal together. So what is it doing in a collection of Italian recipes? Well, I christened it Italian because it tasted like my own mamma's meat soup and I sprinkle mine with plenty of Italian grated cheese. Thanks for letting me go on this one.

¼ cup olive oil

6 short ribs of beef

3 tablespoons all-purpose flour

4 large stalks celery with leaves, washed and
  diced

1 pound can crushed Italian plum tomatoes

4 quarts water

Salt and freshly ground black pepper

1 pound perciatelli, if unavailable, try
  spaghetti

(continued)

1 large onion, peeled and diced

4 boiled potatoes, cooked in skin, then peeled

Freshly grated Pecorino Romano cheese to
   pass at table

In a 6-quart pot, heat the olive oil on moderate heat. Dredge the short ribs in flour and brown well on all sides. Add the celery and sauté for 5 minutes. Add the tomatoes, adjust the heat to a simmer, and cook covered, for 20 minutes.

Add the water, bring to a boil, and stir. Adjust the heat to moderate. Add salt and pepper to taste, and cook, covered, for 1 hour.

Add the raw macaroni and cook al dente, about 15 minutes. Remove from the heat and allow to set for 5 minutes. On table have ready a bowl of chopped onion, a bowl of hot boiled potatoes, and plenty of grated Pecorino Romano cheese. Pour the pasta and short ribs into a large pasta bowl and bring to table.

Pasta Salvatore

(ANGEL HAIR PASTA WITH MUSSELS)

SALVATORE VASSALLO

VERONA, NEW JERSEY

SERVES 2

When I asked my "nephew" Sal for one of his favorite pasta recipes, he replied, "Sure Unc, but I don't have it written down. When I cook, I just cook." One evening, Sal came to visit me with a bagful of groceries. "OK, Unc, I'm going to make that recipe for your book." I watched him carefully as he cooked this dish and made

notes. From what I could ascertain from watching him dig into this seafood medley of pasta and mussels, it's a seafood lover's dream come true.

1 cup dry white wine

8 large cloves garlic, peeled and minced

1 cup olive oil

Salt and freshly ground black pepper to taste

16 large fresh basil leaves, left whole

2 pounds fresh mussels, scrubbed clean under
   cold water

9 ounces angel hair pasta

Freshly grated Pecorino Romano or Parmesan
   cheese to pass at table

Heat the wine in a deep saucepan until it begins to boil. Add the garlic, stir, and cook for 5 minutes over high heat. Lower the heat to medium. Add the olive oil, salt, and pepper, stir, and bring to boil. Add the basil leaves and mussels and cook, covered, for 15 minutes.

Cook the pasta al dente. Drain quickly, so as to leave some water in pasta. Pour into a serving bowl. Pour the mussels and sauce over pasta, toss lightly, and sprinkle with grated Pecorino Romano or Parmesan cheese. Serve immediately.

Ziti San Vito

(LUCIANO'S SPECIAL SAUCE)

LUCIANO VENTRONE

SAN VITO RESTAURANT

BAYONNE, NEW JERSEY

SERVES 4

Luciano and his lovely wife, Maria, warned me ahead of time about the anchovies and tuna fish in this flavorsome Neapolitan sauce because they knew my story about fish. They urged me so earnestly to try it that I did. I couldn't perceive the anchovy; and tuna is the only fish I can eat. Canned tuna, that is. And it must be solid white. I have to tell you the truth. I really enjoyed it, and so will you.

4 tablespoons olive oil

2 large cloves garlic, peeled and minced

4 anchovy fillets

4 tablespoons dry red wine

1 7-ounce can tuna, drained

1 28-ounce can Italian plum tomatoes, drained, juice reserved

Pinch of dried oregano

Pinch of dried thyme

1 tablespoon chopped fresh Italian (flat-leafed) parsley

Pinch of crushed red pepper flakes

Freshly ground black pepper to taste

1 pound ziti or rigatoni

1 tablespoon butter

Parmesan cheese to be passed at table

Heat the oil in a heavy saucepan, add the garlic, and sauté until opaque. Add the anchovies and cook until reduced to a paste. Add the wine, then stir in the tuna, breaking it up. Add the tomatoes, stirring and breaking them up. Gradually, add the juice from tomatoes. Cook over medium heat for 25 minutes. Add the herbs, red pepper flakes, and black pepper, stir, and set aside.

Cook the pasta al dente and drain well. Melt the butter in a large skillet and add the cooked pasta. Add the sauce and mix very well over low heat for 2 to 3 minutes. Serve immediately, and pass the cheese.

Pasta Dishes from the Microwave

Sandro La Bozzeta is the second eldest son of my mother's godchild Marietta. I have known him and his wife Clelia for forty years. Since Marietta considers me her American son, Sandro and Clelia have been my Italian brother and sister.

Clelia hails from Locri, an ancient town founded by Greek colonizers around 2,500 years ago. Locri was renowned for the luxurious presentation of its exceptional cuisine, and Clelia has certainly absorbed her hometown's culinary heritage. The recipes that follow are from her collection.

Beginning this writing project in 1993, I have since visited Italy twice a year for five years to do my research. I often spent time with the La Bozettas where Clelia's Italian cooking has added a new dimension to my Italian cooking, the microwave. I have used every one of the recipes in my own kitchen with great success.

Accustomed to cooking in a traditional manner, during my last few visits to Italy I was surprised to see how often a microwave is used to save time in preparing many recipes. In fact, almost every home has one.

My generous and loving hosts, Sandro and Clelia, very patiently demonstrated how they, like many members of households where both husband and wife must have full-time employment, make use of a microwave oven and thus have to spend less time in their kitchen. This section of the book contains the recipes they shared with me for some wonderful pasta dishes specifically designed for microwave cooking. Al-dente pasta is cooked in the traditional manner, on the stove, while the sauce cooks in a jiffy in the microwave.

Pasta al Brodo di Pollo
(PASTA WITH CHICKEN SOUP)

SERVES 8

This combination of aromatic, steaming, delicious, and warming chicken soup with light egg noodles is tailor-made for a cold evening. It will convince you *that chicken soup with an Italian touch does indeed have some magical curative powers. And it is so easy to prepare.*

2¼ pounds fresh chicken, washed well and
    quartered

1½ quarts water

2 stalks celery, washed and thinly sliced

2 medium carrots, peeled and thinly sliced

Pinch of fresh basil

Dash of dried rosemary

1 teaspoon salt

1 grinding black pepper

12 ounces long flat egg noodles, broken into
    bite-size pieces

Freshly grated Parmesan cheese

Freshly grated black pepper

Place the chicken pieces, 1 quart of the water, and the celery, carrots, basil, rosemary, salt, and pepper into a 5-quart glass casserole. Cover and cook in the microwave at medium (50%) power for 30 to 40 minutes. Mix twice during the cooking.

Remove the bones and skin from the chicken. Dice the meat and put it back into the casserole. Add the remaining 1 1/2 quart of water to the soup. Add the raw pasta. Cover and cook on maximum power for 8 to 10 minutes, until the soup boils. Cook another 7 to 10 minutes. Serve with grated cheese and black pepper.

Salsa al Basilico
(FRESH BASIL SAUCE)

ENOUGH SAUCE TO DRESS 1 1/2 POUNDS OF YOUR FAVORITE PASTA

I *simply adore fresh basil sauce or pesto. The traditional pesto recipe is raw and requires a quantity of grated Parmesan cheese. However, I find that this microwave version is easier for me to digest because cooking the garlic for a bit calms it down. Then, if desired, grated Parmesan or Pecorino Romano cheese may be sprinkled on top of your dish at the last moment before serving. Use the sauce to dress pasta or fish, or stir a good tablespoonful into meat, poultry, fish, or pasta main courses right before serving to brighten the flavor. Your taste buds will thank you!*

2 cups fresh basil leaves packed down,
    washed

3½ ounces fresh parsley, washed

1 cup pignoli (pine nuts) or shelled walnuts

3 small cloves garlic, peeled

2 tablespoons olive oil

Pinch of salt

1 grinding black pepper

Place all the ingredients in a food processor fitted with the steel blade. Process until you obtain a loose and homogenized sauce. Place in a glass container, cover, and cook in the microwave on maximum power for 2 minutes. Store in the refrigerator but allow to warm up to room temperature for 1 hour before using. The pesto can be stored in a tightly closed glass or plastic container in the refrigerator for 2 weeks. It also can be frozen for a year and thawed out for use later. I make mine at the end of the summer when I pick the leaves from my basil plants.

Pasta e Fagioli Porto Rico
(PASTA AND BEANS PUERTO RICO)

SERVES 6

Clelia and Sandro tasted this dish at a beach-front restaurant while they were on vacation in Palma de Majorca. Clelia walked boldly into the kitchen and asked the cook for the recipe. The cook, an Egyptian, pointed to a Goya can of Vienna sausages and said in passable Italian: "You can figure out the rest or go to Puerto Rico, San Juan, Plaza Condado, and ask the cook at the La Concha Hotel." Well, Clelia muttered some "kind words," left, and when back in her own kitchen, came up with this recipe. It is really excellent, if not authentically Puerto Rican.

9 ounces spaghetti, broken into pieces

1 tablespoon olive oil

1 15-ounce can Vienna sausages, diced (Goya is a good brand)

1 medium onion, peeled and diced

1/2 green bell pepper, seeded and diced

1 tablespoon crushed red pepper flakes or cayenne pepper

1 clove garlic, peeled and crushed

2 fresh basil leaves, minced, if unavailable, do not use dried, simply skip the basil

Dash of dried oregano

1 teaspoon salt

2 1-pound cans pinto beans, with their liquid

1 8-ounce can tomato sauce

1 quart hot water

Cook the pasta al dente on the stovetop and drain well. Dress with the olive oil. Set aside. Place in a 3-quart glass casserole the Vienna sausage, onion, green pepper, hot pepper, garlic, basil, oregano, and salt. Cover and cook in the microwave on maximum power for 6 to 8 minutes. Stir twice during cooking. Add the cooked spaghetti and remaining ingredients and stir. Allow to heat through, uncovered, on maximum power for 8 to 9 minutes, stirring twice. Serve.

Minestra con Tortellini e Pollo
TORTELLINI WITH CHICKEN

SERVES 6

A hearty, wholesome, and savory meal for your family is ready to enjoy in about a half hour when you make this dish. Pass some fresh grated Parmesan or Pecorino Romano cheese to enhance the aroma and taste. Serve a crisp green salad dressed with fresh lemon or lime juice and good virgin olive oil. Believe me, they will ask for seconds.

2 tablespoons olive oil

1 medium onion, peeled and finely diced

1 stalk celery, finely diced

1/2 teaspoon dried marjoram

Dash of garlic powder

Dash of dried rosemary

(continued)

Dash of dried thyme

1 pound frozen cheese tortellini, defrosted

2 canned Italian plum tomatoes, drained and chopped

1-pound can white kidney beans (cannellini), drained

1-pound can green beans, drained

4 cups canned clear chicken broth

½ pound cooked skinless chicken breast, diced

In a 3-quart glass casserole, mix the oil, onion, celery, marjoram, garlic powder, rosemary, and thyme. Cover and cook in the microwave on maximum power for 4 to 6 minutes. Stir once. Add all the other ingredients except the diced chicken. Cover and cook on maximum power for 20 to 25 minutes, stirring every 10 minutes. Add the chicken and cover. Cook on maximum power for 5 minutes. Stir and serve.

Fettuccine alla Veneziana
FETTUCCINE VENICE STYLE

SERVES 6

When you bring this dish to the table, it first pleases the eye with glistening pink of the shrimp and the bright green of the parsley against the creamy off-white of the sauce. Then it pleases the nose, with its delicate aroma, and finally the taste buds, with its magnificent flavor. Don't be surprised if your guests break into applause—it's that good.

3 tablespoons butter

1 medium onion, peeled and finely diced

¼ cup dry white wine

1 pound frozen medium shrimp, cleaned and deveined

2½ tablespoons all-purpose flour

1 teaspoon salt

1 grinding black pepper

¼ cup milk, whole or skim

1½ teaspoons half and half (half cream, half milk)

¼ cup chopped fresh Italian (flat-leafed) parsley

Dash of nutmeg

1 pound fettuccine

Place the butter and onion in a 2-quart glass casserole. Cover and cook in the microwave on maximum power for 2 to 3 minutes. Add the wine. Cover and cook on maximum power for 2 to 3 minutes. Add the shrimp, cover, and cook on medium-high (70%) power for 4 to 5 minutes, until the shrimp are opaque, stirring two times. Remove the shrimp with a slotted spoon and set aside. Add into the liquid, the flour, salt, and pepper, then the milk and half and half. Beat with a whisk until homogenized (about 3 minutes). Cook on maximum covered, for 13 to 18 minutes, stirring three or four times, until boiling hot. Add the cooked shrimp and the parsley and nutmeg. Mix well. Set aside.

Cook the pasta al dente on the stove. Drain well. Toss with the sauce and bring to table.

Tagliatelle alla Siciliana
SICILIAN-STYLE EGG NOODLES

SERVES 6

Yes, this is rich, and you will not be hungry an hour later! You will want to accompany it with a glass of hearty dry red wine, maybe two glasses. Afterward, slip into a cozy chair, put your feet up, and perhaps dream that you are on a lovely warm beach in Sicily being mesmerized by the sight and sound of the blue sea lapping gently on the shore. It isn't heaven, but it's as close as you'll come to it in this life. A cup of delicious espresso coffee will bring you back to reality.

1 pound Italian sausage, skinned and
   crumbled
2 medium onions, peeled and finely diced
2 medium carrots, peeled and thinly
   sliced
1 stalk celery, washed and thinly sliced
1 teaspoon olive oil
1 tablespoon butter
3 cloves garlic, peeled and crushed
1 tablespoon dry red wine
1 12-ounce can crushed tomatoes
1/2 cup tomato paste
1 teaspoon dried oregano
1 teaspoon fresh basil
1 teaspoon freshly ground black pepper
1 teaspoon salt
1 pound long, flat egg noodles

Cook the crumbled sausage in a 1-quart glass casserole in the microwave on maximum power for 6 to 8 minutes, stirring only once. Drain and set aside. In a 3-quart casserole add the onion, carrot, celery, oil, butter, and garlic. Cover and cook on maximum power for 5 to 6 minutes, stirring once. Add the wine, cover, and cook on maximum for 3 minutes. Add the rest of the ingredients except the cooked sausage. Cover and cook on maximum for 11 minutes. Now add the sausage. Cover and heat on maximum for 4 minutes. Set aside.

Cook the pasta al dente on the stove and drain well. Toss with the sauce and bring to the table.

Fettuccine al Funghi Freschi e Prezzemolo
FETTUCCINE WITH FRESH MUSHROOMS AND PARSLEY

SERVES 4

This may look like pasta in cream of mushroom soup at first glance, but you'll be convinced it isn't when you savor this delightful combination. The earthiness of the mushrooms exuding their precious liquid will titillate your taste buds and the affinity of the pasta with the sauce will give you gustatory pleasure. This is so simple and yet so good.

9 ounces fresh mushrooms, sliced
1/4 cup chopped fresh Italian (flat-leafed)
   parsley
2 tablespoons olive oil
1 cup half and half
Salt and freshly ground black pepper
12 ounces fettuccine pasta, white or green
1/4 cup freshly grated Parmesan cheese

Place the mushrooms, parsley, and oil in 1-quart glass casserole. Cover and cook in the microwave on maximum power for 2 minutes. Add the half and half, cover, and cook on maximum power for 2 minutes, stirring twice. Set aside.

Cook the pasta al dente on the stove and drain well. Toss with the sauce, salt and pepper to taste, and grated Parmesan cheese.

Fettuccine Verdi con Vitello e Funghi
(GREEN FETTUCCINE WITH VEAL AND MUSHROOMS)

SERVES 4

Veal scallops and mushrooms seem to have been created to be joined together in culinary matrimony. Here this marriage is brought to perfection in blissful harmony with green pasta. A match made in heaven! And what an unforgettable honeymoon of taste. You are really going to like this one. Trust me.

1 tablespoon butter

1 tablespoon olive oil

9 ounces fresh mushrooms, sliced

2 medium onions, peeled and diced

2 tablespoons chopped fresh Italian (flat-leafed) parsley

1 clove garlic, peeled and crushed

2 tablespoons chicken broth, canned or preferably your own freshly made (page 37)

Dash of salt

1 grinding black pepper

1½ pounds veal scallops or veal cutlets

pounded and cut into 1½ inch slices

2 tablespoons all-purpose flour

2 eggs, beaten

½ cup Italian flavored bread crumbs— Progresso brand is satisfactory

1 cup sour cream

Freshly grated Parmesan cheese (optional)

12 ounces spinach fettuccine

Put the butter, oil, mushrooms, onion, 1 tablespoon of the parsley, and the garlic in a 2-quart glass casserole. Cover and cook in the microwave on maximum power for 3 to 4 minutes, stirring once. Add the broth, salt, and pepper. Stir and set aside.

Dredge the veal pieces in the flour. Dip in the beaten eggs, and drain. Place the bread crumbs in a plastic bag, add the veal, and shake to coat. Place the meat in the casserole with the mushrooms. Cover and cook on medium-high (70%) for 35 to 45 minutes, stirring gently twice during the cooking time. Add the sour cream and the rest of the parsley. Stir and set aside.

While the veal scallops are cooking, cook the pasta al dente on the stove, and drain well. Toss with the sauce and, if you wish, sprinkle with grated Parmesan cheese. Bring to table.

Fettuccine con Verdure
(FETTUCCINE WITH VEGGIES)

SERVES 1

When Sandro comes home late from a meeting, he makes this light supper. Pasta for one. There are many

gals and guys out there who live alone. A lot of them simply stop at a take-out eatery or order something to be delivered. Usually the stuff they eat is full of fat and salt. If you are in that number, then this one's for you! If you are fortunate and have others with whom you want to share this, then simply multiply the ingredients by the number of your guests. Either way, it is healthy and delicious nourishment for body and spirit.

1/4 pound fettuccine

1 tablespoon butter or margarine

1 pinch dried oregano

1/4 pound broccoli florets

1/2 small onion, peeled and thinly sliced

2 cherry tomatoes, quartered

2 ounces fresh mushrooms, sliced

1 teaspoon half and half (or milk)

2 tablespoons freshly grated Pecorino
 Romano cheese

1 tablespoon freshly grated Parmesan
 cheese

1 tablespoon ricotta cheese

Pinch of salt

Cook the fettuccine al dente on the stovetop. Drain well. Season with half the butter and the oregano and set aside.

In a bowl, place the remaining butter, the broccoli, and the onion. Cover and cook in the microwave on maximum power for 1 or 2 minutes. Add all other ingredients. Stir and pour over the drained pasta. Pour into a microwaveable serving bowl. Cover and cook at medium (50%) power for 3 to 4 minutes, stirring once in the middle of the cooking time. Let cool for 1 minute and enjoy.

Linguine con Sugo di Vongole
(LINGUINE WITH CLAM SAUCE)

SERVES 2

This is a wonderfully delicious dish to share with your significant other or with someone you wish to become significant. I have a dear friend who swears that when he wishes to impress some interesting gal, he cooks a lovely dinner for her. He claims the results are foolproof—it works 99 percent of the time, but, he says: "You must eat by candlelight and have the charming sounds of a Jimmy Buffet ballad emanating softly from your stereo." Of course, to be politically correct and realistic, this method of wooing also applies to gals who invite guys to supper. Sharing a good meal with someone you hold dear is an equal-opportunity occasion.

4 ounces linguine

2 tablespoons butter or margarine

1 medium onion, peeled and diced

1 tablespoon olive oil

1/2 clove garlic, peeled and crushed

2 tablespoons all-purpose flour

1 tablespoon chopped fresh Italian (flat-
 leafed) parsley, plus 2 additional
 tablespoons for garnish

1 7-ounce can minced clams

2 tablespoons milk

Pinch of salt

1 grinding black pepper

Cook the linguine al dente on the stovetop. Drain well. Cover and set aside.

In a 1/2 quart bowl, place the butter, onion, olive oil, and garlic. Cook in the microwave at maximum power for 1 to 2 minutes. Add the flour and stir. Add the 1 tablespoon parsley, clams, milk, salt, and pepper. Cook at maximum for 1 to 3 minutes, until the sauce is thickened, stirring once or twice during cooking time. Toss the hot linguine with the sauce, garnish with the 2 tablespoons chopped parsley, and serve.

Tagliatelle alla Stroganov
(EGG NOODLES STROGANOV)

SERVES 4

No, *this is not Italian. Yes, it is Russian. But I tasted it and enjoyed it in an Italian kitchen—in Italy yet. Don't allow this recipe's Russian origin to prevent you from trying it. You will be happy with the results. Mamma mia! This is really good.*

 1 pound good lean boneless steak, about 1
   inch thick

 1 teaspoon coarsely ground black pepper

 3 tablespoons butter

 1 pound fresh broccoli florets

 1 small carrot, peeled, washed, and julienned

 2 small onions, peeled and diced

 2 tablespoons water

 2 tablespoons all-purpose flour

 7 ounces hot water

 1 tablespoon ketchup

 1 teaspoon Worcestershire sauce

 1/4 cup sour cream

 12 ounces long, flat egg noodles

Rub butter into steak. Sprinkle both sides of steak with pepper, pressing it lightly into the meat so it will adhere. Grill the steak on both sides on the stove or a grill to the doneness you prefer—rare, medium, or well done. Let the meat rest for 5 minutes. Slice into thin slices and set aside.

Place the broccoli, carrot, and onion in a 2-quart glass casserole. Add the water. Cover and cook in the microwave at maximum power for 6 to 8 minutes, stirring once. Drain and set aside.

Place the flour in a large bowl. Add the hot water. Beat with a whisk and cook at maximum power for 6 to 8 minutes, until the gravy begins to thicken and boil. Beat with the whisk after the first 2 minutes of cooking and every minute thereafter during the cooking process. Add the ketchup, Worcestershire sauce, and sour cream. Beat with the whisk until homogenized. Add the slices of steak and cooked vegetables, and stir. Cover and warm at maximum power for 1 to 2 minutes. Cook the pasta al dente on the stove top, and drain well. Pour the Stroganov over the warm pasta and serve.

Fettuccine con Salsa di Pesce Piccante
(FETTUCCINE IN SPICY FISH SAUCE)

SERVES 4

If *you have a yen for a pasta dish sauced with a denizen of the deep blue sea, this one is going to fit the bill. I heard that! Someone said: "Bill who?" You know what I mean. If you like fish, you'll go bonkers over this. Honest. I wouldn't kid you. You are going to thank me for this.*

1 pound fettuccine or spaghetti

1 tablespoon olive oil

2 tablespoons butter

2 stalks celery, sliced into large chunks

1 medium onion, peeled and diced

1/2 green bell pepper, diced

1 1/2 tablespoons all-purpose flour

Pinch of dried oregano

Pinch of salt

1/4 teaspoon crushed red pepper flakes or
cayenne pepper (If you would like it a little
hotter, increase the hot pepper to 1 full
teaspoon—that's what I do.)

1 grinding black pepper

1 8-ounce can tomato sauce

1 pound Italian canned plum tomatoes,
drained and chopped

12 ounce fillet white-flesh fish (sole, flounder),
skinned, boned, cut into 1-inch pieces

Cook the pasta al dente on the stovetop.
Drain, dress with the olive oil, and keep warm.

In a 2-quart glass casserole, place the butter,
celery, onion, and green pepper. Cover and cook
in the microwave at maximum power for 3 to 5
minutes, until vegetables are just tender, stirring
once. Add the flour, oregano, salt, hot pepper,
black pepper, tomato sauce, chopped tomatoes,
and fish. Cover and cook at maximum power for
10 to 16 minutes, until the fish is tender, stirring
twice during cooking. Add the pasta to the
sauce, toss well, and bring to table.

Tagliatelle al Tonno
(EGG NOODLES IN TUNA SAUCE)

SERVES 4

There is a lot more you can do with a can of tuna than
smothering it with a load of mayonnaise and slapping
it onto a couple of slices of bread. This dish makes your
can of tuna sing operatic arias and raises it to a level of
culinary excellence. I'm not kidding. You are going to
love it.

1 10 1/2–ounce package frozen peas

3 tablespoons all-purpose flour

1 small clove garlic, peeled and crushed

1/4 teaspoon fennel seeds, crushed

1 grinding black pepper

2 tablespoons milk

1 6 1/2–ounce can tuna packed in oil, drained
and flaked

12 ounces long, flat egg noodles

1 tablespoon olive oil

1 medium tomato, seeded and coarsely
chopped

3 tablespoons freshly grated Parmesan cheese

Place the peas in a 1-quart glass casserole.
Cover and defrost in the microwave at maximum
power for 3 to 5 minutes, stirring once. Drain
and set aside.

Put the flour, garlic, fennel seeds, and black
pepper in the same casserole. Add the milk and
stir well. Cook at maximum power for 7 to 9 minutes, just until the sauce begins to thicken and
boil, stirring three times. Add the peas and tuna
to the sauce. Mix well and cover. Cook at maximum power for 3 to 4 minutes, stirring once.

Cook the pasta al dente on the stove. Drain, and toss with the olive oil. Toss with tuna sauce. Garnish with the tomato, sprinkle with the cheese, and serve.

Spaghetti con Involtini di Pollo
(SPAGHETTI WITH STUFFED CHICKEN ROLLS)

SERVES 4

When boneless, skinless chicken breast are on sale, I buy plenty of them. Chicken breasts are so versatile and economical. For many recipes that require highly priced veal cutlets, I simply substitute chicken breasts. The results—as in this dish—are very satisfactory. I promise you. This will be a winner.

2 whole boneless, skinless chicken breasts, trimmed of all fat and tendons, and cut into halves horizontally, thus giving you 4 chicken cutlets
3 1/2 ounces ricotta cheese
2 tablespoons freshly grated Parmesan cheese
1/2 large onion, peeled and thinly sliced
Pinch each of oregano, thyme, and salt
1 grinding black pepper
2 cups canned tomato sauce or marinara tomato sauce (page 50)
3 1/2 ounces mozzarella cheese, sliced as thinly as possible
1 pound spaghetti

Pound the chicken between layers of plastic wrap until thin. Set aside. Place the ricotta, grated Parmesan, onion, oregano, thyme, salt, and pepper in a bowl and mix well. Spread a quarter of the cheese mixture on each of the chicken fillets. Roll up the chicken and seal with wooden toothpicks.

Place the chicken rolls in a small glass baking dish, seam side down. Pour the tomato sauce over them. Cover with wax paper and cook in the microwave at maximum power for 11 to 15 minutes. Turn the dish twice inside the oven for even cooking. Remove the toothpicks. Garnish each chicken roll with mozzarella. Heat at medium (50%) power 2 to 4 minutes, until the cheese melts.

Cook the pasta al dente on the stove. Drain well. Pour into a serving dish, arrange the four chicken rolls (involtini) on top, pour the sauce over all, and serve.

Fettuccine con Pollo alla Cacciatora
(FETTUCCINE WITH CHICKEN— HUNTER'S STYLE)

SERVES 4

Chicken legs are always less expensive than chicken breasts, and they are nice and juicy. Am I starting to follow a pattern of frugality here? No matter. This is a magnificent dish and it won't leave you broke.

8 chicken legs, skinned
Dash of dried oregano

1 medium green bell pepper, seeded and julienned

2 cups canned tomato sauce or tomato sauce
marinara (page 50)

4 ounces mozzarella cheese, thinly sliced

12 ounces fettuccine

Place the chicken legs in a deep square glass dish. Sprinkle with oregano. Cover and cook in the microwave at maximum power for 7 to 10 minutes. The chicken will be half-cooked. Drain and place back in the same dish. Cover with the bell pepper and tomato sauce. Cook uncovered at medium-high (70%) power for 9 to 12 minutes, until the sauce is hot and the pepper is cooked. Cover each drumstick with a slice of mozzarella. Return to the microwave for 1 to 2 minutes at medium-high.

Cook the pasta al dente on the stove. Drain. Arrange the pasta as a nest on a warm serving platter, place the drumsticks in the nest, cover with the sauce, and serve.

Pasta al Pomodoro e Mozzarella

(PASTA WITH TOMATO AND MOZZARELLA)

SERVES 4

Do you like pizza? I don't know many who don't. This dish uses pasta as a crust, topped with an appetizing combination of ingredients. Maybe we should name it Pasta Pizza or Pizza Pasta. Whatever. It's so darn good that I bet you will be making it a lot.

½ pound vermicelli or capellini (very thin
spaghetti)

2 tablespoons olive oil

1 medium green bell pepper, seeded and diced

1 medium onion, peeled and diced

1 cup canned tomato sauce or salsa pizzaiola
(page 48)

3½ ounces pitted black olives, cut into rings

½ pound mozzarella or provolone cheese,
grated

Pinch of dried oregano

Cook the pasta al dente on the stovetop. Drain thoroughly. Heat the oil in a nonstick skillet on medium-high heat on your conventional cooktop. Add the pasta and press down to make a uniform layer. Cook 4 to 5 minutes, until golden brown. Reverse onto a serving dish, browned side up, and set aside.

Place the green pepper and onion in a 1-quart glass casserole sprayed with liquid shortening. Cook uncovered in the microwave at maximum power for 2 to 3 minutes. Set aside.

Pour the tomato sauce over the pasta nest. Garnish with the green pepper, onion, and olive slices. Cover with the grated cheese, dust with the oregano. Heat for 3 to 4 minutes at medium power, until the cheese melts, turning the dish once. Cut into slices and serve.

Sformato di Pasta
(PASTA MOLD)

SERVES 4

Most of the time, the way prepared food looks either attracts you or turns you off. This is a recipe that is as pleasing to the sense of sight as it is to the sense of taste.

1/2 pound spaghetti

1 tablespoon butter

9 ounces Italian sausage, skinned and crumbled

1 medium onion, peeled and diced

1 large green bell pepper, seeded, halved, and coarsely chopped

2 cups canned tomato sauce or Mamma's Tomato Sauce (page 47)

1/4 cup pitted black olives, sliced

1/2 pound mozzarella, sliced thinly

Cook the pasta on the stove al dente. Drain, dress with the butter, and set aside. In a 1-quart glass casserole, crumble the sausage, add the onion and green pepper, stir, and cover. Cook in the microwave for 5 to 6 minutes on maximum power, stirring once during cooking process.

Add the tomato sauce, pasta, and olives. Cover and heat on maximum power for 6 to 8 minutes, stirring once. Cover with the mozzarella. Replace in the microwave without a cover and heat at high power for 2 to 3 minutes, until the cheese melts, turning the casserole once.

Risotti (Rice Dishes)

isotto is a wonderful, delicious, and nutritious dish. Rich, creamy yet al dente risotto is the hallmark of Northern Italian cuisine. The Milanese (people who live in or near Milan) serve risotto as a first course, and follow it with a main course of meat or fish accompanied by vegetables and roasted potatoes, then a salad of radicchio, and then fruit and cheese.

Many are intimidated by risotto, thinking of it as difficult to prepare. Let's lay to rest the notion that you need to have graduated from a culinary college in order to prepare a tasty al dente risotto. Take my word for it, please, risotto isn't difficult at all—provided that you follow a few simple rules.

1. Use only Arborio rice imported from Italy for risotto. If you are unable to purchase it where you live, you can mail-order it from the establishments I mentioned on page 20.

2. Don't overpower the rice with other ingredients; use the amounts indicated in the recipe.

3. Use homemade broth whenever possible. However, a good canned chicken broth (skimmed of any fat) or reconstituted bouillon (Knorr's is very good) will still produce a tasty and satisfying risotto.

4. Stir the risotto constantly with a wooden spoon.

5. Don't overcook it. It should be al dente, so test it by tasting. A risotto will take about 18 minutes to cook once you begin adding the broth.

6. Don't start the risotto until everyone is ready to eat. Once it is al dente, it must be served immediately.

7. Don't make a risotto for more than six people.

Risotto Milanese
(MILAN—STYLE RISOTTO)

SERVES 4

When most people think risotto, this is the classic dish that they think about. It is substantial, colorful, and *pleasing to the taste buds. One forkful or spoonful transports you to Milan. It is a gustatory sensation.*

5 cups chicken stock

2 tablespoons olive oil

1 small onion, minced

2 cups Arborio rice

1 teaspoon saffron (This is a must. It is expensive, but without it the risotto will not be genuine.)

Salt and freshly ground black pepper to taste

1½ tablespoons butter (not margarine!)

4 tablespoons freshly grated Parmesan cheese

Heat the stock in a covered saucepan on high heat. When hot but not yet simmering, reduce the heat to low.

Heat the olive oil in a large saucepan on medium heat. Add the onion and sauté gently for 3 minutes. Add the rice and stir 2 minutes to coat each grain with oil. Increase the heat to medium-high and add 1 cup of the hot broth, stirring constantly until all the broth has been absorbed. Continue to add the stock 1 cup at a time, stirring constantly, until all the stock (5 cups) has been absorbed. This will take about 16 minutes.

Sprinkle in the saffron. Taste for al dente doneness and season with salt and pepper if necessary. Remove the risotto from the heat, stir in the butter and Parmesan cheese, and serve immediately.

Risotto al Funghi
(FRESH MUSHROOM RISOTTO)

SERVES 4

This marvelous dish brings me back to the beautiful day when I visited Parma. It is a jewel of a medieval city that most tourists just don't get to see. In the afternoon I was fortunate enough to join a group of Americans on a trip to a Parmigiano-Reggiano cheese factory on the outskirts of the city. I learned that the production of Parmesan cheese is an ancient agricultural art. That evening, back in Parma, this dish was served, to my delight. I'll never forget it, and I'll never forget Parma.

3 tablespoons finely chopped onion

1 clove garlic, peeled and left whole

3 tablespoons olive oil

1 tablespoon chopped fresh Italian (flat-leafed) parsley

1 tablespoon chopped celery

Salt and freshly ground black pepper

10 ounces fresh mushrooms, sliced thin

1 cup whole milk

1½ cups Arborio rice

4 tablespoons heavy cream

5 cups hot beef stock

1 tablespoon butter

1 cup freshly grated Parmesan cheese

In a 6-quart saucepan, sauté the onion and garlic in the oil on medium-high heat for about 5 minutes. Add the parsley, celery, and salt and pepper to taste. Discard the garlic when it becomes pale brown. Add the mushrooms and cook on low heat for 8 minutes, stirring frequently. Add the milk. Cook for 10 minutes.

Add the rice and cream. Continue to cook by adding hot broth a cup at a time, adding another cup as the broth is absorbed by the rice. Continue to stir and add broth until all 5 cups have been absorbed. This will take about 25 minutes. Now add the butter and Parmesan cheese. Stir in and then serve immediately.

Risotto di Carne
(VEAL RISOTTO)

SERVES 5

This risotto and the two that follow were made for me when I visited my dear La Bozzetta family in Reggio Calabria. Although risotti are characteristic of Northern Italian cuisine, the people of Southern Italy can and do make them expertly.

The base flavor of this risotto is the same as you'll find in Salsa Genovese (page 50). It is light and refreshing. Geni La Bozzetta Stilo made it for us one afternoon and served it as a first course. Well, I was offered a second serving and of course I accepted. Yes, I couldn't even take a nibble of the main course.

6 cups good beef stock
2 tablespoons olive oil
1 tablespoon butter
1 large onion, minced
1/2 pound stewing veal, diced
2 cups Arborio rice
1/2 cup good dry white wine
1/2 cup chopped fresh Italian (flat-leafed)
    parsley

2 teaspoons freshly ground black pepper
Salt to taste
Freshly grated Parmesan cheese to serve at
    table (optional)

Heat the beef stock to a simmer, cover, and leave on lowest heat. Heat the butter in the olive oil in your largest saucepan on medium heat. Add diced veal and the onion and sauté until brown, about 10 minutes. Add the rice and stir to coat every grain with oil, about 3 minutes. Add the wine and continue to cook until almost evaporated, about 8 minutes. Add the parsley, black pepper, and salt.

Now begin adding the hot beef stock 1 cup at a time, stirring until absorbed by the rice. Continue this process until all the broth (6 cups) is absorbed. Remove from the heat and serve immediately.

Purists eat this without adding a thing; wise guys like me will sprinkle on some grated Parmesan and like it better. You'll have to decide whether you're a purist or a wise guy.

Riso al Carciofi
(ARTICHOKE RISOTTO)

SERVES 4

Clelia La Bozzetta drove home from work to prepare supper. As soon as she got through the door, she hurried into the kitchen. As I watched in amazement, she threw this recipe together. Forty minutes later we were sitting at table enjoying this delicately flavored dish.

For this risotto and the next one you may use Amer-

ican rice because they are not true risotti, but risi (rice dishes), so they do not follow the risotto cooking method. I do, and with great success. I use Uncle Ben's Long Grain Converted Rice.

2 tablespoons olive oil

2 cloves garlic, peeled and minced

1 14-ounce can artichoke hearts packed in water, drained (save the artichoke water)

3 cups water

1/2 cup chopped fresh Italian (flat-leafed) parsley

2 cups regular long grain rice

Salt and freshly ground black pepper

Freshly grated Parmesan cheese

Heat the oil in a large saucepan. Sauté the garlic for 5 minutes on medium-high heat. Cut the artichoke hearts in quarters, add to the garlic, and sauté another 5 minutes. Add the artichoke water, the 3 cups water, and the parsley, the rice, and salt and pepper to taste. Stir, and bring to a boil. Lower the heat to simmer. Cover and cook for 30 minutes. Remove from the heat and let stand for 5 minutes. Serve immediately. Pass the Parmesan at table.

Riso con Spinaci
(FRESH SPINACH RISOTTO)

SERVES 4

I was visiting Mimy La Bozzetta Giovanella and after a stupendous dinner, while sipping espresso coffee,

I asked her for a risotto recipe. She cleared the table and said: "Watch me now, Giuseppe, I'll show you." She immediately prepared this dish while I took notes. Even though we were stuffed from dinner, we had to taste-test this attractive riso. It passed the test "plusquam optime" (better than best). Now tell me you don't want to try it.

2 tablespoons butter (don't even think margarine)

1 large clove garlic, peeled and minced

1 pound fresh spinach, washed carefully in cold water, chopped, and left in a bowl of cold water

2 cups long grain rice cooked 20 minutes on simmer in 4 cups water

1/2 cup heavy cream

Salt and freshly ground black pepper

Freshly grated Parmesan cheese

Heat the butter in a medium saucepan and gently sauté the garlic for 6 minutes on medium heat. Lift out the spinach from the cold water and add it to the garlic. Watch out—the butter will spit and splatter when the dripping cold water hits it. Cover the pan and cook the spinach on medium heat for 8 minutes. Add the cooked rice, cream, salt, and pepper. Stir thoroughly and heat through for 5 minutes on simmer. Serve. Pass the grated Parmesan.

Secondi Piatti (Main Courses)

In Italy, the main course is either meat, poultry, or fish. I'm going to leave the fish dishes for the end of this section. As I've said, I don't eat fish and seafood and I have to wear a clothespin on my nose when I'm cooking them, but I'll cook them for my family and friends who love them—and take great pleasure in their enjoyment.

Although veal is undoubtedly the best and favorite meat in Italy, and the ways of cooking it excellent, all the other meats can be found (even horse meat sold at special butcher shops), and Italians offer some interesting and unusual methods of cooking them. These tend to be regional and depend on the type and quality of meat available locally. In Florence the beef is good and the specialty is an enormous sirloin steak grilled over charcoal. In Rome the baby lamb is renowned and Reggio Emilia is famous for its pork, including roast suckling pig and the famous Parma hams (prosciutto).

Many Italian recipes with meat are top-of-the-stove dishes which are very simple to prepare. Many of the recipes in this section are of this type. Roasts and grilled meats are also popular in Italy; the difference is, however, that chops are marinated with oil, herbs, and seasoning before grilling. Roasts of beef, lamb, or pork are studded with slivers of garlic, sprigs of parsley, and spikes of rosemary. Italians also excel in using the less costly cuts of meat and make them tender by cooking them in wine. Meat is very expensive in Italy because most of it is imported. The Italians prefer to use the less expensive fish from their seas and free-range poultry from their countryside for main courses.

Rotolo di Vitello
(ROLLED BREAST OF VEAL)

SERVES 4

When I was visiting the Emilia Romagna region of Italy, I was very fortunate because I made friends of cooks and chefs who cheerfully shared their special recipes with me. When I asked them if I could use their names in conjunction with their recipes in my book, invariably these fine humble men said no. Why? I asked. Just as invariably they claimed that their recipes were borrowed from their wives. So thank you Annamaria, Gioconda, Violetta, and Francesca. These next four recipes are so good that they do not need my introductory words of description or praise. Make them and you will be inspired to describe and praise them with your own words.

1¼ pounds boned breast of veal
¼ cup olive oil
Salt and freshly ground black pepper
6 fresh sage leaves or ½ teaspoon dried
¼ pound boiled ham, chopped
⅓ cup shelled green peas
¼ pound freshly grated Parmesan cheese
1 large egg
Juice of 1 large lemon

Preheat the oven to 375°. Rub the veal with 1 tablespoon of the olive oil and sprinkle with salt and pepper to taste. Combine the sage leaves, chopped ham, peas, Parmesan cheese, and egg by beating together. Spread the mixture over the veal. Roll up the meat tightly and fasten with kitchen string. Place the roll in a baking dish, pour the lemon juice and the remaining olive oil over it, and cook for 1 hour.

Cut the veal into 1/4-inch slices after it has rested for 10 minutes out of the oven. Serve to the pleasure of your table companions.

Bracioline Rustiche
(COUNTRY-STYLE PORK CHOPS)

SERVES 4

I know, I know. I said I wasn't going to say anything about these recipes. I ate these in a charming farmhouse when invited to dine with Giovanni (one of the previously mentioned chefs) and Gioconda's family. Oh! The moist pork chops, the wine, the laughter! What a joyous experience.

2 large cloves garlic, peeled and left whole
4 tablespoons olive oil
4 2-inch-thick rib pork chops
Salt
5 ounces Parmesan cheese, slivered

In a large skillet, sauté the garlic in the olive oil for 5 minutes on medium heat. Adjust the heat to high and add the pork chops, browning them on both sides for 4 minutes on each side. Remove and discard the garlic, reduce the heat to medium, and cook the chops another 10 minutes. Sprinkle with salt, and place slivers of Parmesan cheese over the chops. Cover the pan and cook until the cheese has melted. Serve.

Scaloppine alla Parmigiana
(VEAL SCALOPPINE PARMA STYLE)

SERVES 4

No, this is not what we commonly accept as Veal Parmigiana. It is not the old stand-by of a pizzeria *restaurant's piece of meat (who knows if it's veal, pork, beef, or some unknown horse?) heavily breaded, fried until it is dried out, slathered with pizza sauce, and drowned in mozzarella cheese. This dish is definitely gourmet fare.*

8 veal scaloppine
4 slices good boiled ham (I like Krakus brand Polish ham)
1/4 pound Parmesan cheese, cut into slivers
2 tablespoons butter

Pound the scaloppine 1/8 inch thick between heavy sheets of plastic with a kitchen mallet. Cover each of 4 scaloppine with a slice of ham and slivers of cheese. Top each one with another scaloppine. Seal the edges by pounding with the mallet. Heat the butter in a skillet over medium-high heat and brown the meat on both sides for about a minute each side. Transfer to a warm serving platter and serve.

1/2 cup light cream
Salt and freshly ground black pepper
1 tablespoon balsamic vinegar (not any other kind)
1 pound ground round beef
1 cup freshly grated Parmesan cheese
2 egg yolks

In a skillet sauté the sliced onion in the oil and 1 tablespoon of the butter on medium heat. When the onion becomes a light golden color (in about 8 minutes), add the cream, salt and pepper to taste, and the balsamic vinegar. Stir thoroughly. Cook for another 5 minutes, then set aside.

Combine the ground beef, cheese, and egg yolks. Mix very thoroughly and shape into six oblong patties. Brown them in a skillet with the remaining 2 tablespoons butter. Transfer to a warm platter, pour the sauce over the patties, and serve.

Saporite di Manzo
(BEEF PATTIES PARMA STYLE)

SERVES 4 TO 6

These may look like hamburgers or Salisbury steaks, but believe me, any resemblance is purely coincidental. These transform ground round beef from the ridiculous to the sublime.

1/2 onion, sliced very thinly
1 tablespoon olive oil
3 tablespoons butter

Corona di Maiale Arrostita
(PORK CROWN ROAST ITALIAN STYLE)

ATTILIO (ARTHUR) AND JOSEPHINE FRANCONERI
BAYONNE, NEW JERSEY

SERVES 8

Artie Franconeri and I have been friends since 1945. Artie was nine and I was eight when we went into his "clubhouse," a converted chicken-coop, and smoked our first cigarette. We were sitting against the back wall of the shed, feeling like big shots smoking, when all of a sudden the door burst open and we were doused with a bucket of water by Mr. Franconeri, Artie's father. He had seen smoke wafting out of the cracks of the wooden shed, thought it was on fire and took the appropriate action. Mr. Franconeri started to laugh when he saw his son and Joey Orsini with limp Lucky Strike cigarettes hanging from their lips.

Fifty-four years later, Attilio and I are still the best of friends. He, his wife Josephine, and his sons Anthony and Patrick, are in the Italian manner, part of my extended family.

The Franconeris have a beautiful tradition. On each New Year's Day, all their blood relatives and extended family gather in their family room to feast on the following recipe. Why pork? It is an Italian tradition to eat fatty food on the first day of the year. The fat consumed is a symbol of prosperity and good fortune for the families who share the feast together. Of course, nowadays, we do not eat the fat. Who needs all that cholesterol? But the symbol remains.

One taste of this scrumptious dish and you and your families may make this your family tradition. Buon appetito e buona fortuna!

1 crown roast of pork—consisting of about
    18 to 20 chops
1 lb Italian sausage
1 package seasoned stuffing mix (we use
    Pepperidge Farm)
2¹/₂ cups of chicken broth (page 37 or
    College Inn brand)
2 tablespoons butter
3 tablespoons olive oil
Store bought Italian seasoning
    to taste
2 tablespoons minced garlic

Salt to taste
Freshly ground black pepper to taste

Stuffing:

Remove casing from the sausage and crumble the meat. Sauté the sausage meat in olive oil until brown. Drain and set aside. In a medium pot or saucepan, melt the butter and add the chicken broth and heat. Add the stuffing mix according to package directions and, finally, add the sausage meat and mix well. Set aside.

The Roast:

Preheat the oven to 350°.

While oven heats, coat meat with Italian seasoning, minced garlic, salt and pepper. Place the seasoned roast in a shallow roasting pan. To hold the roundness of the roast while it cooks, place an oven proof cup or bowl in the center of roast. Wrap bone ends in foil to prevent burning. Spoon stuffing into center of roast; do not be concerned if the stuffing overflows the shape holding container. Place in oven and roast until the meat reaches an internal temperature of 170–175 degrees.

Serve with vegetables of your choice and don't forget the baked apples!

Abbacchio al Forno
(ROMAN ROAST LEG OF LAMB)

We have left Emilia-Romagna and come to the Eternal City, Rome.

When it comes to lamb, I can take it or leave it. Most of the time I leave it. But when I was in Rome one Easter season, my nose led me to every other restaurant on the Via Veneto because the aroma wafting from those kitchens was divine. I walked into a trattoria (family restaurant) and ordered the lamb. It was the right decision; it was scrumptious.

1 3-pound leg of *young* lamb
Salt and freshly ground black pepper
3 cloves garlic, peeled and sliced
1 teaspoon dried rosemary
2 tablespoons butter

Preheat the oven to 350°. Rub the leg with salt and pepper to taste and tuck pieces of garlic and rosemary under the skin and around the bone. Let it stand at room temperature for 1 hour. Place with the butter in a roasting pan and roast for 11/2 hours, basting occasionally. Remove, let rest for 10 minutes. Slice and serve.

Scaloppine di Vitello al Marsala

(VEAL CUTLETS IN MARSALA WINE SAUCE)

SERVES 4

Marsala wine hails from Marsala in Sicily—that island of enchantment and mystery. You must use dry Marsala wine in this recipe; the sweet Marsala is meant to accompany a simple dessert of Italian biscotti (plain cookies that you dip into the wine). They say Marsala wine and high-quality veal were meant for each other. After you sample this dish, you'll agree.

2 tablespoons olive oil
8 ounces white button mushrooms, wiped clean
6 tablespoons chicken stock
Juice of 1/2 lemon
8 thin small veal cutlets
Seasoned flour (1 cup all-purpose flour mixed with 1 teaspoon salt and 2 teaspoons black pepper)
2 tablespoons butter, for frying
4 tablespoons dry Marsala wine
1/4 cup chopped fresh Italian (flat-leafed) parsley

Heat the oil in a saucepan, add the mushrooms and shake over moderate heat for 1 minute. Add half of chicken stock and 1 teaspoon of the lemon juice. Stir and set aside.

Pound the veal thinly, sprinkle with the remaining lemon juice, and coat with the seasoned flour. Melt the butter in a large skillet and fry the veal (in a single layer) until golden, about 5 minutes each side. Stir in the Marsala wine, cook for 1 more minute, then dish the veal onto a warm platter. Add the remaining stock to the skillet and let bubble until the sauce is syrupy, about 5 minutes; pour over the veal. Garnish with the cooked mushrooms and chopped parsley. The warm sun of Sicily will shine upon your table.

Piccata di Vitello al Limone
(SCALLOPS OF VEAL IN LEMON SAUCE)

SERVES 3 – 4

The lemon refreshes your tastebuds as well as tenderizing the already tender veal. This is a magnificently simple dish that makes you say: "I should have made more." And your guests will say: "Well, why didn't you?"

> 12 ounces veal cutlet, cut in *thin* 2-inch squares
> Seasoned flour (see page 121)
> 2 tablespoons olive oil
> 3 tablespoons butter
> 2 tablespoons fresh lemon juice
> 1 tablespoon finely chopped Italian (flat-leafed) parsley

Coat the veal with the seasoned flour. Heat half the oil and half the butter in a large skillet and when hot, fry half the veal until golden on each side and cooked through (taste a piece). Remove by pouring onto a platter. Add the remaining oil and butter to the same skillet and cook the rest of the veal in the same way. Add the lemon juice and parsley and replace the reserved veal. Heat gently, stirring to coat the meat with the lemon sauce. Serve at once, with sautéed potatoes and a crisp green salad. Joy! Joy! Joy!

Osso Buco alla Milanese
(VEAL SHANKS MILAN STYLE)

SERVES 6

Osso Buco is as Milanese as the Cathedral of Milan. It and the Cathedral have been there for ages. I tasted it in the Galleria di Milano (the first enclosed shopping mall in the world). I simply had to get the recipe. I asked for the chef. He came out of the kitchen expecting a troublesome customer. When I asked him for his Osso Buco recipe, he smiled, sat down, and said: "I'll give you my mother's recipe, it's better than mine." I wrote the directions on a napkin which I thought later that I had lost. I prayed to St. Anthony of Padua (the finder of lost articles) and found the napkin tucked away in a corner of my suitcase. Thank you, St. Anthony.

> 6 1-inch slices veal shank
> 4 tablespoons all-purpose flour
> 4 tablespoons olive oil
> 2 cups beef stock
> 1½ cups dry white wine
> Juice of 1 lemon
> 1 cup finely chopped fresh Italian (flat-leafed) parsley

Dredge both sides of the veal shanks in the flour. Place the olive oil in your largest skillet on medium heat. (The skillet should be large enough to hold the veal in one layer.) When the oil is hot, place the veal in the skillet and brown both sides, 3 minutes each. Add the stock, lower the heat, and simmer until the stock evaporates. Add the wine and a little more water if necessary. Cover and simmer for 14 minutes; the liquid should be almost completely evaporated. Add the lemon juice, sprinkle with the parsley, and serve on a bed of cooked rice.

Costolette alla Bolognese
(VEAL CUTLETS BOLOGNA STYLE)

SERVES 4

The city of Bologna is the location of the oldest university and medical school in the Western World. It is famous for its unfinished cathedral as well as its wonderful cooking. Other Italians have named the city Bologna La Grassa (Bologna the Fat Lady), but not in disrespect. Just the opposite. It is so named to respect the superiority of its cuisine. When you sample these veal cutlets, you will never forget Bologna La Grassa even if you have never been there.

4 veal cutlets, pounded very thin
Seasoned flour (see page 121)
1 large egg, beaten
Fine white bread crumbs (unseasoned)
3 tablespoons butter
4 thin slices proscuitto or boiled ham
Freshly grated Parmesan cheese
4 tablespoons chicken stock

Coat the veal with the seasoned flour, then dip in the beaten egg and bread crumbs, pressing the coating on firmly. Melt the butter in a flame-proof shallow dish with a cover on medium heat. Cook the veal until golden, about 3 minutes on each side. Lay a similarly sized slice of ham on top of each cutlet and sprinkle thickly with Parmesan cheese, pressing the cheese in with a wide knife or spatula. Stir the chicken stock into the butter in the pan and spoon a little over each cutlet. Cover and cook gently for 5 minutes on low heat, until the cheese is melted.

VARIATION: Prepare exactly as above but place a thin slice of fontina, Swiss or provolone cheese instead of the Parmesan cheese on each cutlet, and allow cheese to melt in a 475° oven for 5 minutes.

Bistecca alla Pizzaiola
(STEAK NAPLES STYLE)

SERVES 3

It is generally accepted that what we know today as pizza originated in Naples. As the story goes, a pizzaiola (the pizza chef's wife) found a quantity of pizza sauce left over and decided to make her tired husband a treat for their late supper. She made this dish for him and he was so happy with it that he kissed her a thousand times. Like with so many Italian folk tales, we have to say: "Se non é vero, é ben trovato" (Even if it's not true, it's still a good story). If you don't get a couple of kisses from your loved one when you make it for him or her, then shame on them!

1 recipe Salsa Pizzaiola (page 48)
3 thin rump or round steaks
Salt and freshly ground black pepper
Olive oil

Prepare the sauce. Season the steaks with salt and pepper to taste. Fry them in a little olive oil until browned on each side. Spread the sauce thickly over each steak, cover the pan, and cook on low heat for 10 minutes. Serve, and be ready for some kisses.

Salsicce alla Romagnola
(ROMAGNA STYLE SAUSAGES)

SERVES 4

The region of Emilia-Romagna is a gourmet's dream come true. Tortellini from Bologna, Parmesan cheese from Parma, prosciutto from Parma, balsamic vinegar from Modena—what more can you ask for? These gorgeous sausages from the countryside, that's what. These are rustic and hearty and almost make you want to live near a pig farm. No kidding, they're that tasty.

1 teaspoon olive oil
1 pound fresh Italian pork sausages (sweet or hot)
1 pound ripe tomatoes, peeled (see Tip, page 32) and chopped
Salt and freshly ground black pepper
1 teaspoon sugar

Grease a frying pan with the olive oil and fry the sausages on low heat until lightly browned, about 10 minutes. Drain off the excess fat, leaving the sausages in the pan. Add the tomatoes and the salt, pepper, and sugar to taste and simmer for 10 to 15 minutes, until the tomatoes are reduced to a sauce. Arrange the sausages in a serving dish and spoon the sauce over them. Serve with a side dish of Spaghetti Agli'e Olio (page 69).

Bistecca alla Pizzaiola d'Elena
(HELEN'S STEAK PIZZAIOLA)

HELEN BARBERIO
BAYONNE, NEW JERSEY

SERVES 4

This mouth-watering recipe comes from the kitchen of Helen Barberio. Helen is a registered nurse who works in the emergency room of Bayonne Hospital. I met this vivacious woman about ten years ago when my brother Oreste escorted her to a family wedding. When they danced together, everyone moved to the edge of the dance floor to watch—they were that outstanding. Helen has become a very dear friend and is an excellent cook. Her kitchen and dining room are absolutely Italian. When you sample this recipe, you will be convinced that Helen should give up nursing and open an Italian restaurant. I would be a regular customer.

6 boneless "chicken"-cut beef steaks, filleted in halves
3 tablespoons olive oil
2 28-ounce cans Italian peeled tomatoes, not drained, squeezed through your fingers
6 cloves garlic, crushed
1/4 cup fresh Italian (flat-leafed) parsley, chopped
1 teaspoon dried oregano
Salt and freshly ground black pepper to taste
1 pound linguine

Heat the oil in your largest skillet on moderate heat. Brown the steaks 3 minutes on each side. Add all the remaining ingredients on top of the steaks. Stir. Cover and cook on low heat for 1 hour. Remove the steaks to a serving dish and keep warm in the 170° oven, until pasta is ready. These are best when served with 1 pound of linguine cooked al dente, drained, and dressed with the steak-tomato sauce. Reserve some sauce to top the steaks.

Salsiccia Fatta in Casa
(HOMEMADE SAUSAGE)

THE REVEREND DEACON DOMINICK RICCIO

HASBROUCK HEIGHTS, NEW JERSEY

YIELD: 10 – 12 POUNDS

Dominick Riccio is a family friend of fifty years. My brother Oreste was best man at his wedding to Claire Isolde and godfather to his son Damon. He answered the call to serve the church over twenty years ago and was ordained a deacon. When he was a very young man, his father, an immigrant from Casoria (Province of Naples), taught him the art of butchering. Dominick worked as a butcher for many years and his homemade sausage is the best I've ever tasted.

Factory-made Italian sausage is filled with fat and chemical preservatives. Buy it, if you must, but here is a flavorful and healthier alternative. If you have a Kitchen Aid mixer, you can purchase their sausage maker attachment and your labor will be much easier. (Follow directions for grinding and stuffing sausage enclosed with attachment.)

3 – 4 boneless pork butts (10–12 pounds)

¹/₄ cup salt

³/₄ cup coarsely ground black pepper, or
   ²/₃ cup hot pepper flakes and ²/₃ cup paprika
   for hot sausage)

1¹/₄ cups fennel seeds

1 container pork casings for Italian sausage
   (available from your butcher or at large
   supermarkets) packed in salt

Trim the excess fat from the pork butts and cut into 1-inch cubes. Grind the meat coarsely, or have your butcher grind it for you. Place it in very large mixing bowl. Add the salt, pepper, and fennel seeds. Mix thoroughly by hand to blend in the spices. Take three or four casings at a time and wash them carefully in cold water. Open the end of each casing and attach it to the cold water spigot to allow water to wash the inside also. Now attach a casing to the end of a large kitchen funnel and stuff with the prepared sausage meat. (The sausage maker adapter of the Kitchen Aid mixer quickly and easily fills the casings.) Repeat with each casing. Any air bubbles in the sausage should be punctured with a kitchen needle. Pack the sausage in 1- or 2-pound batches in heavy freezer plastic; it will keep in the freezer for up to six months. Use in any recipe that calls for Italian sausage.

This may sound like a lot of work and it is; but if you make it a Sunday afternoon family project, your children will have another lovely memory to pass on to their own kids someday. And the taste! The taste of your own homemade sausage will be legendary.

POLLAME
(POULTRY)

Italians have a number of unusual ways of cooking poultry. Chicken may be either free-range or intensively reared in the modern system—both are equally suitable for the various recipes for cut-up chicken cooked with tomatoes, wine, peppers, and onions. In Bologna, where the poultry is particularly good, there are excellent ways of cooking chicken and turkey breasts. Let's get into it.

Filetto di Tacchino alla Parmigiana
(TURKEY CUTLETS PARMA STYLE)

SERVES 4

I sampled this dish in Rimini, a very clean and beautiful city on the Adriatic Sea. Rimini is part of the region of Emilia-Romagna, but I went to a Parmigiano-Reggiano restaurant and got the recipe from a German cook. Go figure! But taste these first, they are ambrosial.

1 pound (4 pieces) turkey cutlets
1 large egg, beaten
1 cup plain bread crumbs
2 tablespoons olive oil
1 tablespoon butter
5 ounces Parmesan cheese, cut into thin slices

Preheat the oven to 400°. Dip each turkey cutlet on both sides in the egg and then the bread crumbs. Heat the oil in a skillet on medium heat and fry the cutlets on both sides, 5 minutes each side. Butter a baking dish, transfer the cutlets to it, cover each with the slivers of Parmesan cheese, and cook for 10 minutes. Serve immediately.

Petti di Pollo alla Bolognese
(CHICKEN BREASTS BOLOGNA STYLE)

SERVES 4

I told you that Bologna has outstanding food, and this recipe proves my point. The Bolognesi take ordinary ingredients and, like the alchemists of old, try to turn lead into gold. The alchemists never succeeded, but the Bolognesi do.

4 skinless, boneless chicken breasts
Seasoned flour (see page 121)
3 tablespoons butter
4 slices boiled ham
4 tablespoons freshly grated Parmesan cheese
8 stalks fresh asparagus, cooked al dente, for garnish

Flatten the chicken breasts between heavy plastic sheets with a kitchen mallet and coat with the seasoned flour. Melt the butter in your largest skillet and cook the chicken breasts on gentle heat, turning several times, until golden, about 10 minutes. Lay a slice of ham on each piece of chicken, sprinkle thickly with the Parmesan cheese, and spoon some of the butter in the pan over each. Cover the skillet and cook for 5 minutes. Arrange the chicken on a serving platter and pour the remaining butter and pan juices over it. Garnish with the asparagus stalks.

Petti di Pollo di Marsala
(CHICKEN BREASTS WITH MARSALA)

SERVES 4

This is a Sicilian variation of the above recipe. Of course, a Sicilian will say that this version far surpasses the Bolognese recipe. You decide for yourself.

4 skinless, boneless chicken breasts
Seasoned flour (see page 121)
3 tablespoons butter
4 tablespoons dry Marsala wine
4 tablespoons chicken stock
Juice of 1/2 lemon
4 tablespoons freshly grated pecorino
    cheese

Flatten the chicken breasts between heavy plastic sheets with a kitchen mallet and coat with the seasoned flour. Melt the butter in a large skillet and cook the chicken over gentle heat, turning several times, until golden. Pour the Marsala over the chicken and let bubble on high heat for 1 minute. Add the lemon juice. Cover each breast with the grated Pecorino cheese and moisten with the chicken stock. Cover the pan and cook gently on low heat for 5 minutes. Transfer the chicken to a serving dish, pour the pan juices over it, and serve.

Petti di Pollo al Antonio
(ANTHONY'S PERFECT CHICKEN BREASTS)

SERVES 4

Here's Anthony Oswald again, folks! You already know this is going to be special. By the way, Anthony's mom, Norma, is Italian. Could it be that is where Anthony inherited his cooking talents? Please, don't ask me again! He is not accepting any more marriage proposals. He invented this recipe one night at my home and we've repeated it innumerable times since.

2 boneless, skinless chicken breasts, filleted
    to give four cutlets
Seasoned flour (see page 121)
3 tablespoons butter
Juice of 1 medium lemon
3 ounces dry white wine
3 teaspoons capers
1 clove minced garlic
1 6-ounce jar roasted red peppers, drained,
    sliced 1/4 inch wide, and dressed with
    1 tablespoon olive oil

Remove any visible fat or connective tissue from the chicken and pound thin (about 1/8 inch) between sheets of heavy plastic with a kitchen mallet. Dredge the chicken cutlets in the seasoned flour. Melt the butter in a large skillet on medium heat. Sauté the cutlets about 3 minutes on each side. Add the lemon juice, white wine, capers, and roasted peppers. Adjust heat to high and reduce the sauce for 3 minutes. Transfer the cutlets to a serving platter, spoon the sauce over them, and serve.

Petti di Pollo Veneziano

(CHICKEN BREASTS VENETIAN STYLE)

SERVES 8

It was August 1965; my brother Oreste and I brought our mamma to Italy because she had not returned since she had emigrated from Reggio Calabria forty-five years prior. We had a blast in Reggio Calabria because we were the house guests of Marietta La Bozzetta, Mamma's godchild. After ten glorious days, we had to depart from Reggio to Rome by train in order to connect with another train to Venice, our final destination. After a long, long exhausting train ride we arrived to the wild, chaotic mobs of Termini Station in Rome. We had thirty minutes to catch our train to Venice. Oreste and I, laden with five heavy suitcases, told Mamma to follow us as we rushed to our next train. You guessed it—we lost our mamma. I asked a policeman if he could help us. "Abbiamo perso la nostra Mamma!" (We lost our Mamma!), I said. He smiled and took us to the Lost and Found Department. Mamma was there, weeping and shaking. When she saw us she yelled: "Non vogqhiu stari ccani chiu, piqghiamu u lariuplanu e iamonindi a casa!" (I don't want to stay here anymore, let's take the plane and go home!). She calmed down, we caught the next train to Venice, and arrived at the Danieli Palace Hotel in time for supper. We were served this recipe. Oreste and I almost swooned with ecstasy when we tasted it. Mamma wouldn't touch it—it looked so colorless. She ordered minestrone soup and so we all were happy. When I would make it at home, Mamma would make herself spaghetti alla marinara instead. But that was Mamma. Believe me, this dish will make you rapturous.

2 pounds boneless, skinless chicken cutlets, cut into 2-inch pieces

1 cup seasoned flour (see page 121)

1/2 cup olive oil

3 medium onions, peeled and thinly sliced

1 1/2 pounds fresh white mushrooms, thinly sliced

2 cups dry white wine

5 cups cooked rice

1 1/2 pounds shredded mozzarella cheese

2 tablespoons butter

1/2 cup chopped fresh Italian (flat-leafed) parsley

Preheat the oven to 350°. Dredge the chicken pieces in the seasoned flour (I put the flour in a large plastic food bag, drop in the chicken, close the bag, and shake it well). Heat the olive oil in a large skillet on moderate heat. Quickly brown the chicken on both sides in batches. Remove with a slotted spoon and set aside. Sauté the onion in the same oil for 8 minutes. Add the mushrooms and sauté for 5 minutes. Return the cooked chicken to the skillet, add the wine, and simmer on low for 10 minutes.

Mix the cooked rice well with 1 pound of the shredded mozzarella cheese. Press this mixture into a well-buttered baking dish. Pour the chicken and sauce on top of the rice and smooth with a spatula. Sprinkle the remaining 1/2 pound shredded mozzarella over the top. Cover with aluminum foil and bake for 30 minutes. Remove from the oven and let rest for 5 minutes. Slice and serve. You'll need a crisp green salad dressed with olive oil and lemon juice to accompany this luxurious dish.

Tacchino Arrosoto Ripieno
(ROAST STUFFED TURKEY)

SERVES 6

How would you like a holiday turkey that gobbles with an Italian accent? Well, we have one for you in this recipe. Cooking a turkey in this manner takes this American bird to the shores of Italy and makes him sing an Italian serenade. This gobbler would be just as at home steering a gondola in Venice as driving a Ford on an interstate highway in the good old U.S.A. Here is the best of both worlds; America's native bird cooked in an Italian manner.

    1 6-8 pound turkey (OK, it's small, but it's
        tender)
    Salt and freshly ground black pepper
    20 large pitted black olives, chopped
    20 roasted chestnuts, skinned and chopped
    1 pound fresh Italian sweet sausage, skinned
    4 slices fatty bacon
    1 tablespoon all-purpose flour

Preheat the oven to 325°. Wash the turkey under cold running water and pat dry with paper towels. Season the inside of the bird with salt and pepper. Mix the olives, chestnuts, and sausage meat together and stuff the turkey. Place the turkey on a rack in a roasting pan, lay the bacon strips across the breast, and roast the bird for 2 1/2 hours or longer according to the size of the turkey—use a meat thermometer.

When the turkey is cooked as indicated on the meat thermometer, remove the bacon, crumble it, and add it to the pan juices. Sprinkle the breast with the flour, return the turkey to the oven, and cook until the skin is golden brown and crisp, basting it at intervals. Serve as usual, using the pan juices as a light, tasty gravy.

PESCE
(FISH)

It is almost impossible in a cookbook intended for use outside of Italy to do justice to Italian fish dishes. It is not that the cooking methods are unusual, but the varieties of fish available are quite different; even within Italy they vary from coast to coast.

When staying anywhere on Italy's seacoast, it is always interesting to visit the fish markets in the early morning. The markets of Genoa and Venice are particularly worthwhile for they offer a fascinating spectacle of unusual species, bizarre shapes, and splendid colors. Boxes of writhing eels lie side by side with whole tuna, piles of pale pink scampi (only on the Adriatic coast), scarlet and gray mullet, spindly crabs, black and purple mussels on the Tyrrhenian coast.

Pesce alla Pizzaiola
(FISH IN TOMATO SAUCE)

SERVES 4

When I visited Positano (near Naples) with my brothers Oreste and Anthony, we walked down the *narrow streets of this charming fisherman's village to the beach. It was a beautiful evening and the view of Positano from the beach was like looking at a pyramid of twinkling lights climbing fantastically up the side of a mountain. We walked over to an open-air restaurant and sat down. My brothers ordered this dish and wolfed it down while I was very happy with my Pasta al Pesto. Rusti and Toto insisted that I ask for the recipe for their dish. I asked and the chef happily shared it with me. We became instant friends and the espresso with Sambuca was his little gift to us. Enrico Gennarino, this is your wonderful recipe. Again, I thank you.*

4 portions any white fish, skinned
1 bay leaf
1 cup chopped fresh Italian (flat-leafed) parsley
5 tablespoons olive oil
Seasoned flour (page 121)
2 cloves garlic, peeled and crushed
1 14-ounce can peeled Italian plum tomatoes, chopped, with their liquid
Salt and freshly ground black pepper
Sugar

Lay the fish with the bay leaf and half of the chopped parsley in a shallow dish and pour the olive oil over. Leave the fish for 2 hours in the marinade, turning once. Drain and dry the fish, reserving the marinade, then coat with the seasoned flour. Strain the marinade into a large skillet and heat on medium-high until hot. Fry the fish until golden on both sides and cooked through, about 8 to 12 minutes depending on thickness. Remove the fish with a slotted spoon, arrange on a serving dish, and place in a warm oven on its lowest setting to keep warm.

Add the garlic to the oil remaining in the skillet and cook on medium-high heat for 5 minutes, then add the tomatoes. Cook on high heat until the liquid is evaporated and the tomatoes are reduced to a rough puree, about 10 minutes. Season to taste with salt, pepper and sugar. Pour the sauce over the fish, sprinkle with the remaining 1/2 cup chopped parsley, and serve immediately.

Zuppa di Pesce alla Messinese

(FISH SOUP MESSINA STYLE)

SERVES 4

Messina *is a port city in Sicily that lies directly across from Reggio Calabria and is easily reached by hydrofoil in 10 minutes. During one of my stays in Reggio, my "compare," Sandro La Bozzetta, took me for a special treat in Messina. It was then that he discovered to his amazement my sad aversion to fish and seafood. The special treat was this Zuppa di Pesce that he ordered in one of his favorite restaurants. Sandro, gentleman that he is, said: "No problem, Giuseppe. You'll have a beautiful plate of Rigatoni Marinara with a scoop of their ricotta. I'll take the rest of the Zuppa di Pesce home to Clelia; she loves it." We were both content with his resolution of the problem. When we got back to Reggio, Clelia gave me this recipe.*

5 tablespoons olive oil
1 medium onion, peeled and thinly sliced

1 rib celery, thinly sliced

2 cloves garlic, crushed

1 tablespoon chopped fresh Italian
    (flat-leafed) parsley

8 ounces canned peeled tomatoes, chopped,
    with their liquid

1/3 cup dry white wine

1 1/4 cups water

Salt and freshly ground black pepper (or if you
    like it hot, 1 tablespoon crushed red pepper
    flakes)

1 small mackerel, gutted and trimmed

1 8-ounce piece halibut

2 flounder fillets

6 ounces frozen small shrimp, thawed

4 slices buttered Italian bread

Heat the oil in a wide, deep saucepan on low heat and fry the onion, celery, and garlic until soft and golden, about 8 minutes.

Add tomatoes with their juice, and the wine, water, and salt and pepper to taste. Simmer for 15 minutes. Meanwhile, skin the fish if necessary, cut the mackerel into thick slices, the halibut into bite-size chunks, and the flounder into 1-inch strips. Add all to the broth, add a little more water if necessary (the fish should be covered with liquid), and simmer gently for 10 minutes. Add the shrimp and heat for another 4 minutes.

Meanwhile, fry the bread slices in a nonstick skillet until crisp and golden, then put one in the bottom of each soup bowl. Pour the fish soup over the bread, dividing it evenly among the bowls. Sprinkle fresh parsley leaves and serve.

Merluzzo Gratinato
(BAKED WHITING)

SERVES 4

Whiting was my mamma's favorite fish because it was mild and juicy and cooked quickly. I wanted to try it several times, but I lost my nerve. Marietta La Bozzetta made this dish for my friend Peter Gaglioti, who accompanied me on one of my visits to Reggio Calabria. For me, she made a fabulous Zucchini Parmigiana. Peter said the fish was awesome.

1 pound whiting, cut into 4 portions

6 tablespoons olive oil

6 anchovy fillets

1 tablespoon chopped fresh Italian
    (flat-leafed) parsley

1/2 teaspoon freshly ground black pepper

1 cup plain bread crumbs

2 tablespoons olive oil

1 lemon, quartered, for garnish

Preheat the oven to 375°. Place the fish in a baking dish oiled with 1 tablespoon of the olive oil. Make a paste from 3 tablespoons of the olive oil and the anchovies, parsley, and black pepper. Spread the paste over the fish. Cover with the bread crumbs, then sprinkle with the remaining 2 tablespoons olive oil. Bake for 20 minutes, until golden. Garnish with the fresh lemon quarters.

Triglie alla Calabrese
(MACKEREL CALABRIAN STYLE)

SERVES 4

Geni La Bozzetta Stilo is the youngest child of Marietta La Bozzetta. She is really into cooking and loves to please her family. She generously gave me this recipe and asked me to let her know how my family liked it. I made it for some friends and they raved about it. I hope you will too. Let me know, and I'll let Geni know, OK?

3 tablespoons olive oil

1 small onion, peeled and chopped

1 small rib celery, sliced

2 cloves garlic, peeled

¼ cup chopped fresh Italian (flat-leafed) parsley plus an additional ¼ cup for garnish

1 pound ripe tomatoes, chopped

Salt and freshly ground black pepper

4 small or 2 medium-sized mackerel, scaled, gutted, washed, and dried

Chop the onion and the tomatoes and slice the celery. Heat the olive oil in a saucepan and fry the chopped onion, whole garlic cloves, sliced celery, and first 1/4 cup parsley for 8 minutes. When all begins to soften and color, add the chopped tomatoes and salt and pepper to taste. Cover the pan and simmer very gently for 30 minutes.

Press the sauce through a sieve into a shallow flame-proof baking dish. The sauce should be rather thin; if too thick, add spoonfuls of water. Check the seasonings and correct if necessary. Arrange the mackerel head to tail in the sauce. Cook over low heat until tender, about 20 minutes, basting with sauce frequently. Serve hot in the same baking dish, garnished with the additional parsley. When they smack their lips, you'll know it's as good as Geni's.

Contorni (Side Dishes)

The range and variety of vegetables grown in Italy is enormous. Italy is changing with the rest of our world, so it's not only Italian wives but also husbands who shop daily for their "verdure." They take infinite pains to select firm unblemished specimens, usually preferring the smaller to the larger in the belief that youth, tenderness, and delicacy of flavor are found together. As well as all the usual green and root vegetables, finocchio (fennel), carciofi (artichokes), and wild funghi (mushrooms) are commonplace in Italy.

Although a few potatoes and sometimes a green vegetable or salad are served with roasts, it is more usual for vegetables to be eaten as an introductory course, often before the meat. The term for such a dish is *contorno*. Vegetables of all kinds are often served: stuffed artichokes, small zucchini, eggplants, tomatoes, peppers, and onions among others. Vegetables are seldom, if ever, just boiled but are usually tossed in a skillet with butter or olive oil, seasonings, herbs, and, of course, garlic.

ZUCCHINI

One of the most delicious of all vegetables, zucchini are green summer squash, best when 4 to 6 inches long. They are cooked unpeeled, fried in various ways, stewed, stuffed, or used in omelets, risotti, soups, or sauces. One pound of small zucchini will serve 3 to 4.

Zucchini Fritte
(FRIED ZUCCHINI CHIPS)

There are many ways of frying small zucchini. Here is the simplest way.

Small zucchini
Seasoned flour (see page 121)
Olive oil

Cut the zucchini into small chips, 1/4-inch-thick rounds or 1/4-inch-thick lengthwise slices.

Just before cooking, shake them in a plastic food bag with the seasoned flour, then fry them in deep hot olive oil until golden, about 3 minutes. Drain on paper towels and serve immediately.

Are you or your kids addicted to calorie- and fat-laden potato chips? Kick the habit and try these nutritious and tasty zucchini chips instead; you'll thank me.

Zucchini al Burro
(BUTTERED ZUCCHINI)

SERVES 3 – 4

This is a simple vegetable dish that goes well with about any main course.

1 pound baby zucchini
Salt
2 tablespoons butter

Cut the zucchini into 1/4-inch rounds. Sprinkle evenly with a little salt. In a wide saucepan with a lid, melt the butter on medium heat. Add the zucchini rounds and stir to coat them evenly with butter. Cover the saucepan and cook on very low heat until tender, about 10 to 12 minutes. Shake the pan now and then to prevent sticking. Serve hot, with the butter in which they were cooked.

Zucchini Ripiene
(STUFFED ZUCCHINI)

SERVES 4

This is a side dish that I have often used instead of a main course. A few slices of crusty Italian bread and a glass of red Italian wine is all you need to keep the zucchini company.

4 zucchini, about 6 inches long
1 small onion, sliced
1 carrot, sliced
$^1/_2$ bay leaf
$^1/_4$ teaspoon dried thyme
1 cup chicken stock, boiling hot

Stuffing:

1 tablespoon butter
1 large onion, chopped
1 clove garlic, crushed
1 pound small white mushrooms, finely chopped
8 ounces ripe tomatoes, peeled (see Tip, page 32), drained, and finely chopped
Salt and freshly ground black pepper
1 cup boiling chicken stock

Preheat the oven to 375°. Cut the zucchini in half lengthwise, and scoop out the centers with a teaspoon leaving a 1/8-inch wall of flesh. Blanch in boiling water for 2 minutes, remove, and plunge into ice cold water to stop the cooking. Remove and let drain and cool.

Next, prepare the stuffing. Melt the butter in a saucepan and on low heat fry the onion and garlic until soft, about 5 minutes. Add the mushrooms and cook, stirring frequently, for 4 to 5 minutes. Add the tomatoes with salt and pepper to taste, and simmer until the stuffing becomes fairly dry, about 8 to 10 minutes. When cool, press the stuffing into the hollow centers of the zucchini. (You may have leftover stuffing; just sauté it for 1 minute in olive oil and spoon it into the pan in between the zucchini).

Arrange the onion, carrot, bay leaf, and thyme on the bottom of a greased baking dish, lay the stuffed zucchini on top, and cover with the boiling stock. Cover and braise for about 20 to 30 minutes. Pour a little of the reduced cooking liquid over the stuffed zucchini before serving.

FINOCCHIO
(FENNEL)

The bulbous root of fennel is used a great deal in Italian cooking. It has an anise or licorice flavor and a crisp texture like celery. It is often eaten at the end of a meal to help digestion. Sometimes it appears as an antipasto and small quantities are added to give "bite" to mixed salads. It is also cooked, usually in boiling salted water, and then sliced and served hot with olive oil and lemon juice.

Finocchio al Forno
(GOLDEN BAKED FENNEL)

SERVES 4

Clelia La Bozzetta made this once for me as a side dish to a roast beef. I ate one slice of beef and pigged out on the baked fennel. This is a dish that you want to eat until it's all gone. Superb.

> 2 small young fennel roots
> 1¹/₂ tablespoons butter
> 2 tablespoons whole milk
> 2 tablespoons freshly grated Parmesan
>   cheese

Preheat the oven to 400°. Remove any coarse outer leaves and cook the fennel in boiling salted water for about 20 minutes. Cut vertically into four slices and arrange in a shallow baking dish in which 1/2 of the butter (4 1/2 teaspoons) has been melted. Pour the milk over the fennel, sprinkle heavily with the grated cheese, and dot with the remaining butter. Bake until golden, about 20 minutes.

Crocchette di Patate Ripiene
(STUFFED POTATO CROQUETTES)

SERVES 4

I was in Agrigento, Sicily, on a warm January day (yes, warm, about 70°) and returning from a walking tour of the Valley of the Temples. My tour guide was a distinguished white-haired gentleman, a native of Agrigento and a doctor of anthropology by the name of Pietro Arancio. We clicked. He asked me to talk to him in my first language, Reggio Calabrian, and invited me to lunch. We walked into a sidewalk café and Pietro ordered a couple of these delectable croquettes. The food, the wine, and the conversation turned a chance meeting into an enduring friendship.

2 pounds potatoes, peeled

1 tablespoon butter

2 ounces onion, finely chopped

2 cloves garlic, crushed

1 tablespoon chopped fresh Italian
   (flat-leafed) parsley

2 eggs, lightly beaten

1 cup freshly grated Pecorino Romano
   cheese

Salt and freshly ground black pepper

1/2 pound provolone cheese, cut into 2-inch
   cubes

1 egg, beaten, for coating

Fine dry plain bread crumbs

Olive oil or vegetable oil for frying

Cook the potatoes in boiling salted water until tender, drain, and allow to dry. Melt the butter in a small pan and on low heat fry the onion, garlic, and parsley for 5 minutes. Mash or whip the dried potatoes, then add the eggs, grated cheese, and salt and pepper to taste; add onion mixture; mix until smooth.

Using a large soup spoon, form the potato mixture into egg-sized balls. Make a large hole in the center of each with your thumb, insert a chunk of provolone cheese, and close the potato ball over the top. When all the croquettes are formed, place in the refrigerator on a cookie sheet (don't let them touch each other) for 1/2 hour.

Finally, coat each croquette in egg and bread crumbs and deep fry until golden brown. Let them cool off a bit before you bite into them or you'll burn your mouth. These are great to accompany any meat or poultry main course.

Peperoni Ripieni di Riso
(BELL PEPPERS STUFFED WITH RICE)

SERVES 4

Did you ever eat a stuffed pepper in a diner? I have. The pepper was half-cooked and the stuffing was hard-packed steamed flavorless hamburger meat. Aagh! Now, these stuffed peppers, which I ate in Sorrento, made me get up from the table and dance a lively tarantella. The elegant lady who cooked them, Antonella Migliaccio, was pleasantly startled when I kissed her on both cheeks and asked how she prepared them.

4 large green or red bell peppers

5 tablespoons olive oil

1 small onion, finely minced

6 ounces pancetta or unsmoked bacon, diced

1 8-ounce can peeled plum tomatoes

Salt and freshly ground black pepper

6 ounces cooked rice

Preheat the oven to 350°. Cut the top off each pepper, and discard the seeds and pith. Drop the peppers into a large pan of boiling water and simmer for 5 minutes, then drain. Meanwhile, heat 2 tablespoons of the olive oil in a saucepan on low heat and fry the onion for 5 minutes. Add the pancetta and fry another 2 minutes, then add the tomatoes, squeezing them through your fingers, and their juice. Season with salt and pepper to taste, and simmer for 3 minutes. Add the cooked rice and stir until the liquid has been absorbed, about 8 minutes.

Stand the peppers upright in a deep baking

casserole and fill them with the rice mixture. Pour the remaining olive oil over the peppers. Bake, covered, for 40 minutes. Serve hot. This side dish can easily become a main course.

cover the pan, and cook gently for 10 minutes. Add the tomatoes and salt and simmer, stirring occasionally, for 30 minutes. Serve hot or cold, alone as an antipasto, or as an accompaniment to chicken or meat.

Peperonata
(BELL PEPPERS STEWED WITH TOMATOES)

SERVES 4

When I was in Sicily, I was almost overcome by the beauty and charm of the village of Taormina, from which you can see the smoke and fire of Mount Etna. When my stomach grumbled and said: "It's time to eat," I walked into the nearest simple trattoria and ordered a veal cutlet milanese. It arrived accompanied with this delectable peperonata. I returned to that trattoria for four evenings in a row, became friends with the owner, Turrido Belantoni, and ate peperonata to my heart's content.

4 large green or red bell peppers
4 tablespoons olive oil
$^1/_2$ medium-to-large onion, sliced coarsely
1 pound ripe tomatoes, peeled (see Tip, page 32) and quartered
2 level teaspoons salt

Cut the peppers in half lengthwise, and discard the seeds and pith. Cut the peppers into 1-inch-wide strips and rinse under cold water. Heat the oil in a saucepan and on low heat fry the onion about 5 minutes. Add the peppers, stir,

Budino di Patate
(MASHED POTATO PIE)

SERVES 4

We are going to Parma for the next four recipes. They are substantial vegetable dishes that are reflective of Parma's agricultural society. This first dish was prepared for me in Reggio Calabria by my precious surrogate mother, Marietta La Bozzetta. Our own (U.S.) version of mashed potatoes is very good, but this Parmesan version is a flavorsome change.

4 medium-sized potatoes
2 cups freshly grated Parmesan cheese
2 eggs
1 cup milk
Salt and freshly ground black pepper
6 tablespoons butter

Preheat the oven to 400°. Boil the potatoes until tender. Drain, peel while still hot, and mash in a large bowl. Add the cheese, eggs, milk, salt and pepper to taste, and 5 tablespoons of the butter. Mix thoroughly. Transfer to a baking dish smeared with the remaining 1 tablespoon butter and bake for 30 to 35 minutes, until the top is browned.

Carote Dorate
(GOLDEN CARROTS)

SERVES 4

*W*e have all been told since we were kids that eating carrots will benefit our eyes. "You never saw a rabbit wearing glasses, did you?" We have heard recently about beta-carotene and antioxidants being the natural enemies of carcinogens. In other words, carrots are good for you. This recipe will have you eating carrots not so much for the benefits to your health, but because they taste so darn good. They are great as a side dish to poultry.

1 pound carrots
¼ pound butter (you can use low-fat or
    no-fat margarine here, it's OK)
Salt
¼ cup half and half or light cream
2 eggs (Egg Beaters are OK too)
¼ pound freshly grated parmesan cheese
    (no substitutes)
¼ pound boiled ham, diced

Preheat the oven to 400°. Peel the carrots and cook them in boiling water for 4 minutes. Drain when still very firm and cut into slices. Heat the butter in a skillet over high heat. Add the carrots, sprinkle with a little salt, and sauté for 1 minute. Transfer to a bake-and-serve dish. In a bowl, beat the eggs with the cream, Parmesan cheese, and diced ham. Spread the mixture over the carrots and bake for 20 minutes.

Melanzane alla Parmigiana
(EGGPLANT PARMIGIANA)

SERVES 6

*T*he tantalizing "eggplant parm" with which we are all familiar is a Southern Italian adaptation of this authentic original from Parma. Frankly, I like this one better because it's tastier and much lighter.

4 medium-sized eggplants
Salt and freshly ground black pepper
1 cup all-purpose flour
Olive oil for frying
2 tablespoons butter
½ cup canned peeled Italian plum tomatoes
1 cup freshly grated Parmesan cheese
12 fresh basil leaves

Preheat the oven to 400°. Peel the eggplants and slice them lengthwise 1/4 inch thick. Set the slices in a colander, sprinkle with salt and let stand for 1 hour. Pat the slices dry and dredge them in the flour. Fry in a large skillet in very hot oil until golden brown on both sides, about 3 minutes each side.

Grease a bake-and-serve dish with 1 tablespoon of the butter. Line the bottom of the dish with fried eggplant slices. Top this layer with some of the tomatoes squeezed through your fingers, add some Parmesan cheese, freshly ground pepper, a few basil leaves, and dots of butter. Continue building up layers of eggplant, tomatoes, cheese, and basil leaves. Dot the top layer with the remaining butter and bake for 15 minutes. Allow to cool and settle for 10 minutes, then slice and serve.

Asparagi alla Parmigiana
(ASPARAGUS PARMA STYLE)

SERVES 4

I love young pencil-thin crisp asparagus, parboiled for just 2 minutes, drained, and dressed with extra-virgin olive oil and lemon juice. Here's another recipe that will make your asparagus splendid.

    2 pounds young fresh asparagus
    4 tablespoons butter
    1 cup freshly grated Parmesan cheese

Preheat the oven to 400°. Trim and peel the root ends of the asparagus. Place lengthwise in a baking dish greased with 1 tablespoon of the butter. Dot the asparagus with the remaining butter. Sprinkle with the cheese and bake until the top forms a light brown crust, about 20 minutes. Serve immediately.

Spinaci alla Ragusana
(SPINACH RAGUSA STYLE)

SERVES 3

Ragusa, in Sicily, was a stronghold of the Arab domination of the island nation. This recipe clearly reflects the Arab influence in the use of raisins and nuts. If your kids resist eating spinach, try this one on them and they'll be asking: "When are we going to have spinach again?"

    1 ounce sultana raisins (white or purple)
    1 1-ounce slice boiled ham

    1 10-ounce box frozen spinach
    1 tablespoon butter
    Salt and freshly ground black pepper to taste
    1 level tablespoon pignoli (pine nuts) or slivered almonds

Soak the raisins in warm water until they are plump, then drain. Cut the boiled ham into strips. Cook the frozen spinach according to package directions, drain thoroughly, and squeeze dry. Melt the butter in a skillet on moderate heat and fry the ham for 2 minutes, add the spinach, stir well, and season to taste. Stir in the drained raisins and the nuts, cover the pan, and cook on low heat for 5 minutes. Serve.

Broccoli di Rape
(BROCCOLI RABE)

SERVES 4

On page 85 there is an exquisite recipe for broccoli rabe with pasta. Follow the recipe for the broccoli but omit the pasta and you will have a vegetable side dish that goes very well with Italian sausage or roast pork.

Funghi Ripieni
(STUFFED MUSHROOMS)

SERVES 4

Mushrooms prepared in this manner can be used as a side dish to accompany meat or poultry, as a main course, or as *an antipasto (appetizer). They're so savory that no matter how many you make, you'll wish you had made more.*

12 large cup-shaped mushrooms

4 tablespoons olive oil

2 cloves garlic, crushed

1 small onion, finely chopped

¹/₄ cup fresh Italian (flat-leafed) parsley, chopped

¹/₄ cup fresh plain bread crumbs

2 strips cooked bacon, crumbled

¹/₄ cup freshly grated Parmesan cheese

Salt and freshly ground black pepper

2 tablespoons chicken stock

Preheat the oven to 375°. Wipe the mushrooms. Remove the stems and mince them. Heat 1 tablespoon of the olive oil in a small saucepan and fry the garlic, minced mushroom stems, and onion gently for 5 minutes. Stir in the parsley, bread crumbs, bacon, and cheese, and salt and pepper to taste. Add just enough chicken stock to moisten and bind the stuffing.

Spoon the stuffing into the mushroom caps. Pour about 2 tablespoons of the olive oil into a shallow baking dish, arrange the mushrooms in a single layer, and drizzle a few drops of olive oil over each of them. Bake for 20 minutes.

Pomidori alla Siciliana
(SICILIAN-STYLE TOMATOES)

SERVES 4

Randazzo is a mountain town situated on the sloping approach to the summit of Mount Etna, Europe's most active volcano. The people who live under the volcano enjoy its soil enriched with minerals because the vegetables that grow in it are magnificent. The dark side of the situation is that Mount Etna could destroy their lives with no warning. The people are profoundly religious and stage an awe-inspiring procession every August 15, the feast of the Assumption of the Virgin Mary. Twenty-five children representing God, the angels, and saints are secured to a fifty-nine-foot-tall mast on a four-hundred-year-old shrine which is pulled through the town by seventy boys. The crowds throw candies to the children from their balconies to sustain them through the two-hour procession. It was here that I tasted these tantalizing stuffed tomatoes. Unforgettable Randazzo and unforgettable tomatoes. I thank the Creator for both.

4 large firm ripe tomatoes, even sizes

5 tablespoons olive oil

1 small onion, finely chopped

2 ounces pitted black olives, chopped

4 anchovy fillets, chopped

1 tablespoon chopped fresh Italian (flat-leafed) parsley

1 level tablespoon capers, drained

1 ounce plain bread crumbs

¹/₄ cup freshly grated Pecorino Romano cheese

Preheat the oven to 350°. Cut the tomatoes in half horizontally and scoop out a little of the center. Chop the top halves of the tomatoes and reserve. Heat the oil in a small saucepan and cook the onion gently for 8 minutes. Add the chopped olives, anchovies, parsley, capers, rest of the tomato pulp and reserved chopped halves, bread crumbs, and cheese to the onions, mixing well.

Stuff the tomatoes. Arrange in an oiled baking dish and bake for 30 minutes. Let cool for 1/2 hour and serve as a side dish to a meat, poultry, or fish main course, or as an antipasto.

Pomidori col Riso alla Romana

(RICE-STUFFED TOMATOES ROMAN STYLE)

SERVES 4

Every time I visit Rome, I pay a visit to the Capuchin Franciscan Cemetery at the end of the Via Veneto going toward the Piazza Barberini. The top end of the Via Veneto begins at that gorgeous park, the Villa Borghese. I walk the avenue made famous in Fellini's film La Dolce Vita. *It is the avenue of charming outdoor cafés, exclusive shops, luxury hotels, and crowds of tourists trying to catch a glimpse of movie stars, artists, and powerful politicians. But toward the end of this avenue symbolic of temporary material values stands the Capuchin Cemetery housed in what is called "The Bone Church." When you enter, you are shocked into recalling lasting spiritual values. You view hundreds of skeletons belonging to the former inhabitants of the Franciscan Friary (monastery) attached to the church. Human bones artistically decorate the walls, the ceilings, and the altars of the cemetery. As you leave there is a sobering sign that reads: "What you are, we once were, what we are now, one day you will be."*

Right across from the Church is an outdoor restaurant where these stuffed tomatoes are served cold as appetizers or as an accompaniment to roast meats. I enjoy them and thank God that I'm still alive.

4 very large firm tomatoes
3 ounces uncooked rice (I prefer Uncle Ben's)
1 large clove garlic, crushed
1 tablespoon olive oil
6 fresh basil leaves, or 1/2 teaspoon dried
1/4 teaspoon freshly ground black pepper
1 level teaspoon salt

Preheat the oven to 350°. Cut the tops off the tomatoes in one piece and reserve them. With a teaspoon, scoop out the pulp into a bowl, discarding the hard central core but retaining all the juice and seeds. Add the rice, garlic, olive oil, basil, pepper, and half the salt to the tomato pulp, and mix well. Sprinkle the inside of the tomatoes with the remaining salt and place in an oiled baking dish.

Fill the tomatoes with the rice mixture with all its liquid (there must be plenty of liquid for the rice to absorb during cooking). Replace the tops of the tomatoes ensuring that no rice is exposed. Cover and cook for 1 hour.

Melanzane Ripiene all' Amalfitana

(STUFFED EGGPLANT AMALFI STYLE)

SERVES 4

The only way to drive to Amalfi from Naples is to endure the torturous serpentine and frightening Amalfi drive. It is a road carved into the sides of mountains and outcroppings of steep cliffs with the blue Mediterranean Sea hundreds of feet below the edge of the sharply winding road. But the precious gem of Amalfi is your reward for the hair-raising ride. Amalfi suffered many Saracen (Arab) invasions during its long and colorful history, and the Saracen influence is clearly seen in the raisins in this recipe. This sensational dish is best when served at room temperature.

2 large eggplants, unpeeled

6 tablespoons olive oil

1 small onion, finely chopped

4 ounces long-grain rice

1¼ cups chicken stock

1 ounce seedless raisins

2 ounces freshly grated Pecorino Romano cheese

1 large tomato, peeled (see Tip, page 32) and chopped

4 large pitted green olives, cut into rings

Salt and freshly ground black pepper to taste

Preheat the oven to 350°. Cut the eggplants in half horizontally, scoop out the flesh, and chop it finely. Heat 2 tablespoons of the olive oil in a saucepan and on low heat fry the onion for 5 minutes. Add the rice and stir for 2 minutes, then add the stock, cover the pan, and simmer on lowest heat for 20 minutes. Add the raisins, cheese, tomato, olives, salt, pepper, and chopped eggplant flesh.

Stuff the eggplant mixture lightly into the eggplant halves and arrange in a shallow baking dish. Drizzle the remaining olive oil over them, cover the dish, and bake for 1 hour. Serve hot, room temperature, or cold. They are phenomenal.

Cavolofiore alla Romagnola
(CAULIFLOWER ROMAGNA STYLE)

SERVES 4

This is a rustic recipe that reflects the intensely cultivated countryside of Emilia-Romagna. When I collected this recipe, I was told the following story: Two women got on a bus to Bologna. They were from the same village but didn't know each other very well. They were about the same age but from different social classes. One was a peasant dressed in widow's black, the other, the wife of a landholder. She was rich, dressed elegantly, and smelled of very expensive perfume. They took the only two remaining seats, which were next to each other. The elegant lady moved close to the window to avoid contact with the poor peasant. The peasant lady, trying to be pleasant, remarked to her rich companion: "Your perfume smells wonderful, what is it?" The elegant lady haughtily responded: "Chanel Number Five, $150 an ounce." The poor peasant lady, full of country wisdom, said nothing. Ten minutes later, the peasant lady quietly relieved herself of flatulence. The elegant lady sniffed, turned to the poor woman, and asked: "What is that?" The peasant responded, "Cauliflower, $.45 a pound." Both women arrived in Bologna a little wiser from their encounter. God does use the lowly to confound the proud.

1 medium-sized cauliflower

1 tablespoon butter

3 tablespoons olive oil

1 clove garlic, crushed

2 tablespoons chopped fresh Italian (flat-leafed) parsley

Salt and freshly ground black pepper to taste

6 tablespoons water
1 level tablespoon tomato puree
Freshly grated Parmesan cheese

Divide the cauliflower into individual florets, wash, and drain. Heat the butter and oil in a saucepan and fry the garlic and parsley for 4 minutes on low heat. Add the cauliflower, stir and cook for 8 minutes on medium heat, then add the salt and pepper, water, and tomato puree. Cover the pan, and cook on low heat for 25 minutes. Turn into a serving dish, sprinkle with grated cheese (as much as you prefer), and serve hot.

Insalate (Salads)

Salads are popular throughout Italy and none more so than a plain green salad or a simple mixed salad (insalata mista). The position of a salad in a meal is a very moveable feast—it may appear as an antipasto, it may accompany roast meat, or most traditionally, it may be served alone after the meal. A variety of salad vegetables is used, sometimes of a local character such as the unusual salad greens and radishes grown around Treviso near Venice. Quite a number of salads contain fish, cheese, poultry, or meat and can be served as an antipasto or, in larger quantities, as a light main course. Fresh prime vegetables such as asparagus, green beans, or Calabrese broccoli are often cooked, allowed to become cold, and then served alone dressed with seasoned olive oil and lemon juice.

A typical salad dressing consists of three parts olive oil to one part lemon juice or wine vinegar, plus salt and pepper and a crushed garlic clove. Chopped fresh herbs, mashed anchovies, freshly grated or slivered Parmesan or Pecorino Romano cheese are sometimes added.

INSALATE DI EMILIA-ROMAGNA (SALADS FROM EMILIA-ROMAGNA)

These first four salads are from Emilia-Romagna, the region that happily houses the city of Parma, whose cheese, Parmigiano-Reggiano (Parmesan), is world-renowned. I am going to allow these brilliant salads to speak for themselves. Make them. Enjoy them. Listen carefully and they will whisper terms of endearment into your ears and spirit.

Insalata di Formaggio
(CHEESE SALAD)

SERVES 4

¹/₂ pound Parmesan cheese, cut into slivers
1 green or red bell pepper, roasted (see page 55) and cut lengthwise into strips

(continued)

2 ounces pitted green olives, chopped

1 cup diced celery

2 tablespoons olive oil

1 tablespoon balsamic or red wine vinegar

Salt and freshly ground black pepper to taste

Combine all the ingredients, toss, and serve.

Insalata Mista

(MIXED SALAD)

SERVES 4

1/2 pound romaine lettuce, torn in pieces

5 red radishes, sliced

1 rib celery, diced

1 carrot, peeled and diced

1 small bulb fennel, sliced thin

4 ounces Parmesan cheese, cut into slivers

2 tablespoons olive oil

1 tablespoon balsamic or red wine vinegar

Combine all the ingredients, toss thoroughly, and serve.

Insalata di Carciofi e Formaggio

(ARTICHOKE AND CHEESE SALAD)

SERVES 4

2 raw artichokes, pared down to the tender hearts and cut into very thin lengthwise slices

1 tablespoon fresh lemon juice

1/4 pound Parmesan cheese, cut into thin slivers

3 tablespoons extra-virgin olive oil

Salt and freshly ground black pepper to taste

Sprinkle the artichoke slices with the lemon juice. Combine with the other ingredients, toss, and serve.

Insalata di Finocchi

(FENNEL SALAD)

SERVES 4

2 fennel bulbs, cut into very thin slices

1/4 pound Parmesan cheese, diced

Salt to taste

1 tablespoon fresh lemon juice

3 tablespoons olive oil

Combine all the ingredients, toss well, and serve.

Insalata Mista del Contadino

(PEASANT'S MIXED SALAD)

SERVES 4

Escarole is a lowly, misunderstood green that is often passed by in favor of more expensive and biting greens like arugula or radicchio (OK, radicchio isn't green, but you get my point). It is fabulous cooked and com-

bined with white kidney beans (canellini) or in a chicken soup. Here it is used as a bittersweet lettuce.

1 medium-sized head escarole

½ green or yellow bell pepper, seeded and thinly sliced

½ fennel bulb, shredded

2 large tomatoes, sliced

4 radishes, sliced

3 tablespoons olive oil

1 tablespoon red wine vinegar

1 clove garlic, crushed

Salt and freshly ground black pepper to taste

Wash and crisp the escarole under cold running water. Tear into fairly large pieces and put into a salad bowl with the bell pepper, fennel, tomatoes, and radishes. Mix the oil, vinegar, garlic, and seasoning together and, just before serving, sprinkle the dressing over the salad and toss lightly.

Insalata di Broccoli
(BROCCOLI SALAD)

SERVES 3

This is a quick version of the fresh broccoli salad my mamma used to make. She would drop the fresh broccoli into boiling salted water and blanch it for three minutes, then drain it while it was tender but still crisp.

1 10-ounce package frozen broccoli spears

3 tablespoons olive oil

1 tablespoon fresh lemon juice

Salt and freshly ground black pepper to taste

Cook the broccoli for the minimum time indicated on the package; drain and cool. Mix together the oil, lemon juice, and seasoning and pour over the broccoli just before serving.

Insalata di Baccala
(SALAD OF COD FISH)

SERVES 3

This dish is found on many Italian family tables at the Christmas Eve supper. On Christmas Eve most Southern Italians serve as many as thirteen different fish and seafood dishes. Since Christmas is the Feast of the Incarnation, which celebrates the Christian belief that God took on human flesh, the Italians traditionally abstain from eating flesh meat to state their belief. The number thirteen is in honor of the Twelve Apostles and Jesus

1 pound cod fillet, frozen or fresh

4 tablespoons olive oil

Salt

3 ounces black olives (Gaeta or oil-cured)

3 ounces green olives

1 lemon, cut into quarters

Poach the cod fillet in a little salted water for about 12 minutes. Remove all the skin and bones, coarsely flake the fish, and while still hot, dress with the olive oil and season to taste with salt. Cover the fish and leave until cold. To serve, pile the fish on a dish; arrange the olives in the center and the lemon quarters around the edges of the dish. The lemon is squeezed over the fish just before eating.

Insalata di Manzo Lesso
(COLD BEEF SALAD)

SERVES 4

My mamma used to make this unusual salad with the beef she used to make meat soup. It frugally stretched the meat into two uses. You may use the beef used to make Pasta Daniele on page 97.

12 slices boiled beef, cold
2 large potatoes, cooked firm
Salt and freshly ground black pepper
4 tablespoons olive oil
1 tablespoon red wine vinegar
1 small onion, diced
1 tablespoon capers, chopped
1 tablespoon chopped fresh Italian
   (flat-leafed) parsley

Cut the meat and potato into 1/4-inch dice. Put a little salt and pepper into a small bowl, add the oil, vinegar, onion, and capers and mix thoroughly. Add the meat and potatoes, and toss together lightly. Pile the meat on a serving dish and scatter the chopped parsley over it. Surprisingly good.

Insalata di Riso e Pollo
(RICE AND CHICKEN SALAD)

SERVES 4

Do you have leftover chicken from yesterday's supper? No problem. Use it in this delightful salad.

2 cups water
1 cup long-grain rice
3 tablespoons olive oil
1 tablespoon fresh lemon juice
Salt and freshly ground black pepper
Grated nutmeg, to taste
1 cup cooked chicken meat, left over from
   Mamma's Chicken Broth (page 37), diced
2 ribs celery, finely sliced
5 ounces cooked green peas
Crisp romaine lettuce leaves

Bring the water to a boil, add the rice, and cook on simmer, covered, for 20 minutes. While still hot, toss the rice with the oil, lemon juice, and seasonings. Add the chicken meat to the rice with the celery and peas. Cover and set aside for an hour so the flavors blend. To serve, line a salad platter with lettuce leaves and pile the chicken and rice mixture over the lettuce.

Insalata di Pomodori
(TOMATO SALAD)

SERVES 4

For this salad use under-ripe tomatoes, which remain crisp even when cut and dressed. The touches of green in the salad look attractive too. This is terrific in the summer when you pick the tomatoes from your own garden.

6 large firm tomatoes
1 medium onion, diced
Salt and freshly ground black pepper
$1/4$ teaspoon dried oregano

4 tablespoons olive oil
12 fresh basil leaves, chopped

Cut the tomatoes into quarters and the quarters into halves. Put into a salad bowl. Add the diced onion, salt and pepper to taste, oregano, and oil. Toss lightly. Set aside for 1/2 hour. Sprinkle with chopped basil and serve. Meravigliosa!

Frutte—Dolci—Noci (Fruit—Desserts—Nuts)

Fresh fruit is served at practically every meal in Italy. In summer, the market stalls piled high with fruit offer a mouth-watering sight to natives and tourists. The scarlet–fleshed watermelons jostle with flowing oranges, green and purple figs, mountains of strawberries, peaches, apricots, and plums, not to mention apples, pears, raspberries, and tiny Alpine strawberries. Although fruit is frequently eaten "just as it comes," there are many ways of presenting it a little differently. For instance, strawberries sprinkled with sugar and balsamic vinegar, sweet Marsala wine, or lemon juice; mixed fresh fruit with a flavoring of liqueur. And of course, there are fruit ices. Italy is the birthplace of ice cream and the variety of ice cream recipes is a revelation. Happily, many of them can be made at home simply and successfully.

The desserts in this section I collected from among the treasures kept and produced in the humble kitchen of Geni La Bozzetta Stilo. Geni lives in Reggio Calabria very near her mother, my surrogate mamma, Marietta La Bozzetta, the eighty-eight-year-old godchild of my beloved mother. All the recipes were chosen for their flavor and simplicity. You may notice that this section is quite brief. This is because I am not really "into" desserts. However, if you are, and you would like more sweet treasures from my Italian repertoire, you can find eighteen different dessert recipes in my book *Father Orsini's Italian Kitchen* (New York: St. Martin's Press, 1991).

Pesche al Vino Bianco
(PEACHES IN WHITE WINE)

For each person, skin a ripe peach and slice it into a glass of sweet white, still or sparkling wine (Asti Spumante is my preference). Leave for 5 minutes before serving. Then eat the peach and drink the wine. You'll be temporarily transported into the next world. But only temporarily. We still have to serve the last course of the meal, which we will discuss in the next chapter.

Insalata di Arancie e Banane
(ORANGE AND BANANA SALAD)

SERVES 4

6 seedless oranges, peeled and thinly
  sliced
4 bananas, thinly sliced
⁵/₈ cup powdered sugar
¹/₄ cup sweet white vermouth
2 tablespoons maraschino liqueur

In a glass bowl, arrange alternate layers of
oranges and bananas, finishing with a layer of
orange. Sprinkle with the powdered sugar, sweet
white vermouth (Martini and Rossi), and
maraschino liqueur. Chill for a few hours before
serving. Simply ambrosial.

Fragole al Marsala
(STRAWBERRIES WITH SWEET
MARSALA WINE)

SERVES 3 – 4

1 pound small ripe strawberries
2 teaspoons powdered sugar
6 tablespoons sweet Marsala wine

Arrange the strawberries in a glass bowl.
Sprinkle with the powdered sugar and Marsala.
Chill for several hours before serving. When you
taste it, be ready to climb Mount Zion with
Moses and receive God's Revelation.

Gelato di Tutti Frutti
(MIXED FRUIT ICE CREAM)

SERVES 6

*You do not need any special equipment to make this
exceptional homemade ice cream. It is more like an ice
cream fruit cake. If you like fruitcake as I do, you will
go bonkers over this ice cream.*

The Custard:
  3 egg yolks
  3 ounces granulated sugar
  3 drops vanilla extract
  1¹/₄ cups milk

The Cream:
  ¹/₂ pint heavy cream
  1 13-ounce package candied fruit and peel
  ¹/₂ cup toasted almonds, coarsely chopped

Put the yolks in a bowl with the sugar and
beat until creamy and thickened. Add the
vanilla. Heat the milk in a saucepan almost to a
boil on moderate heat, and add by tablespoonful
to the egg mixture, stirring constantly with a
wooden spoon. When all the hot milk is incorpo-
rated into the egg mixture, rinse the saucepan
and strain the custard into the same saucepan.
Cook on low heat, stirring constantly, until the
mixture thickens enough to coat the spoon (*do
not allow to boil*).

Place the custard into the refrigerator and allow
to cool 1/2 hour. Pour into a segmented plastic ice
cube tray or trays and freeze until firm but not hard
(about two hours); turn into a mixing bowl.

Whisk the cream in another bowl until very

thick. Fold the candied fruit and chopped nuts into the cream. Then fold the cream mixture thoroughly into the custard. Turn into a non-stick bread pan and freeze until firm.

To serve, unmold the ice cream by dipping the pan into warm water and turning it over onto a serving dish. Slice and expect a standing ovation from your guests.

Granita di Caffe
(COFFEE WATER ICE)

SERVES 4

When my brothers Oreste and Anthony and I made our pilgrimage to Reggio Calabria a year after my mother's death, I was moved to tears as I watched my brothers kneel and kiss the "sacred" ground where our mother, father, and two oldest brothers, Leo and John, were born. During our visit, every day at about four P.M., we would stop at an ice cream shop called "Da Cesare" and order this scrumptious coffee water ice.

> 3 ounces good ground Italian espresso coffee
> (I use Lavazza brand) as it comes from
> the can
> 3 ounces sugar
> 3³/₄ cups boiling water

Put the coffee and sugar into a small saucepan. Pour on the boiling water, stir, and cover. Allow to stand until quite cold. Strain through a clean muslin kitchen towel into a metal or plastic tray. Freeze without stirring for 2 hours. It will be fairly solid mush. Spoon into dessert glasses and serve. If

you wish, you may top it with whipped cream (the real stuff, please!—not the artificial substitute).

Coppe Mascarpone
(CREAM CHEESE CUPS)

SERVES 4

Mascarpone is Italian cream cheese that is available in Italian specialty food shops, but plain cream cheese works well in this dessert and is not overpriced as is the imported cheese. This is a light and yummy dessert that is especially welcome after a heavy meal.

> 8 ounces cream cheese
> 2 eggs, separated
> 4 teaspoons sugar
> 2 tablespoons unflavored brandy
> 1 cup fresh strawberries or raspberries

Push the cheese through a wire-mesh sieve into a bowl and beat with the egg yolks and sugar until light (no lumps). Stir in the brandy. Whisk the egg whites until very stiff, then fold lightly into the cream. Pile into individual glass dessert cups and stud the surface with berries.

Noci
(NUTS)

At most holiday dinners, after the fruit or dessert has been served, a huge basket of mixed unshelled nuts is placed on the table. Nut crackers are provided and there are always dried figs which are split open by hand and stuffed with freshly shelled nuts. The table is cleared while the nuts and figs are being eaten. This is a pleasant, restful time of conversation and fellowship. Then, unobtrusively, the last course arrives at table—the formaggi (cheeses).

Formaggi (Cheeses)

A slice or two of cheese is served at the end of a meal; the cheese brings the Italian formal dinner to a close.

Italians are serious about their cheeses and have established government guidelines controlling the ingredients and production of many types of cheese. The authority is the Denominazione di Origine Controllata, meaning Determination of Origin under control, or DOC. The DOC also certifies wines. DOC-certified wines are guaranteed to be made using the grapes of a particular region under strictly controlled conditions, which ensure their purity and authenticity.

In this section, I will discuss the most commonly used Italian cheeses, describe them, perhaps share some of their history, and recommend the wines that go best with them. Welcome to the fascinating world of Italian cheeses.

ASIAGO

This cheese originates from the area after which it is named: the Asiago high plateau in the region of Trento-Alto Adige. This is not by accident. The area has the rich soil and excellent pastures essential to the quality and peculiar characteristics of the cheese. As early as the year 1000, the plateau was renowned as a grazing place for flocks of sheep. The elderly mountain dwellers still use the dialect term *pegorin* (sheep's milk cheese) to refer to today's Asiago, though it is now made exclusively of cow's milk. It is excellent as a table cheese—rich in proteins and low in fat. When it is ripened for more than two years it is called stravecchio (very old) and can also be used for grating. It is an indispensable ingredient of many typical dishes of the region, such as polenta seasoned with butter and asiago, raviolini and sopa coda.

Asiago can be mild to sharp tasting, depending on maturity, and calls for high-quality red wines.

RECOMMENDED WINES:
Cabernet Colli Berici
Gave del Friuli
Valpolicella Classico

CACIOCAVALLO

This is a drawn-curd cheese typical of Southern Italy. The cheeses are usually about six pounds, spherical in shape, and narrow-necked at the top. They are left to mature two or more years, then the cheese is covered with molds on a hard and shiny rind. When cut, the paste (the inner cheese) is a golden-yellow with small slits oozing oil. The aroma is intense and lingering; the taste, full and mellow. The best caciocavallo is found in the regions of Molise, Campania, Basilicata, and Calabria.

There are a few different explanations of the origin of the name caciocavallo. Some authorities think that in ancient times the cheese was made from horse milk, thus *cacio* (from the Latin "caseus"—cheese) *cavallo* (horse). Others believe that the name refers to the system of drying the cheeses suspended one on each side of a pole (a cavallo). Whatever. It is a wonderful table cheese and can be used in many recipes calling for cheese. The imported cheese is expensive but well worth it.

RECOMMENDED WINES:
Ciró Classico Rosso
Aglianico del Vulture

FONTINA

It is difficult to speak of the region of Valle d'Aosta and of its cheese without speaking of its mountains. The region is surrounded by an impressive, unbroken sequence of mountains, valleys (valle), pastures, and forests. It is no wonder that its inhabitants have always been centered on cattle-breeding and the transformation of milk into cheese. The existence of a flourishing cheese-making activity is well documented since ancient times.

Since this cheese was officially declared DOC in 1955, fontina is the cheese of Valle d'Aosta. Fontina is rich in taste, aroma, and texture. Maturation lasts an average of five months, after which the cheese acquires its sweet delicate taste and soft-textured, easily melted paste (inner cheese). It is the main ingredient of fonduta, the regional dish par excellence of the Valle d'Aosta. Made with milk, butter, and eggs, as well as a good deal of fontina cheese, this substantial dish has a creamy and thick consistency. However, fontina is known best as an unsurpassable table cheese which goes well with a full-bodied red wine. The cheese has a 45 percent fat content, but the old mountain people of Valle d'Aosta, some of them over ninety, seldom renounce their daily ration.

RECOMMENDED WINES:
Valle d'Aosta Chambave Rosso
Valle d'Aosta Pinot Noir
Valle d'Aosta Donnas

GORGONZOLA

There are many folktales about the origin of this cheese, especially in Lombardy and Piedmont. According to the most popular story, Gorgonzola was the result of carelessness. An absent-minded cheese maker hung up a bundle of curd to drain and forgot all about it. The following day he put it together with the morning curd, hoping perhaps that curing might repair his mistake. When he cut the cheese across, however, to his surprise he found that it was veined inside with a greenish mold not at all pleasant to look at. It should be said, if the story is true, that he sampled it and found it so good that he taught others to repeat his "mistake." The cheese is named after the village of Gorgonzola near Milan.

Today the cheese is made by the addition of penicillium spores, which are responsible for the characteristic green veins of the paste (inner cheese). Gorgonzola has a considerable fat and protein content, and contains vitamins (A, B_1, B_2, and D) and minerals as well. It is easily digested because of the important proteolytic action performed by penicillium molds during the maturation process. It is one of the most popular cheeses in Italy. Over three million 12- to 24-pound blocks of this cheese are produced yearly. The taste is "sweet" as well as strong, and connoisseurs suggest that it is best eaten with a fresh or toasted homemade bread. Gorgonzola can be used in many ways in gastronomy, from appetizers to first and second courses and the last course after dessert. It is the principal ingredient of many sauces and dips with the addition of butter or cream. As I heard a proper Englishman vacationing in Stresa comment: "It's a lovely cheese, yes. Very lovely." I agree with the chap, totally.

RECOMMENDED WINES:

Bramaterra

Ghemme

Picolit

MOZZARELLA DI BUFALA

This marvelous cheese is made most authentically from the milk of the water buffalo. A presidential decree of September 28, 1979, states that "mozzarella di bufala is a fresh, drawn-curd cheese, made directly from whole cow-buffalo's milk carefully selected to ensure freshness and wholesomeness." Most buffalo farms are in Southern Italy, near Naples. When this cheese is made truly and only of cow-buffalo milk, it is porcelain-white in color, spherical, with a very thin, shiny, and glossy rind, neither slippery nor crinkled, and with a rather springy body in the first eight to ten hours. When cut across, a whitish whey-smelling milk ferment oozes out.

The taste of true mozzarella di bufala is pleasantly sourish with a faint mossy smell which recalls the humid grazing of buffaloes, for which water is essential since they do not have sweat glands.

What we know in the United States as mozzarella is made from cow's milk and should be used exclusively for pizza and pasta dishes. Mozzarella di bufala is a superb table cheese and eaten with no accompaniment.

RECOMMENDED WINES:

Asprigno di Aversa (red)

Falerno del Massico (white)

PARMIGIANO-REGGIANO

Careful choice of the raw material is an essential part of production of this world-renowned cheese. The milk must come from perfectly healthy cows fed basically on fodder from meadows with various grasses or alfalfa, never silage. The official production area is Parma, Emilia, Modena, and Bologna (on the left of the Reno River) and Mantua (on the south of the Po River).

This cheese has a very long history in fact and in fiction. There are documents and decrees going back to Charlemagne in 781 and as recent as 1955 concerning Parmigiano-Reggiano. From the time the milk gets to the cheese factory and the cheese gets to the market and is certified for sale, at least eighteen months have elapsed.

The texture of Parmigiano-Reggiano is unmistakable: granular and flaky, with a particular fragrance and delicate bouquet. It is excellent when used as a condiment (on top of pasta, rice, and soups), and is a valuable ingredient in many dishes, and especially as a substantial antipasto together with fresh fruit, nuts, and a high quality red wine. The cheese has been scientifically analyzed and judged to be the richest in proteins and the lowest in fat and cholesterol of all European cheeses.

RECOMMENDED WINES:
  Chianti Classico
  Colli di Parma Rosso
  Monica di Sardegna

PECORINO ROMANO

Pecorino is the generic term for any cheese made of sheep's milk. In Italy there exist many varieties of pecorino, each characteristic of specific areas or of particular breeds of sheep. Pecorino Romano, however, occupies a special place, if for no other reason than volume of sales. Originally it was made in the Argo Romano (the countryside around Rome), after which it is named. It is probably one of the oldest cheeses in the world and is essentially the same as was made by the shepherds of Latium two thousand years ago. The surrounding countryside of Rome was the birthplace of this cheese, but the island of Sardinia has become the most important location of production.

Pecorino Romano is cylindrical and usually weighs 44 to 66 pounds. The rind is straw-yellow in color. The white paste (inner cheese) is compact, fragrant, and piquant in taste. Tests carried out on the product ready for sale show a humidity content (water) of 32 percent, fat content 28 to 29 percent, proteins 25 to 28 percent, and a good amount of calcium.

Pecorino Romano is a table cheese very much appreciated for its strong taste. When used for grating it is the indispensable ingredient of many Central and Southern Italian dishes. In regard to its "marriage" with wine, the rule that sharp, long-cured cheese should be accompanied by red wines holds.

RECOMMENDED WINES:
  Velletri Rosso
  Brunello di Montalcino
  Carignano del Sulcis Rosso

PECORINO SICILIANO

Never was there a term more generic for cheese than *pecorino,* especially in Sicily, a land of lacerating conflict and mixed civilizations; a continent more than an island, a place where the mingling of different races and cultures has resulted in a mixture of languages, a medley of words and phrases. In Sicily this cheese takes on many forms, appearing under different names depending on the villages you go through, whether it is the hills and mountains of the interior or the undulating plains close to the sea.

Pecorino is not just a cheese (indeed, *the* cheese). It is emblematic of Sicily, the embodiment of the contradictions and the heavy burden of history with which the island is laden. Pecorino is the Sicilian himself. It is always called tumazzu or cacio as the ancestors called it. It is a cheese that exudes history, tears, and blood, and is imbued with the exhausting labor of finding sufficient grazing for sheep.

This wonderful cheese is made exclusively of sheep's milk and sometimes whole grains of black pepper are added to the paste before the process of maturation. Then it is called pippato, and is my favorite Sicilian pecorino. It is used as a table cheese as well as a grating cheese.

RECOMMENDED WINES:
Etna Rosso
Cerasuolo di Vittoria

PROVOLONE

Provolone is a drawn-curd cheese of Southern Italian origin. It comes from the Basilicata region, more precisely from the province of Potenza. The name is probably of Neapolitan origin; "prova, provola" means "taste it, try it." Locally, this cheese takes on many names which describe its size (provole, provolette, giganti, and mandarini—tangerine size).

It is made from whole pasteurized cow's milk. The taste varies depending on the type: dolce (mild) or piccante (sharp). Both are used as table cheeses at the end of meal or as an ingredient in pasta dishes. It melts easily and combines perfectly.

RECOMMENDED WINES WITH *Mild Provolone:*
Colli Orientalli del Friuli
Chardonnay Gave del Friuli
Pinot Bianco
Fiano di Avellino

RECOMMENDED WINES WITH *Sharp Provolone:*
Ghemme
Arurasi
Velletri Rosso
Bonarda

RICOTTA

Ricotta is a rich, commonplace cheese readily available at your supermarket. The Italian government wisely withheld DOC certification from a cheese that can be and is readily made at home. It is delicious eaten by itself, but more often it is used in hundreds of pasta recipes.

Epilogue

It was a bitter-sweet experience writing this book. Doing the research was a blast, but writing the comments brought back many memories of dear people who have died since I met them.

My first love is God, then my mother, and then Italy and its cuisines. I guess it's because I'm Italian.

My fond hope is that you get to know me through my books. Perhaps this short poem will help you understand who Father Joe Orsini really is. It was written by Gaspare Lo Bue in the Sicilian language, and it has become my daily prayer before I celebrate Mass.

Accept me as I am
Bread of Life within this Tabernacle
I am here.
I am here at your door like a beggar seeking help.
My heart is darkened and all bound up.
It is like a twisted ball of barbed wire, and I feel it
*   deep within me.*
My heart is pinched, afraid and attacked.

The coldness is beginning to penetrate my bones.
Take me by the hand,
Show me the road I must travel.
Wash me with your blood,
*   forgive me of my sins.*
Just one more time I want to eat the Bread of Life
*   like I used to do when I was innocent so many*
*   years ago.*
I know I am not worthy,
*   but I . . . if I am truly repentant . . .*
*   show me your mercy, oh my dear God.*
I beg your mercy!
Accept me the way I am.

Well, my friends, dinner is over. Let's have our espresso coffee and Sambuca liqueur. I hope we can get together again soon to enjoy one another's company in the intimate and sacred setting of our homes, sharing the food of our tables. "Ossa benedica" (May you be blessed).

—FATHER JOE ORSINI

Appendix: Italian Family Christmas Memories

The season of Advent is the season of preparation for Christmas, when people all around the world anticipate and commemorate what they believe is the pivotal event in the history of humankind—an event that took place 2000 years ago, the birth of Jesus of Nazareth through the vehicle of the Virgin Mary. Christmas, in the language of the church, is called the Feast of the Incarnation, when the second person of the Blessed Trinity, the Savior and Redeemer of the human race took on the burden of human flesh. Incarnation in simple terms means "to become flesh."

Curiously, the Christian church prepares us for the celebration of Christ's first coming to earth with a reference to Christ's second coming in the gospel reading for the first Sunday of Advent. The point made in the reading is the unpredictability of the second coming—"No one knows the day nor the hour" (Mark 13:33–37). That being so, it makes sense to be ready at every moment of our lives. This is God's will and as Dante stated: "In His will is our peace."

The mass for the monday after the first sunday of Advent sounds the theme of the Advent season: the second coming of the Lord will take place in the last day of the history of humankind when the peoples "from the east and the west shall assemble . . . at the *banquet* in the kingdom of God." The *bread and wine* which become the body and blood of Jesus at every mass is a foretaste of the *banquet* which we eagerly await after human history as we know it comes to an end and we enter the "new heavens and the new earth" planned for us by our loving father, God, through his son Jesus Christ. Please take note of the word "banquet" and the elemental foodstuffs "bread and wine."

There is one Advent season that I shall never forget. The year was 1943. World War II was raging in Europe and in the Pacific. My brother John, a soldier, was in the midst of fierce battles in Belgium. My mother and father listened daily to the Italian language newscasts on the radio and heard how their beloved Reggio Calabria was suffering death and destruction from the constant bombing by the Allied Forces. Their hearts were torn with worry about my brother John and the relatives they had left behind in Reggio Calabria nineteen years earlier.

I was only six years old and didn't quite understand all that was happening. I remember that papa and mamma spent every evening baking Italian Christmas cookies and allowing my brothers, Oreste, Anthony, and Dominick, and my sister Evelyn, and me to roll out the dough. My father, Giuseppe, worked as a longshoreman at the Pennsylvania Railroad Terminal in nearby Jersey City. In the early morning of November 17, 1943 I remember hearing my papa and mamma in the kitchen as she pleaded with him not to go to work that day. She had a premonition that something terrible would happen to him. Papa said, "Carmela, I must go to work or the kids won't eat." I scrambled into the kitchen and took my privilege as the baby of the family to climb on my papa's lap and drink tiny spoonfuls of his Italian coffee. He always made coffee before he attended mass and received Holy Communion: this was papa's daily routine. That morning he shared one of the biscotti he baked the previous night with his youngest son, me.

Mamma kept me home from school that day because she didn't want to be alone. At precisely 3:00 p.m., a kindly Bayonne police officer knocked on our door. I clung to her apron as he told my mother that her husband had been in a serious accident at work. Mamma knew immediately that papa was dead. She screamed, *"é morto, mio marito é morto!"* (My husband is dead!) She collapsed. A few minutes later our small rented apartment was filled with our Italian neighbors. The policeman came back and gave the details to

my oldest brother, Leo. Indeed, Giuseppe Orsini was crushed to death in an accident at work.

My very strong and courageous mamma decided to make the coming Christmas very special for her children, even though my papa would be missing. We all went to midnight mass, and then Mamma began to deep-fry the traditional Christmas Eve zeppole, a treat enjoyed by Calabrian families from Reggio. Our entire family assembled in the kitchen, hovering close to Mamma, impatiently waiting for the first batch to be done, and hardly allowing them to cool before we gobbled one.

Mamma's eyes were brimming with tears as she served her children zeppole that papa had taught her how to make when they were first married.

Here is Papa and Mamma Orsini's recipe for zeppole, which I have modernized a bit.

Zeppole

YIELD: 20 – 25 ZEPPOLE

1 package active dry yeast, or 2¹/₂ teaspoons of either Red Star or Fleischmann's dry yeast.

1¹/₄ cups lukewarm water

3 cups all-purpose flour

¹/₄ teaspoon salt

1 cup vegetable oil (for frying)

In a large measuring cup, dissolve the yeast with 1/4 cup lukewarm water. Measure the flour and salt onto a large wooden pastry board. Make a well in the center of the flour and gradually add the dissolved yeast and the remaining water. Pull the flour with your fingers into the liquid. Knead for 8 minutes until the dough is smooth and elastic. Put the dough into a lightly oiled bowl, turn to coat with oil, and cover with a thick towel. Let the dough rise in a warm place for 2 hours—it will double in size. Pinch off a piece of the dough the size of a golf ball, stretch it with your fingers into a 2 by 5-inch rectangle and place it on wax or parchment paper. Repeat the process until all the dough is used. Then simply fold each rectangle to make plain zeppole.

Fry briskly in very hot oil (350°), a few at a time without crowding. Turn until all sides are golden and crisp, about 3 to 4 minutes. Remove with a slotted spoon and drain on paper towels. Keep fried zeppole warm in a 170° oven until all are cooked. For plain zeppole, sprinkle with powdered sugar while they are still hot.

Serve them to your family and guests as you celebrate a southern Italian Christmas Eve antipasto.

VARIATION: If you wish you may place one or two drained anchovies in the center of each zeppola, fold over, twist, and pinch all edges tightly.

GIFTS FROM THE HEART— HOMEMADE ITALIAN CHRISTMAS COOKIES

If your home is like my residence, then at this time of year your mailbox overflows with mail-order catalogs, department store flyers and local shop notices that presuppose you never learned basic arithmetic and can't do addition.

"Less than two weeks left for Christmas shopping!" they say. Radio and television newscasts join in the chorus: "You'd better get to the stores now, don't be a last minute Christmas shopper!"

Wise shoppers bought their gifts at last year's sales at the end of January and saved tons of money. Even wiser shoppers will buy their friends and relatives my book, *Italian Family Cooking,* and save them as gifts for next Christmas. That would make me very happy because I would consider your purchase of my book a belated Christmas gift to me. Yes, you are right, Father Joe is always thinking. But it is important you know that whatever royalties I receive from my books I donate to charities.

There is a tradition in my family that probably began with my grandparents, was passed on to my parents who passed it on to their children (my brothers and sisters), and is still carried on by my fifteen nieces and nephews and twenty-three grand–nieces and nephews. The best gifts that one can give are family love and loyalty as expressed in the southern Italian manner: with food that serves as a bond that holds families together. At Christmas time that means baking dozens and dozens of Italian cookies whose sweetness is an expression of family love that makes life together very special

We southern Italians begin our relationships as friends. Soon those friends become members of our extended families. At Christmas time we like to demonstrate to our dear ones that they are truly appreciated, so we spend hours in our kitchens preparing special cookies (biscotti) that take a great deal of time and effort. We then give tins or trays of biscotti that we made with care and love to our relatives and friends, and this says more about our feelings for one another than simply buying them gifts from a store or a catalog.

I remember when I was a child, as soon as Thanksgiving Day was over, my papa and mamma spent every evening together making Italian Christmas cookies for all our *comari* and *compari*—either the godparents of their seven children or simply close friends of our family. The variety of biscotti they made were dazzling: Almond cookies, Anise cookies, Mostaccioli (Calabrian chocolate cookies), Crispelle (fluffy fried pastry chips), Amaretti (Macaroons), and Biscotti Di Regina (crispy sesame seed cookies). Papa stored these biscotti in brown paper shopping bags, carefully folding the tops of the bags several times to make them air-tight, and hid them in the coolest and darkest places in our home. He always warned us kids not to open the bags because these biscotti were Christmas gifts for our friends. The week before Christmas he would call us all into the kitchen and show us the biggest bags of cookies. This bag, he would tell us, was the most special one because it was for our landlords, the Amato family. With a broad smile on his face, he would fold the top of this bag only once and hide it in the pantry outside the kitchen door. He would warn us with a serious look, "Don't you dare touch these biscotti or you'll be sorry!"

When we thought that Mamma and Papa weren't looking, my brothers, my sister, and I would borrow a few biscotti every day from that forbidden bag. When Papa got home from work on the day before Christmas Eve, he loudly announced that he was going to get the Amato family's bag of biscotti and deliver them to Sam and Santuzza. We children watched with trepi-

dation as he entered the pantry to retrieve the huge paper sack of cookies. "Marrona mia! The bag is empty. Somebody ate all the biscotti. Who could have eaten them all?" We kids were practically wetting ourselves with fear. He then came back into the kitchen with one empty bag and one full one. He sweetly smiled at each one of his kids and said, "Santa Closi (Santa Claus) came early this year and ate his whole bag of biscotti, but he left another full bag for the Amatos, Grazie a Dio!"

We kids were so relieved that we confessed to Papa that we ate all the biscotti. Papa said, *"Sugno contento. Voi siti bravi e onesti fighioli e to papá e mammá vi vogghiuno tanto beni."* (I'm happy. You are good and honest kids, and your papa and mamma love you very much.) *"Sta sera facimo i pretrali!"* (Tonight we'll make petrali [fig, raisin, and nut filled cookies].) These were our favorite Christmas cookies.

Petrali

YIELD ABOUT 12 1/2 DOZEN COOKIES

Pastry:

4½ cups all-purpose flour

3 teaspoons baking powder

⅔ cup granulated sugar

¾ teaspoon salt

1 tablespoon freshly grated orange zest (peel)*

---

*Wash the orange well, and grate only the skin being careful not to get any of the white bitter pith beneath the skin.

1¼ cups softened unsalted butter or 3/4 cup
   plus 3 tablespoons light olive oil.

1⅓ cups cold water

Filling:

1¼ cups dried figs, stems removed

1¼ cups seedless raisins

½ cup semi-sweet chocolate bits

¾ cup almonds (shelled)

¾ cup walnuts (shelled)

¼ cup honey

2 tablespoons freshly grated orange zest
   (peel)

1 tablespoon cinnamon

powdered sugar for sprinkling

Pre-heat oven to 400°.

In a large mixing bowl, add most of the flour, the baking powder, sugar, salt, and orange zest. With a pastry blender, cut in butter or olive oil. Add the water gradually and mix with your fingers until the dough holds together. If sticky, add remaining flour. Put on a lightly floured surface and knead for 4 to 5 minutes. (I use my Kitchen Aid mixer. I pour all the ingredients in the bowl and mix with the paddle until the dough is formed. Then I change to a dough hook and knead on number 2 speed for 5 minutes). Put dough in a lightly greased bowl, turn to coat, cover and refrigerate while making the filling.

Fit food processor with metal blade. Add figs, raisins, almonds, and chocolate bits. Pulse until contents are chopped into 1/4 inch pieces. Add honey, orange juice, orange zest and cinnamon. Pulse for one second 4 times.

Pull the dough to stretch it. Roll it into two long rectangles, about 1/8 inch thick and 9 inches wide. Divide the filling between each rectangle and spoon filling down the center of each one. Fold the dough over the filling. Seal tightly with the tines of a fork. Bake each log on a greased cookie sheet for 30 minutes. When cool, cut into 1-inch slices. Save in a tightly covered cookie tin. Sprinkle with powdered sugar before serving.

THE CHRISTMAS TREE AND THE NATIVITY SCENE IN THE ITALIAN MANNER

The tradition of the Christmas tree began in the dark misty forests of the Germanic pre-Christian Druids and was part of their Pagan celebration of the Winter Solstice. When these same Germanic and Celtic Pagans were converted by the early missionaries sent by Rome to their lands, the wise missionaries transformed the Pagan practice of decorating an evergreen tree into a Christian symbol. The evergreen tree now represented the eternal life won for us by the first coming of Jesus, the son of God, into our world to bring us the good news of universal salvation through his sacrificial execution on the tree of the Holy Cross. The decorations of lights and garlands became symbols of the resurrection of Jesus and our own resurrection to come at the end of time.

The Christmas tree tradition eventually spread all over Christian Europe and eventually into Italy. But one Italian, Francesco Bernardone, whom we know as St. Francis of Assisi, was uncomfortable with the Pagan origin of the Christmas tree and invented an Italian Catholic symbol of the birth of Jesus Christ. He planned and organized a living tableaux dramatizing St. Luke's story —that of Christ's birth in an animal stable in a cave on the outskirts of Bethlehem. In the woods near Assisi, he gathered people and live animals to depict the Nativity. He constructed an altar and asked a priest to celebrate midnight mass right in front of the first Presepio, Creche, or Nativity Scene—to help the mostly illiterate peasants understand the tremendous significance of the birth of Christ through the Blessed Virgin Mary.

The event was so dramatic and moving that the members of his order, the Friars Minor (The Franciscans) spread its use throughout Italy, then France, and eventually throughout the world wherever Franciscan missionaries were sent.

In later centuries the Nativity scenes became beautiful works of art in wooden sculptures and ceramic figures. The most remarkable ones were created in southern Italy, especially in Naples, Calabria, and Sicily.

Today, in most Christian homes the Presepio, Creche, or Nativity Scene is in a special place of honor reserved for it beneath the Christmas tree.

In both Italy and in Italian parishes in our own country the Nativity Scene is placed, significantly, right in front of the main altar of the church, and Christmas trees adorn the spaces behind or on the side of the altar.

The manger is usually empty until the beginning of midnight mass on Christmas Eve. The churches are muted and darkened. Then, to the Christmas hymn *Tu scendi dalle stelle* (You come down from the stars), written by the founder of the Redemptionist Order, St. Alfonso Liguori, the pastor carries the figure of the baby Jesus in a solemn procession down the center aisle of the church and places the statue of the infant Jesus in the manger. Now all the lights of the church are switched on to signify that the Light of the World, the Savior Jesus, dispels all darkness and the beautiful mass begins.

When I was a young priest in the many parishes I served, there were literally dozens of phone calls from parishioners every Christmas Eve afternoon until right before midnight mass asking the same question, "what time does midnight mass begin?" We in the rectory knew that the phone calls came from what we called "C and E Catholics," that is, Christmas and Easter Catholics whose only contacts with the church were on these two great feasts. I would thank God that these twice-a-year church attending Catholics were at least coming to midnight mass and that perhaps they would now become weekly members of mass every Sunday.

Please remember that back then Christmas Eve was a day of abstinence from eating meat. This tradition of abstaining from meat on Christmas Eve reflected the fact that the son of God, Jesus, became incarnate (that means he took on flesh), and it was only proper and respectful not to eat animal flesh (meat) on that special day.

One year, when I was a parish priest in a predominantly Sicilian-Italian-American parish, I was introduced to a delicious Sicilian custom. I was invited to a wonderfully warm Sicilian-American's home after midnight mass to partake of their post-midnight mass feast.

The matriarch of the family, Nonna Carmelina Girgenti, served huge platters of her homemade sweet and hot grilled sausages surrounded by a medley of roasted green, red, and yellow bell peppers mixed with crisp roasted potatoes. Huge loaves of homemade Sicilian semolina bread artistically twisted and covered with crunchy sesame seeds were on the table. Gallons of her husband Carmelo's ruby red wine, made in his basement in October, were gathered on the floor right next to his chair at the table.

What a feast! What joy! What family love! Even today, many years later, my post-midnight mass feast is a huge sandwich of good grilled sausage smothered with al dente bell peppers and crisp roasted potatoes washed down with Sicilian red wine. By the way, my grandfather, Don Letterio Amore, was a Sicilian from Messina. I'm proud to say I am part Sicilian, and am therefore entitled to celebrate Christmas Sicilian style.

A CALABRIAN CHRISTMAS EVE

If n most southern Italian homes, both here and in Italy, Christmas Eve demands observing two absolute rules: the first requires the family to gather around the dining room table for a feast of fish; the second is attendance as a family at midnight mass.

An old Calabrian proverb *"U pisci nata sempri: 'nta l'acqua, 'nto L'ogghiu, e 'nto vino"* (The fish swims always in water, in oil, and in wine) is truest on Christmas Eve.

For innumerable centuries the ruggedly beautiful coastline along the Tyrrhenian and Ionian Seas of Calabria has provided Calabrians with a wealth of seafood. Almost twenty percent of all the worlds swordfish are still harpooned off the coast of Bagnara Calabria and in Scilla, both of which are in the province of Reggio Calabria. The same techniques that were used by the Greek colonists who came to this enchanting land as far back as 12,000 BC are still used today to harvest these great fish. Each morning, as the mists of dawn slowly rise, small fishing boats can be seen bringing in their daily catch from the previous night's hunt for swordfish.

The ancient Romans had access to a large variety of fish, but because of the impossibility of transporting freshly caught fish inland to the city of Rome, the fish were dried in the sun and/or salted to preserve them for later use. This tradition continues today with Baccalà (dried, salted cod).

Today, most fish in Italy are only hours out of the water when bought at the Pescevendoli (fresh fish stands) and cooked both in the home and in restaurants. Very recently, the Italian government has cracked down on restaurants that try to pass off frozen fish as fresh. A law was passed that causes restaurants to list their fish dishes in prominent print to indicate whether the fish they serve is fresh or frozen. This would be a good law in our country also, because frozen fish and seafood do not taste the same as fresh and once defrosted, become very soggy. It is your right as a consumer in a restaurant to ask your waiter if the seafood or fish you are about to order is fresh or frozen. In some authentic Italian restaurants, both in Italy and in the U.S.A., live selections can be made from a clear glass water tank; in others, the preparation and cooking of your choice of fish can be viewed from start to finish. If both of these opportunities are available in your seafood and fish restaurant, you will know that when your meal is set before you there will be no fish smell at all.

Traditionally, southern Italians who live on the coasts of the regions of Molise, Campania, Puglia, Basilicata, Calabria, Sicilia, and Sardegna, may consume on Christmas Eve either seven different fish dishes (symbolizing the seven sacraments), or nine (to symbolize the Trinity multiplied by three) or, finally, thirteen (to symbolize the twelve Apostles and Christ).

Many varieties of fresh Italian fish are available in the United States: swordfish, fresh tuna, anchovies, sea trout, clams, sardines, mussels, red mullet, squid, octopus, prawns, crab, eel, sole, whiting and either fresh or dry salted cod.

Each region that I named above has its own recipes for preparing fish. Most of them are simple preparations that allow the fresh, subtle flavor of the fish to remain intact. Only fish that is not fresh is smothered with sauces or overpowered with too many flavors to mask its age.

It is best to purchase fish the day you plan to serve it. The flesh beneath the shiny skin should be white and firm and have absolutely no odor. The eyes should be clear and bright. Rinse immediately in cold water, pat dry with paper towels, place on a platter and cover loosely with paper towels, *not* plastic wrap. Have your fish monger scale and gut the fish when you buy it. If you want it skinned and filleted have your fish seller do that too.

When baking fish, remember that your oven's heat will sap most of the fish's natural moisture. To prevent that, brush lightly with olive oil and coat with breadcrumbs seasoned with minced fresh garlic, freshly grated Parmesan or pecorino cheese and salt and pepper to taste. The rule for baking fish is, if it is thick, bake at 350°F; if thin bake quickly at 425°F.

Do not overcook!

If you would like to make the traditional Calabrian Christmas Eve baked cod with potatoes and tomatoes (Baccalà Agghiota), then purchase your dried/salted cod three days before cooking. Try to get pieces uniform in size. Put the pieces in a large pan, cover with cold water, and refrigerate. (Cover the pan tightly with plastic *and* aluminum foil, or your refrigerator will be filled with a very strong fishy smell. Soak for three days to remove salt. Turn pieces periodically and change the water every six hours. On the third day, the cod will be plump, soft, fleshy and well hydrated. Rinse under cold running water, drain and pat dry, then try the following recipe.

Baccalà Agghiota

SERVES 6

1 pound dried cod processed according to directions above

2 tablespoons olive oil

3 medium potatoes, peeled and diced

2 medium onions, peeled and diced

1 16-ounce can Italian peeled plum tomatoes with their juice, coarsely chopped

½ cup seedless raisins, plumped in warm water, drained

¼ cup pignoli (pine nuts) lightly toasted in dry skillet on stove

2 tablespoons capers, rinsed and drained

¼ cup green olives, brine-cured, pitted and
  sliced
½ cup washed and chopped Italian (flat leaf)
  parsley
1 teaspoon salt
1½ teaspoons freshly ground black pepper

Pre-heat oven to 325°

Remove any skin and bones from fish, dry
with paper towels and cut into 6 pieces.

Grease a 9-inch by 12-inch deep ovenproof
dish with olive oil (1 tablespoon). Layer 1/3 of
the potatoes, 1/2 of the onions, 1/2 of the cod,
and 1/2 of the tomatoes. Sprinkle with 1/2 of the
parsley. Add raisins, pine nuts, capers, olives,
and the rest of the potatoes, onions and cod. Pour
in the rest of the tomatoes, season with salt, pepper, and remaining parsley. Drizzle 1 tablespoon
olive oil over the top and bake uncovered for 45
minutes. Remove from oven, and let rest 10
minutes. Serve in soup bowls and have plenty of
crusty Italian bread available to scoop up sauce.

Remember, at least 6, 8, or 12 more fish or
seafood dishes are going to follow in this same
meal. Enjoy and *buona natale*! (A blessed Christmas to you all!)

THE TRADITION OF CHRIST-
MAS GIFTS

Many years ago, Italian children didn't
receive Christmas season gifts until the
eve of the Catholic feast of the Epiphany, which
takes place on January 6 according to the
Church's calendar. In the Italian language

Epiphany is translated into *Befana*. The day is
also called the feast of the Holy Magi.

Epiphany comes from a Greek word that
means disclosure or manifestation. In this case it
refers to the disclosure that the child born of the
Virgin Mary in Bethlehem was indeed the Mes-
siah, the long awaited king of the Jews, the Savior who would free the Jewish people from the
oppression, bondage, and slavery imposed upon
them by the Gentile invaders of the Holy Land.

This disclosure or manifestation could have
been done in many ways: through a vision, an
angelic messenger, or a divine proclamation. But
God chose a star, and three Wise Men to understand it. The star of Bethlehem heralded the
greatest event of all ages—the birth of Jesus
Christ. It was not uncommon in ancient countries of the East to seek knowledge through the
position and brilliance of the stars. God wanted
to tell the Wise Men of the birth of his son, and
He did so in a way they would understand: a new
star in the heavens.

They followed the star to Bethlehem, and each
brought a significant gift. The gift of gold signi-
fied the Christ child's kingship; the incense pro-
claimed His divinity; and the myrrh, a rare
perfume used in embalming the dead, represented His humanity and acceptance of His sacrificial death. (This is the origin of giving gifts to
children during the Christmas season.) The
Magi, as non-Jews, represented the gentile world,
which would also be saved and redeemed by this
King of the Jews who is the Savior of all who
would come to believe in Him.

Many centuries later, when Italy was invaded
and dominated by Pagan Germanic and Celtic
barbarian tribes, these tribes brought their

Pagan religious beliefs with them. One of these beliefs was that there were evil and, in contrast, kindly witches. After these tribes were converted to Christianity, most of their Pagan beliefs were retained and "Christianized." Bad witches became those who gave their souls to Satan. Good witches became saintly creatures whom God used to help His people.

In northern Italy, which was peopled by these former Pagan Teutonic and Celtic tribespeople, one of their good witches was transformed into La Befana, a kindly old witch whom God used to bring gifts to children on the eve of the Feast of the Epiphany in remembrance of the gifts brought to the Christ child by the three Wise Men from the East.

Today in Italy, the tradition of La Befana has almost disappeared and now Italian children receive their Christmas season gifts through the personage of Saint Nicholas of Myra on Christmas Eve.

Saint Nicholas of Myra (a town in present day Turkey) was a bishop and is undoubtedly one of the most popular saints to be honored in the Western world. In English speaking countries, his memory has survived in the unique personality of Santa Claus—the rotund, white-bearded gentleman whose laughter captivates children the world over with promises of gifts on Christmas Eve. His legend as the jolly red-suited Father Christmas who lives at the North Pole and travels the skies of the world in a gift-laden sleigh pulled by flying reindeer, and who climbs down chimneys and deposits Christmas gifts to sleeping children is celebrated even in non-Christian Japan.

In actuality, Saint Nicholas was a bishop in the third century who lived a saintly life, but popular legends tell charming stories about him. The most famous is that a man of Patra, a town in Nicholas' diocese, lost his fortune and because he was unable to support his three unmarried daughters, planned to let them become prostitutes to support themselves and him. Nicholas heard of this man's intentions and secretly threw three bags of gold through a window into their home, thus providing dowries for the girls who could now honorably marry.

Nicholas died in 345 AD and his body was buried in the Cathedral of Myra. There it remained until 1087, when seamen of Bari in Italy, seized his bones and took them to their town. From that time, St. Nicholas was known as San Nicola di Bari (St. Nicholas of Bari.)

Our present day version of Saint Nicholas came to America in a distorted fashion. The Dutch Protestants carried a popularized version of the saint's life to New Amsterdam (now New York City), which portrayed Nicholas as nothing more than a Nordic magician and wonder-worker. Our present day conception of Santa Claus grew from this version. Saint Nicholas, the real one, was a holy bishop and should be admired as a Saint of the Catholic Church—not the jolly old Saint Nick from the long poem "A Visit from St. Nicholas." The only food I can think of that is connected to this story are the proverbial milk and cookies that kids leave for Santa to strengthen him for his hard work every Christmas Eve.

Christmas is a special season for the world, both Christian and non-Christian, because it inspires the dream of peace for all of us who inhabit this planet and believe in the essential goodness of humankind.

Index